Shakespeare's liminal spaces

Manchester University Press

Shakespeare's liminal spaces

Contesting authority on the early modern stage

Ben Haworth

MANCHESTER UNIVERSITY PRESS

Copyright © Ben Haworth 2024

The right of Ben Haworth to be identified as the author of this work has been asserted in accordance with the Copyright, Designs and Patents Act 1988.

Published by Manchester University Press
Oxford Road, Manchester M13 9PL

www.manchesteruniversitypress.co.uk

British Library Cataloguing-in-Publication Data
A catalogue record for this book is available from the British Library

ISBN 978 1 5261 6592 3 hardback
ISBN 978 1 5261 9553 1 paperback

First published 2024
Paperback published 2026

The publisher has no responsibility for the persistence or accuracy of URLs for any external or third-party internet websites referred to in this book, and does not guarantee that any content on such websites is, or will remain, accurate or appropriate.

EU authorised representative for GPSR:
Easy Access System Europe – Mustamäe tee 50,
10621 Tallinn, Estonia
gpsr.requests@easproject.com

Typeset by Newgen Publishing UK

Contents

List of figures	*page* vi
Acknowledgements	vii
Prologue	viii
1 In search of the liminal: The theoretical landscapes of power	1
2 Between ocean and land: 'The guiled shore to a most dangerous sea'	36
3 Subversive sylvan settings: Dark humours and the theatrical forest	80
4 Corrupted Eden: The liminal garden and cultures of resistance	120
5 Theatres of war: Shakespeare's ideological battlefields	163
Conclusion	204
Bibliography	208
Index	217

Figures

1.1 *Las Meninas* (1656), Diego Rodríguez de Silva y Velázquez. Source: Museo Nacional del Prado.   *page* 2
2.1 Title page from John Dee's *The General and Rare Memorials pertayning to the Perfect Arte of Navigation* (1577). Source: British Library.   42
2.2 'The Abbess Appears' Act 5, Scene 1 in Theodore Komisarjevsky's 1938 production of *The Comedy of Errors* in Stratford-upon-Avon. Source: RSC archives.   53
3.1 Polly Findlay's *As You Like It*, for the National Theatre in 2015. Source: National Theatre archives.   89

Acknowledgements

I am infinitely grateful to 'P&P', Peter J. Smith and Peter Kirwan, for their patience, erudition, good humour, skilful direction and their benevolent help and advice. I also owe a debt of thanks to Jonathan Dollimore whose scholarly largesse and gracious manner extended to being cornered at a conference, a conversation that developed my own approaches to his substantial theoretical contributions. So too is Duncan Salkeld to be thanked for his liberally allowing me to pick over much of his outstanding, yet at the time unpublished, research. I would also like to thank the English Faculty at Nottingham Trent University, particularly those such as John Goodridge, Sarah Carter and Sharon Ouditt who encouraged, corrected and guided me throughout my formative years of research. The collections at the Shakespeare Birthplace Trust were also an outstanding help and it is with gratitude I think of Roslyn Sklar and Paul Edmondson who let me rummage through the vaults in search of inspiration. None of this would have been possible without the backing of the Arts and Humanities Research Council and the Midlands3Cities scheme that funded the entire venture and provided support throughout the pandemic.

Finally, I would like to thank my most excellent wife, Aisha, who put up with my numerous crushing bouts of self-doubt, my almost constant distraction, patiently listening to me proofread, offering exceptional feedback and providing an atmosphere of calm in which I could work. Thank you, and sorry.

Prologue

Colin MacCabe: [Raymond Williams] wrote several novels, one of which, *A Border Country*, is a really very good one, [...] it's a very autobiographical novel and it's about him growing up in a Welsh working class community.

Michael Rosen: And perhaps he discovered, by calling it *Border Country*, that other great word – *liminality* – which I think academics are very fond of these days.

Laura Wright: No, that's one Colin chucked out![1]

It is perhaps not surprising that 'liminality' was omitted from Colin MacCabe and Holly Yanacek's *Keywords for Today: A 21st Century Vocabulary* (2018), an attempt to update Raymond Williams's seminal *Keywords: A Vocabulary of Culture and Society* (1978). Indeed, Michael Rosen's over-emphasised use of 'liminality' in his BBC Radio 4 programme and Laura Wright's reply hinted at it being the butt of a joke, possibly for its overemployment, even misuse, in academic jargon.

'Liminality' and 'liminal' are words anchored in the dense theoretical language of anthropology and the arts, and have not, nor may ever, make the crossing into popular language. As if to drive this point home, liminality is central to this book, an academic concept applied to a, by now, familiar academic field – Shakespearean studies (one can already visualise the disdainfully arched eyebrows and derisive eye-rolls of MacCabe, Rosen and Wright). However, the ensuing chapters seek to establish the concept of the liminal as having considerable traction, and contest such views of liminality as an academically elitist term. Rather, they explore the perception, production and power of the liminal on Shakespeare's early modern stage both as a means to address issues in the social and cultural spheres and as a way of challenging the very structures that endeavoured to define and shape behaviours and ideologies in early modern England.[2]

In addressing the liminal, this study looks at the material and metaphorical representations of actual physical geographic spaces employed by Shakespeare to set the scene in ways that drew on their contemporary cultural significances. In recent years there has been a flurry of academic activity at the Shakespearean coalface as the rich conceptual seam of space, place, landscape and environment has been exposed and mined. Following on from John Gillies's seminal work on *Shakespeare and the Geography of Difference* (1994), in which he addressed Renaissance attitudes towards geography and their expression through the agency of the early modern stage, there have been numerous forays into the way Shakespeare and his contemporaries created their worlds to reflect contemporaneous cartographic and social anxieties. Oxford University Press's recent series on early modern literary geographies has produced a number of insightful publications that explore the phenomenology of space. Developing the theory of psychologist James J. Gibson on approaches to visual perception, Andrew Bozio's *Thinking through Place on the Early Modern English Stage* (2020) introduces the idea of environmental cognition under what he terms as 'ecological thinking'. He defines this methodology as 'a mode of cognition in which an environment – defined as the physical, social, and cultural surroundings of an individual creature – functions as both the object and medium of thought'.[3] In terms of early modern theatre, Bozio asserts that interpretation and interaction with staged spaces rely not just on physical laws but on 'the thoughts, feelings, and actions of the creatures who navigate these terrains'.[4] There are two elements he feels should be considered in the understanding of dramatic settings within the playhouse – that of the players whose task it is to engage with a specific place, and that of the playgoers who must imagine themselves within or in relation to such places. Chris Barrett's *Early Modern English Literature and the Poetics of Cartographic Anxiety* (2018) taps into the means by which certain writers turned the intellectual and scientific developments of the day into cultural capital, effectively generating 'a literary discourse that productively complicates concepts of allegory, analogy, metaphoricity and literality, description and detail, bibliographic materiality, and the other essential aspects of poetry and poesis'.[5] Richard Wilson's *Worldly Shakespeare: The Theatre of our Good Will* (2016) and Stuart Elden's *Shakespearean Territories* (2018) plot the way technological advances in navigation and cartography, as well as territorial politics, were articulated on the stage and page. In many ways, Wilson's and Elden's works build on *The Cultural Geography of Early Modern Drama, 1620–1650* (2011), Julie Sanders's excellent work on reconsidering dramatic geographies as embodied spaces, as well as the collection of essays in *Literature, Mapping and the Politics of Space in Early Modern Britain* (2001) that explored 'spatial paradigms' and their incumbent 'metaphorical and/or physical boundaries' to establish what is described as 'a metaphorical currency in cultural discourse that transcends the immediacy of any direct spatial experience'.[6]

What these approaches to Shakespeare's dramatic geographies reveal is the existence of a heightened social sensitivity among early modern audiences to the geopolitical state of affairs in the Renaissance world. What is more, this awareness was meaningfully translated onto the stage in the form of setting and metaphor. Yet it is not enough simply to demonstrate the presence of such dramatic and literary devices, or the audience awareness of such strategies. In his germinal study of the cultural politics of the early modern stage, Louis Montrose cut to the very core of the purpose of theatre – its power to question and the question of power. In *The Purpose of Playing* (1996), Montrose stirred the theoretical waters that were both shared by, yet equally divided, new historicists and cultural materialists – the potential for the playhouse, a 'marginal site of performative authority', to exert pressure on the 'official centres of political and cultural authority', namely the Court and the Church.[7] Since the emergence of these two movements that rose from Foucauldian philosophies on the circulation of power within social structures, there has been a primary point of contention that has alienated their adherents, namely: is the presence of subversive content and dissident undercurrents in literature and drama allowed and therefore contained within the centralised structures of authority, or do such transgressive elements in fact exert pressure on and potentially alter these social, political and religious states?[8] This question of containment, raised by new historicists and cultural materialists, still lies unanswered, and for the most part such debates have reached something of a stalemate. This book not only seeks to engage with this debate, but to moot a resolution to the long-standing dispute over the movement of power and the potential for subversion in both mental and physical representations of place, space and location.

One might ask, what is distinctly Shakespearean about these liminal spaces? Did not his predecessors, collaborators and other contemporary dramatists also use setting and geographic inference to layer and complicate meaning within their various texts? Indeed, there is nothing markedly 'Shakespearean' about the use of liminal spaces. Where possible there are references throughout this volume to Shakespeare's precursors and contemporaries that speak to a tradition of using certain spaces and settings, and their attendant cultural significances, within their plays. Christopher Marlowe used a tiny Mediterranean island in *The Jew of Malta* (c.1590) years prior to the island settings of Shakespeare's *Othello* (c.1603) and *The Tempest* (c.1610). The liminal setting augments the frictions created within Marlowe's play with its concomitant cultural, racial and religious diversity. Francis Beaumont's *The Knight of the Burning Pestle* (1607) radically subverts all notions of social station in its innovative and profound experiment in breaching the barrier between audience and stage, a dramatic pretension that displayed the writer's understanding of the power of liminal spaces to upset the status quo. In a similar manner to Beaumont's meta-theatrical approach, Ben Jonson's *Bartholomew Fair* (1614) begins with a deliberate disruption of stage space – playing on the barriers between the imagined locus of the play and the present physical and political spaces occupied by the audience. Jonson then proceeds to develop the setting of the fair, throwing together London's diverse cultural composites in a liminal space for the purposes of satirising early modern English society. These brief examples of the use of liminal setting and space are but a small selection in what could be constituted a dramatic convention throughout this period, rather than a Shakespearean singularity.

However, there are several reasons why the primary focus throughout these pages is on Shakespeare's use of this literary and dramaturgical practice. First, it became clear, very early on, that the sheer range and variety of liminal spaces in Shakespeare yielded more than enough material for a considerable body of research. Shakespeare's broad corpus revealed a peculiar use of battlefields, of complicated and nuanced garden settings and imagery, of forests altering the behaviours of those who entered them, and the repeated juxtaposition of sea and shore. Furthermore, his deployment of these liminal spaces exposed a rich vein of social engagement, displaying concerns over religious freedoms, patriarchal privilege and social hierarchies. Recent forays into the significance of setting such as 'The Early Modern Literary Geographies' series (published by Oxford University Press) take into account the contribution of multiple authors from the period in order to trace historical questions and the treatment of geopolitics and ecologies. Yet there has been little on exploring one author's literary and dramatic deployment of liminal spaces. A single-writer focus allows the means to investigate authorial strategies in the literary exposure and dramatic depictions of these particular questions.

Moreover, whilst similar studies could be made of other authors, given the centrality of Shakespeare to the core theoretical models employed within these pages – especially new historicism and cultural materialism – focusing on Shakespeare facilitates a more direct confrontation of the existing theories and histories. From Dollimore and Sinfield's *Political Shakespeare* (1985) to Greenblatt's *Shakespearean Negotiations* (1988), the battlefield has already been chosen for those who would bring to bear new approaches to an already crowded field of critical theory centred almost exclusively on Shakespeare. Thus, where I refer to Shakespeare's liminal spaces it does not suggest the playwright's monopoly or invention of the literary concept, but rather the means by which the writer engaged with and applied this device within his works, and how its use relates to Shakespearean critical traditions on the containment of power.

The significance of setting

Drawing attention to the inaccuracy of many of the manuscripts and print documents available to Shakespearean scholars, Michael Hattaway notes that 'it is impossible to postulate a definitive version of a lot of Elizabethan plays, and that characters and even plots were correspondingly fluid'.[9] Hattaway's seemingly innocuous observation actually highlights several critical points. The first is that, once a play had been submitted to the Master of Revels to be vetted or vetoed, the subsequent end product, the performance, potentially nuanced the original ideas expressed within the text. Also, as plays were recycled and reused, shared between companies, resurrected to tie in with current affairs, they were likely to be subject to either unintentional or deliberate alteration. This is not the subject of this monograph. However, it does lay the groundwork for the arguments that follow. Whilst parts of a play's text might be changed, and a performance might be manipulated to allude to a particular event, there were certain dramatic elements that would potentially remain fixed. In establishing a foundation of meaning, one of these crucial constants was the setting.

Bringing together the early modern dramatic interpretations and interrogations of the environs through staged spaces and the complicated cartographic and cultural discourses that shaped Shakespeare's settings offers a unique vantage point from which to re-evaluate the politics of power. In particular, it is important to examine his choice of specific settings that explored the edges of authority – the borders where centralised order and the expression of individual or collective autonomy form a dialogue of resistance. These liminal spaces and their attendant social significances and metaphorical meanings form the focus for understanding how the expression of power is far more fluid, and thus harder to contain, than might previously have been assumed.

This book focuses on the frameworks Shakespeare employed to situate his plots, the dramatic devices that reference specific locations, either to these places' physical representations, or to their respective cultural signifiers and metaphors. I propose that such settings carried with them connotations that would have resonated with Shakespeare's audiences, creating associations with and connections to contemporaneous social issues. Liminal spaces, such as the margins of the shore that are subject to the vicissitudes of tides and the vagaries of the changeable seas and elements, are not simply coincidental locales, but rather are ideally suited to stage the frictions between opposing ideological standpoints and the internal struggles between human nature and conformity with the centralised authorities of Church and Court. The forest that lies at the edge of civilisation comes to represent the darker side of humanity and an escape from conventional systems of governance that in turn promotes alternative models of power. Shakespeare's garden settings sit cheek by jowl with the home and its patriarchal seat of dominance and serve to lay open the possibility of dissident behaviours and radical rethinking of social norms. The numerous battlefields form naturally liminal settings that throw kings and commoners together, upsetting established hierarchies and destabilising the very foundations of monarchical authority. As such, settings take on a far greater significance than might initially be imagined – potentially facilitating more nuanced interpretations of scenes and revealing dissident narratives that challenge the structures of early modern society.

Yet before settings themselves can be interrogated, it is important to establish just what liminality is, its origins in terms of anthropological understanding and its role as a theoretical basis for approaching literature and drama. In this regard, the first chapter lays the groundwork for understanding just what early modern English society looked like, from its centralised pillars of Church, Court, Law and systems of patriarchal control, to its margins and how control was negotiated within such structures. It also looks at the means by which combining concepts of the liminal and the mutability of social control forces a reappraisal and adjustment in the way we view containment of culturally subversive elements. Developing the models of performance theory outlined by Robert Weimann, the representation of authority on the stage can be seen to be a material expression as well as a metaphysical or conceptual manifestation – friction and conflict embodied in the uniquely divided stage space and the way the actor moves though such spaces and interacts with his audience. However, performative elements, cultural frameworks and all their attendant theoretical debates must be historically contextualised – and it is through Shakespeare's use of setting that a new approach to the dynamics of power is revealed.

Beginning with Shakespeare's marine imagery and the friction between sea and shore, the second chapter addresses the concepts of national identity and 'otherness', with the oceans an uncontrollable force that mirrors the inward motivations of humanity and the coastline as a symbol of the limit of human control. This chapter develops John Gillies's notion that Shakespeare created dramatic literary geographies, and argues that the playwright often utilised the metaphoric inferences of such settings, juxtaposing city and sea to play on the resistance inherent in such liminal spaces. Ambiguity, conflict and subversion are the by-products of the contrasts of sea and shore, and a consideration of parallels the poet created between the imagined theatrical spaces of islands, Mediterranean cities and the familiar realities of one of the greatest maritime cities of its day, London, highlights the presence of opposition with which his audiences would have been all too familiar. *The Comedy of Errors* forms a case study for these cultural conflicts as Ephesus epitomises everything from England's monarchical systems of power to the recent upheavals in religious ideologies, the patriarchal hierarchy to the disparity between social classes.

The third chapter moves under the boughs of Shakespeare's sylvan worlds. Reflecting on contemporaneous historical and social contexts, this chapter demonstrates how the prevailing conceptualisation of forests shaped the dramatist's works. It also addresses more recent critical approaches to these topographies, overturning ideas of the existence of such forest spaces as the locus of benign transformation. Rather, Shakespeare's woodland realms constitute paradoxical spaces that serve to conceal those who enter from the disapproving judgments of society yet equally unravel and amplify their inner character in a process of carnivalesque inversion. Parodies of centralised power structures exist within Shakespeare's woods, the dramatic capital of such familiar settings effectively becoming the means to satirise and subvert the social, religious and juridical institutions of authority by which early modern society was regulated and maintained. As a liminal space, both geographically and within the collective cultural consciousness, Shakespeare's forest becomes a testing ground for alternative models of power, a landscape that allows, even promotes, aggressive change, resistance and rebellion.

Shakespeare's cultivated spaces – parks, gardens, orchards and vineyards – are the focus of the fourth chapter. Initially, such spaces may not appear to be liminal as the human control over the wilderness could make them seem cultivated and contained. However, in exploring the significance of such spaces, particularly in the rich literary traditions that incorporate biblical imagery and Church doctrine through to horticultural metaphor, it becomes apparent that the garden is one of the most semantically complicated settings used by the writer in terms of the sheer scope and nuance of what it may embody. The garden is indeed a liminal space, rendered so by its links both to the domicile, of which it is an extension, and to the wilderness, where it originates. The imagery of encroaching weeds and seasonal cycles creates a uniquely slippery space in which power is constantly in flux, progressions of life and death, youth and decay, the battle between nature and culture played out within its bounds. As a metaphor for control, Shakespeare's garden presents a very cynical vision of the systems of societal jurisdiction that focuses not so much on the outward order but on the fundamentally negative, fallible and corrupt aspects within such structures. This, in turn, raises thought-provoking questions about the negotiation of power, emphasising the flaws in such models of governance and inevitably resulting in repetitions of Edenic expulsion into the wilderness of humankind's postlapsarian condition.

The final chapter delves into the early modern cultural significance of the battlefield, its theatrical representation, and the means by which vast armies could, or could not, be rendered on the stage. The battlefield is ostensibly the exemplary liminal space, its physical, geographical, temporal and ideological properties rendering it the ultimate place of contestation and subversion, ideally suited to dissident narratives. In considering the contemporaneous cultural, political and religious resonances of war, it can be demonstrated that staging battles could present the means by which social institutions and their unavoidable ideological derivatives were challenged. Chivalry, heroics and the justification for conflict, far from being homogeneous models anchored in historical fact, are challenged and inverted. I would argue that Shakespeare presents us with alternative histories, and that the battlefield ironically offered the playwright a unique space in which to introduce carnivalesque subversion. War was traditionally the arena of masculine power and chivalric proficiency. Yet, as the chapter demonstrates, in many of Shakespeare's battle settings such ideological mores are in fact subverted, as indeed are their incumbent social orders and values. With these theatrical re-enactments or reinterpretations of history, Shakespeare raises the question of remembrance – how the retelling of history shapes, and indeed challenges, social identity.

What can be seen from the development of Shakespearean critical approaches throughout the past century is a move towards acknowledging and understanding the cultural power and agency of theatre. This study aims to look back at Shakespeare's dramatic texts and at the liminal settings that allow deviation from contemporary socio-political models. By paying particular attention to the extremities of hierarchy that are peculiar and particular to these spaces, I will argue that a place within a structure of power, especially one at the margin, has the potential to upset, destabilise and challenge the social stasis. I aim to show that the deliberate inclusion of liminal spaces in Shakespeare's plays effectively gave those in such settings a voice that could be used to apply pressure to the social order by creating new power dynamics and undermining received ideologies.

Notes

1 'Raymond Williams' Keywords', *Word of Mouth*, BBC Radio 4, 23 October 2018, www.bbc.co.uk/programmes/m0000t6v [accessed 15 Dec. 2020].
2 This research does not look at the modern dissemination of drama. Rather it strongly challenges any idea that early modern theatre foreshadowed some of the class-based and elitist associations of modern theatre. There is an argument that has been made for the democratisation of theatre as the advent of Covid-19 has shut theatres, forcing the broadcasting of drama in new forms that have expanded its potential audience. Yet despite recent observations that 'coronavirus may have brought the theatrical and scholarly communities together in unexpected ways', implicit within such a statement is the demarcation of two communities neither of which represents the public at large. It is the latter community, or rather, its early modern counterpart, which is central in the focus of this book. See Peter J. Smith, Janice Valls-Russell and Daniel Yabut, 'Shakespeare under Global Lockdown: Introduction', *Cahiers Elisabethains: A Journal of English Renaissance Studies,* 103 (2020), 101–110, p. 108.
3 Andrew Bozio, *Thinking through Place on the Early Modern English Stage* (Oxford: Oxford University Press, 2020), p. 2.
4 Ibid., p. 3.
5 Chris Barrett, *Early Modern English Literature and the Poetics of Cartographic Anxiety* (Oxford: Oxford University Press, 2018), p. 2.

6 Andrew Gordon and Bernhard Klein (eds), *Literature, Mapping and the Politics of Space in Early Modern Britain* (Cambridge: Cambridge University Press, 2001), pp. 6, 7.
7 Louis Montrose, *The Purpose of Playing* (Chicago: University of Chicago Press, 1996), p. xi. Montrose here builds on Leonard Tennenhouse's work, *Power on Display: The Politics of Shakespeare's Genres* (New York: Methuen, 1986), which explores the complexities of cultural discourse within Shakespeare's plays.
8 Regarding the circulation of social energies, see Stephen Greenblatt, *Shakespearean Negotiations* (Oxford: Oxford University Press, 1999).
9 Michael Hattaway, *Elizabethan Popular Theatre* (London: Routledge & Kegan Paul, 1982), p. 55.

1

In search of the liminal: The theoretical landscapes of power

In 1656 the Spanish painter, Diego Velázquez, created what has become one of the most enigmatic artworks to come out of the Renaissance – *Las Meninas* ('The Ladies-in-Waiting'; see Figure 1.1).[1] Pablo Picasso was inspired to paint no fewer than 58 artistic interpretations of *Las Meninas* in 1957, using them as a means to comment on the contemporary political condition of Spain. In 1966, Michel Foucault devoted the entire first chapter of *The Order of Things* to a compelling and detailed examination of Velázquez's painting, concluding that it constitutes a representation of representation itself.[2] Quite simply, Velázquez created a metacritical experiment with space – one that challenged the viewer and that, although the word would not have existed in common parlance at the time of its creation, implicitly references the concept of liminality in its execution.

Within *Las Meninas* Velázquez depicts himself, the painter, poised with brush and palette, looking out of the picture, directly at the viewer. The activity of the central figures of the Infanta with her attendant maids, dwarf, chaperone and dog is strangely upset by the stare of the artist that connects directly with the observer – making them aware of the space they inhabit outside of the painting and unsettlingly drawing them into the scene. There is the suggestion of others present yet hidden within the setting, revealed only by mirrors. These mirrored images may well be the King and Queen, oddly diminished by the small size of their reflections in comparison to the other figures in the painting. And at the back, a doorway frames a man in the act of parting a curtain that divides the darkened room from sunlit stairs. He stands half-turned on the steps, neither

Figure 1.1 *Las Meninas* (1656), Diego Rodríguez de Silva y Velázquez.

coming nor going, provocatively giving us a view of something beyond the ordered, staged and central scene. This is the liminal, the space between spaces, that which is on the edge. Foucault marvelled at this artistic representation of a 'spectacle-as-observation', questioning, 'what is there, then, we ask at last, in that place which is completely inaccessible because it is exterior to the picture, yet it is prescribed by all the lines of its composition?'[3] He noted that 'the centre is symbolically sovereign' but that the painter and 'visitor' on the steps place pressure on this centralised authority.[4] What we can conclude is that Velázquez plays with these liminal spaces, breaking borders, threatening the equilibrium, alluding to things outside a certain order. This is the concept of liminality that lies at the heart of this book.

Before engaging with the way Shakespeare used the liminal properties of certain settings to challenge the social status quo, it is important we navigate the theoretical landscapes that have shaped the politics of power within Shakespearean studies over the past century. This chapter seeks to trace the emergence and increasing significance of liminality from its anthropological roots as well as the idea of early modern English society as envisioned by early twentieth-century scholars up until the appearance of cultural materialism and new historicism in the 1980s. In regard to the latter theoretical movements I posit that the issues surrounding the expression and containment of potential subversion in Shakespeare's dramatic works must be re-examined in the light of more current understandings of the interchange and negotiation of authority on the stage. This chapter's navigation of definitions and theories surrounding both liminality and the expression and movement of power sets the terms for the rest of this book, stressing the importance of the liminal in redressing the dissident themes.

Beginnings

Liminality is a term that has had considerable use since its inception just over a century ago. It first appears in anthropologist Arnold Van Gennep's *Les rites de passage* (*The Rites of Passage*) (1909) and is best summed up in the *Oxford English Dictionary*'s definition of 'a transitional or indeterminate state between culturally defined stages of a person's life; *spec.* such a state occupied during a ritual or rite of passage, characterized by a sense of solidarity between participants'. Liminality, and the liminal, as both words and concepts, have since made their way from cultural anthropology into almost every field of social sciences, arts and science, appropriated to describe persons and objects, places and ideologies, that occupy the margins, interstices and peripheries of established schemes.

However, for liminality and the liminal to exist there must first be structure, a hierarchy that establishes the boundaries and definitions to which a society must conform. Developing the ideas of Van Gennep in social anthropology and the liminal, Victor Turner published several books during the 1960s and 1970s that examined the role of ritual in society. His studies led him to formulate hierarchic configurations in social groups that negotiated power and established what would come to be recognised as normative behaviour. For Turner, the centre is comprised of institutions or persons of authority who stipulate standards and regulations, and dictate what is acceptable behaviour for the larger, weaker *communitas*, comprised of those subject to rule, the civilian populace. As a whole, with centre and periphery in dialogue, we possess what might be simply called 'society'.

Yet society is a very inexact term. Social anthropologist Claude Lévi-Strauss defined society or societal structure as 'entities independent of man's consciousness of them (although they in fact govern men's existence), and thus as different from the image which men form of them as physical reality is different from our sensory perceptions of it and our hypotheses about it'.[5] As such there exist certain incompatibilities, contradictions and ambiguities as the individual and the social interact. Turner expanded on the idea of society being a complex structured concept as he describes it both as 'a differentiated, segmented system of structural positions (which may or may not be arranged in a hierarchy)', and also 'a homogenous, undifferentiated whole'.[6] The smallest social unit, the individual, is thus divided, adopting roles or a persona that subscribes to and integrates with the systems and structures of society whilst potentially maintaining an element of exceptionality. Such duality becomes the basis for ambiguity, with both the potential to conform to as well as to challenge the status quo.

What social anthropologists to date have described is a constant dialogue between the periphery and the centre, a negotiation that ultimately reinforces the status quo or facilitates change. This negotiation takes place when pockets, groups or individuals who do not fully fit, either by accident or design, into the structure of society, draw attention to disparities, to flaws, or to the necessity for change. It must be stated that these challenges are not always positive but that the very action of drawing attention to the limits of society prompts a response from the central institutions of authority – to either absorb these behaviours in a new definition of the socially acceptable, or to resist and crush the emergent rebellious ideologies. These 'liminars' are the drivers of change, of challenge, of transition from one state to another. Turner describes such persons as placing emphasis on 'spontaneity, immediacy, and "existence"'.[7] He goes on to say, 'those who "opt out" of the status-bound social order and acquire the stigmata of the lowly, dressing like "bums", and itinerant in their habits [...] stress personal relationship rather than social obligations'.[8] Whilst the contemporaneous hippy movement of the 1960s no doubt influenced his description, Turner's observations are sound in principle. Structure is rooted in history, tradition and, ultimately, the past. *Communitas*, Turner asserts, is of the present, the now. From this model then, we may assume that liminality may become the vehicle for change, driving towards future possibilities.

Turner states that liminality bears a certain anonymity that produces faceless neophytes – blank canvases on which society can leave its impression. Thus, liminality brings with it a certain ambiguity. Liminal characters, having a foot in the worlds of both centralised social norms and the other, are not easily placed, less likely to receive the impression of society, in fact, somewhat immune to its effects. They display a resistance to 'status incumbency and roleplaying' as they attempt to rid themselves of these clichés, instead instituting or promoting new relations, and a shift in the dynamics of power.[9] In many ways the liminal figure represents the *communitas*. Interestingly, from the point of subversion, or at least potential subversion, Turner notes that the '*communitas* has an aspect of potentiality' in that it is open to explore conditional or imaginary situations.[10]

There exists an element of embryonic subversion in the marginal that explores the limits of societal stricture, one that, given time, may well grow to break through the established norms and effect a shift in the social bedrock. Both temporary and permanent liminality foster change, which in turn repositions the centre of the structure. One such example is that of the contemporary influence previously marginalised gay communities have had on the edifices of Church and State – now being 'absorbed' within certain episcopal polities and public institutions no longer as outsiders but as policy-makers.[11]

Turner's model is of interest when applied to English Renaissance society, and particularly the place of the stage within the societal hierarchy. To some extent the dialogue between the inner, established, and hence the strongest structure of society, and its outwardly weak, binary outside – those pushed to the margins of society – is mediated, or at least expressed, through dramatic representation. As Stephen Mullaney demonstrated in *The Place of the Stage* (1988), the early modern English theatre was itself a liminal place, both physically and metaphysically; London's theatres were for the most part situated on the outskirts of the city, creating temporary dramatic worlds that reflected and commented on the systems and protocols of early modern society. Within these timber, plaster and thatch structures, and within the texts performed on their stages, existed liminal spaces – forests, seas, battlefields and gardens, in which characters could either resist or reinforce accepted social behaviours, playing with the balance of power imposed by centralised hierarchies. The stage also became the means to give a voice to liminal characters: radicals, witches, mendicants, the poor, fools, folk-tale peddlers and artists. Their value as characters within the writers' arsenal is that 'they all fall in the interstices of social structure, are on its margins, or occupy its lowest rungs' and hence are ideally situated to probe and even challenge societal norms.[12]

Yet Turner also proposes that liminal rituals such as the theatre ultimately *reinforce* the status quo, 'bringing social structure and *communitas* into right mutual relation again'.[13] Since the 1980s, new historicists have taken this theoretical standpoint – that social tensions were effectively purged through cultural rituals such as the feast of fools, skimmington rides and theatre, such activities effectively 'resetting' the structure. However, Turner does admit that there is a possibility for complication and exception to this rule. Where centralised structure and *communitas* collide there is the potential for disruption that results in change as these two forces, inner and periphery, are compelled to engage and relate.

What the liminal describes is a place outside of or in-between societal structures. From a social perspective it describes a state apart or detached from the centre, the established norms or status quo. However, as with Van Gennep, Turner also speaks of liminality as expressed in transitional rituals that take an individual or a social group from one stage of life into the next. In terms of early modern drama, these rituals may be seen as the processes by which a citizen passes from one role into the next – the married woman into the widow, the child into the adult, the prince into the king. Turner's anthropological research led him to conclude that rituals reflect the very deepest values of a society no matter how 'simple' or complicated such a society may be. As a result, his ideas began to move towards a more ambiguous view of the liminal in the 1970s. *Dramas, Fields, and Metaphors: Symbolic Action in Human Society* (1974) reflected a leaning towards the liminal being a potentially subversive state rather than simply a ritual transition between socially predetermined positions.

> Without liminality, program might indeed determine performance. But, given liminality, prestigious programs can be undermined and multiple alternative programs may be generated [...] The result of confrontations between the monolithic, power-supported programs and their many subversive alternatives is a sociocultural 'field' in which many options are provided.[14]

The idea of the liminal offering 'alternatives' or 'options' to the subscribed or programmed societal structures was a subtle but ultimately dramatic shift that acknowledged the power of the margins over the centre, effectively to transpose the centre from its position and facilitate social change. As Turner expresses it, 'yesterday's liminal becomes today's stabilised, today's peripheral becomes tomorrow's centred'.[15] What this implies is that there is constant movement, a flux of power between centre and periphery rendering implausible any ideas of an immovable, concrete base of power at the axis. Raymond Williams noted this fluidity reflected within the arts as residual, dominant and emergent hegemonies that challenged static Marxist approaches to cultural superstructure and saw cultural output as a means to challenge the status quo, not simply reflect it.

Viewing the liminal less as a subscribed transition and more as a radical or subversive process opens up new avenues of literary criticism and theory when it comes to early modern theatre. As theories such as new historicism and cultural materialism emerged in the late 1970s, the question of possible subversive undercurrents in the writings of Shakespeare and his contemporaries began to be explored. However, an understanding of the function of the liminal within Shakespearean drama is not really possible without first understanding both the development of and changes to early modern societal perceptions and secondly the role that the various literary expressions – masques, poetry, pageants, plays and popular entertainment – played within such a structure.

Early modern society and culture

Up until the latter half of the twentieth century, liminality, or for that matter subversion, in Shakespearean drama, was largely overlooked. A. C. Bradley, E. M. W. Tillyard and Derek Traversi each contributed considerable research in critical approaches to early modern dramatic texts and understanding of the socio-political environment in which these texts existed. Though their works have for the most part been superseded by modern theorists, consideration of their stance on the construction of early modern society and the function of theatre and the arts within it serves as a valuable exercise in revealing not just the emergence of the liminal, but also the subtle yet pervading influence of contemporaneous socio-political circumstance on their theoretical stance.

Mikhail Bakhtin spoke of the 'sin of anachronism', a tendency to examine texts from current perspectives rather than their contemporary contexts.[16] To some extent it is impossible to examine texts within a completely hermetic environment, devoid of external socio-political factors. Yet this is the very approach A. C. Bradley took in his series of lectures published in 1904 under the title *Shakespearean Tragedy*. Bradley's research involved a detailed comparison of four of Shakespeare's tragedies. Searching for patterns, structures, substance and parallels within Shakespeare's texts, Bradley attempted to distil the writer's 'dramatic view', distancing himself from attempts to discern the personal beliefs of the man, or a picture of the world in which he wrote. Yet Bradley was forced to confront 'inconsistencies and contradictions', noting that 'questions are suggested to the reader which it is impossible for him to answer with certainty'.[17] Such 'defects' were put down to 'indifference or want of care', a result of the pressures to sate the public's increasing demand for theatrical works.[18] Without consideration of external factors such as historical, political, religious, social and cultural contexts, Bradley's approach is limited in its awareness of subtleties, ambiguities and paradoxes within Shakespeare's tragedies. For Bradley, the only structure he offered more than a cursory glance at is that of 'moral order', which he saw as the 'ultimate power in the tragic world'.[19] Though his stance was quite obviously reductive, he acknowledged the divisions and complexities of the sixteenth-century inner person but failed to see any connection within the plays to the contestation of moral, social or political orders. It was not until E. M. W. Tillyard's *The Elizabethan World Picture* appeared in 1943 that a concerted effort was made to acknowledge early modern drama within synchronous socio-political contexts.

Written and published at the height of the Second World War, Tillyard's landmark book reflects a national concern for the conflict enveloping the globe, and the yearning for a return of structure, balance and harmony. Looking to Shakespeare's use of the elements, spheres and hierarchies within his works to create a pleasing symmetry, Tillyard misses any satirical edge that destabilises the balances of power. His epilogue is a wistful and regretful reflection on the failures of Europe's educated to recognise and apply the 'Elizabethan habit of mind', ignoring which he feels has 'helped not a little to bring the world into its present conflicts and distresses'.[20] Tillyard conducts an exercise in coherence and conformity within Elizabethan England that draws on the medieval and classical aspirations of cosmic harmony, clearly delineated hierarchies and corresponding planes of the divine, universal, body politic, humankind and lower creations that are referenced throughout contemporaneous literature and echo the speech by Ulysses to Agamemnon in *Troilus and Cressida*:

> The heavens themselves, the planets and this centre
> Observe degree, priority and place,
> Insisture, course, proportion, season, form,
> Office and custom, in all line of order
>
> (1.3.85–88)

For Tillyard, as for the honey-tongued Prince of Ithaca, the early modern world reflected the heavenly order, a sacred social structure with clearly demarcated hierarchical bounds, roles and responsibilities.

> How could communities,
> Degrees in schools and brotherhoods in cities,
> Peaceful commerce from dividable shores,
> The primogenitive and due of birth,
> Prerogative of age, crowns, sceptres, laurels,
> But by degree, stand in authentic place?
> Take but degree away, untune that string,
> And, hark, what discord follows!
>
> (1.3.103–110)

In such hierarchical structures there is little room for chaos or conflict, and Tillyard rarely speaks of discord, his examples either sanitised or used to illustrate their providential elimination or containment within the divine order. So too are ambiguity, satire and subversion conspicuous by their absence from his work, positions that would threaten clearly defined harmonies and hierarchies. There is the implication that all, from the educated to the illiterate, were submissively cognisant of their position within the system, the planes of existence, the chain of being and the cosmic dance.

Despite coming under considerable fire for his somewhat rigid and simplistic Elizabethan social vision, Tillyard may well have been correct in his belief in a central ideology that was promoted by the twin structures of monarchy and Church and filtered through various systems of education and cultural production. Sir John Davies, lawyer, politician and poet, addressed his exegetical epic *Nosce Teipsum* (1599), 'To My Most Gracivs Dread Soveraigne', followed by nine stanzas of alternate rhyme praising the Queen's nobility. What is noteworthy in this overt literary panegyric is the heliocentric, hierarchical model Davies employs:

> To that cleere maiestie which in the North
> Doth, like another Sunne in glory rise;
> Which standeth fixt, yet spreads her heauenly worth;
> Loadstone to hearts, and loadstarre to all eyes.[21]

Elizabeth's majesty is likened to a second sun, an established, unfailing natural source of life and daily order, supported and sustained by none other than 'the finger of the Almightie's hand'. For Davies, the physical realms mirror the heavenly, divine dispositions. His poetry focuses on the natural order, the unity of the inner workings of humankind with the divine model, whether it is the refining of the soul in *Nosce Teipsum* or his metaphorical moral masterpiece *Orchestra* (1596) which sought to align the hierarchies of contemporaneous society with the divine as a reflection of cosmic balance.

Thus, it comes as no surprise that Tillyard concluded *The Elizabethan World Picture* with an analysis of John Davies's *Orchestra*. He describes the poem as 'the perfect epitome of the universe seen as a dance'.[22] Opening with a deferential dedication to Elizabeth I, the poem unfolds as a dialogue between Antinous and Penelope, the former employing formidable rhetoric yet ultimately failing to persuade Odysseus's faithful wife to dance with him. Antinous's argument centres on the cosmic harmonies that display all the metaphorical signifiers of a dance. However, the true significance of the poem is in its expanded metaphorical connotations. Subtitling *Orchestra* 'A Poeme of Dauncing', Davies used the idea of the rhythms and patterns of a dance to illustrate the harmony a society may experience through each person knowing their respective role within it.

Though written considerably earlier than Davies's poem, and in the reign of Elizabeth's father, Sir Thomas Elyot's *The Boke of the Governour* (1531) used the same metaphor of dance to signify the complementary roles of a man and woman both within matrimony and also within society at large.

> These qualities, in this wise beinge knitte to gether, and signified in the personages of man and woman daunsinge, do expresse or sette out the figure of very nobilitie; whiche in the higher astate it is contained, the more excellent is the vertue in estimation.[23]

Virtue, nobility and the higher (e)state of humankind, a term suitable in its doubled reference to the individual and the body politic, are encapsulated in Elyot's dance, and it is this same philosophy or 'intellectual framework' that is central to the imagery within Davies's *Orchestra*.[24] David Underdown describes this ideal as a 'belief in a divinely ordained cosmic order, linking the entire universe from inanimate matter to God himself, provid[ing] every individual with a natural place or degree' as in the position and function of a dance.[25]

However, the Tillyardian vision of the construction of early modern society and its support within the arts meets with a problem in the assumption that it was readily subscribed to at the peripheries of society. Tillyard's neat hierarchical pyramid of the *communitas* in deference and agreement with the centrally prescribed creeds and directions of Church and Court reduces the artistic output of such a society to reflection of, rather than response to, social issues. Effectively, Shakespeare and his creative contemporaries are reduced to Marxist mirrors of the State, their literary endeavours justified in terms of reinforcing a principal shared ideal. Tillyard's model has been something of an easy target for critics who have unpicked his attempt to justify the order of a fully subscribed Elizabethan worldview as somewhat quixotic, mirroring contemporary national concerns with war-torn Europe.[26]

Derek Traversi's *An Approach to Shakespeare* (1938) reflects fewer of the European tensions of his contemporaries. Having felt that the Victorian methods of character-focused analysis that led to 'errors of misplaced emphasis' had been exhausted, Traversi opted to look at early modern drama in terms of dramatic action.[27] His tentative foray into alternate methods of interpretation saw him abandoning what he saw as the myopic 'card index' approach and 'mechanical collation and counting' to which his forebears had resorted, with a focus on 'the poetry as a living and dynamic whole'.[28] Traversi's idea was that a reader must pay attention to the various external social factors that gave greater understanding to the plays. According to Traversi, dramatic realities are only evident when we remember that 'the individual word cannot be considered apart from the verse'.[29] Sadly such perspectives did not stretch to include historical, political and social contexts that may give Shakespeare's texts a deeper complexity. What's more, there is a paucity of such examples within his critical writing and little is done to establish any idea of the socio-political setting in which Shakespeare's plays were first written and performed. Twenty years on, Traversi published *Shakespeare: 'Richard II' to 'Henry V'* (1957), showing a persistent reticence in committing to situating these plays within contemporaneous social contexts. Yet he remains unconcerned with delving too deeply into early modern socio-political backdrops, claiming that 'there is a very real risk that erudition, in relating these plays to their period, may end by obscuring their true individuality, the personal contribution by which they live as works of art'.[30] Like Tillyard, Traversi takes a top-down view of society, either unwilling to take a more controversial line or simply unaware of the possibility. He writes:

> The royal office is assumed to be divinely instituted, the necessary guarantee of order in a state nationally and patriotically conceived; the political thought expressed in these plays combines the fervent nationalism of the day, fostered for practical ends by the ruling dynasty, with sacramental notions of monarchy more venerable than itself.[31]

Despite Traversi's occasional attempts to ascertain Shakespeare's personal beliefs and agendas – and even the reception given by Renaissance London audiences to his material – there is no mention of potential dissident themes, or of early modern theatre's liminal position in relation to society.

Alternate socio-cultural models

A more nuanced theory of the mechanics of society and the role which the arts played arrived just before the Second World War in Mikhail Bakhtin's thesis on the satirical writings of the early modern French writer François Rabelais. Though his writings remained 'undiscovered' until the early 1960s, they have since climbed to the pinnacle of academic thought on carnival, laughter, subversion and interpretations of Renaissance texts and society. At once one is made aware of the liminal, of the pressure the margin exerts on the central structures of society. Explaining carnival, Bakhtin asserts that it does not exist separate to or outside of life, as an art form or temporary display. Rather, it is expressed as belonging to 'the borderline between art and life', and represents a 'universal spirit' that fosters and generates 'the world's revival and renewal, in which all take part'.[32] Humour is central to the idea of carnival and thus clowns and fools in many ways embody the spirit of carnival, liminal characters who negotiated the borders of art and social life. Bakhtin goes on to explain the problem of controlling carnival within societal structure as a fully regulated and sanctioned event or process, as it exists above such structures, sanctioned 'by the highest aims of human existence, that is, by the world of ideals'.[33] As such, carnival might be viewed as complicating Tillyardian visions of early modern hierarchy and order as it is playful, manifesting itself in festivity, laughter and satire.

It must be stressed that, despite Bakhtin's assertion that a critic's socio-political environment and personal agendas or experiences should not affect their perspective of texts and events, there is an argument to be made that this is an almost impossible task. Bakhtin's involvement in *Voskresenie*, the group of academics and professionals whose ideas of communism strayed from the accepted model, had resulted in six years of exile in Kazakhstan. Publishing a theory that appeared to run contrary to prevailing Party principles in its subversion of the status quo was a dangerous endeavour and thus Bakhtin is cautious to promote the idea of the true power of carnival, of the effect of the marginal has on the centre. Anatoly Lunacharsky, the first People's Commissar of Education, had already written on satire as the means temporarily to relieve social frustrations and avert rebellion and revolution, a 'release valve' idea that conformed to socialist ideals. However, Bakhtin tentatively suggests a greater power, one that exists outside of state-sanctioned ideologies, that creates a dialogue between the centre and periphery and exerts its influence through the possibilities created by inversion, parody and laughter. Attempting to contain these ideas within medieval and early modern contexts, he constructs another world, Rabelais's world, where parody is not parody: 'we must stress, however, that the carnival is far distant from the negative and formal parody of modern times'.[34] These qualifying statements may be interpreted as an attempt to appease those whose socialist sensibilities might be offended by the real implications of carnival and its modern contexts – that which even Bakhtin previously states is central to 'human existence' and 'universal'.

These implications revolve around the infringement of boundaries as the chief function of carnival – inversion, subversion and play. As such, the grotesque takes precedence over the normal, fantasy over reality. Hence, hierarchies are upset and the social order is deconstructed and refashioned as a parody of itself. Rabelais, Cervantes and Shakespeare are listed as pre-eminent in their ability to use carnival and the grotesque within their works. For Bakhtin this is a positive, regenerative act, without any sinister or, as defined from the centre, any seriously subversive undertone. He describes the Renaissance grotesque world as free of gloom, something that 'liberates the world from all that is dark and terrifying; it takes away all fears and is therefore completely gay and bright'.[35] However, it is hard to associate such positive, regenerative ideals with the disturbing images Puck describes at the end of *A Midsummer Night's Dream*, or the pathos of Feste's close to *Twelfth Night*. Comic inversion, the grotesque and the carnival spirit dominates these plays, yet their conclusions ambiguously carry bitter reflections that fail to resonate with the upbeat style of parody and play Bakhtin initially describes. There is, however, the idea of something more destructive at work in carnival as Bakhtin references the work of Wolfgang Kayser, the literary critic working in the wake of Sigmund Freud. Kayser likened the carnivalesque spirit to the id, 'an alien, inhuman power, governing the world, men, their life and behaviour', and though Bakhtin disagrees on the more sinister definition of carnival, he does draw attention to laughter, a human quality, as the means to dispel fear and seriousness.[36] In marrying the idea of the destructive id with the grotesque humour of the carnivalesque we begin to understand how the human spirit is prone to parody, to playful subversion and even to the darker side of dissidence that springs from an unconscious internal pressure to rebel against societal structures and strictures.

It is important to clarify that, when the terms 'carnivalesque' and 'carnival' are used within this volume, they must be differentiated from the medieval and early modern ritual of carnival. Carnival generally refers to the annual festivities engaged in throughout medieval and early modern Europe that culminated on Shrove Tuesday. It was an occasion in which the world was inverted for a time – the peasant became a prince; the acolyte a bishop; and the apprentice usurped the master. This well-documented social tradition was adopted for a time in England as the Twelfth Night celebrations – a festival of reversal, of the subversion of the societal status quo, a transitory suspension of societal and social borders in which the lines between rich and poor, male and female, masters and servants became blurred. To date, there is a substantial body of research by scholars who have looked at carnival's historical, political, social and religious ramifications, not to mention the violence that often resulted from the temporary release of social constraints.[37] It is important to note that carnival was allowed, it was a sanctioned festivity that had clear temporal boundaries imposed by the structures of power. Thus, some have argued that carnival was in fact not at all subversive as it was both legitimated and contained by higher authorities. Social dissent may have revealed itself but such temporary displays were ultimately quashed and life would return to its normal routine with its recognisable hierarchies and rules.

There is a difference between the festivities of 'carnival' and the 'carnivalesque'. One was a festival that served as a precursor to Lent; the other is the spirit of resistance, the animating principle behind carnival behaviours. This motivating force, or 'carnival nucleus' as Bakhtin describes it, manifests itself in a constant pushing of boundaries, testing the limits and exploring the liminal spaces between authoritarian structures and their alternatives.[38] This essence of opposition forms the basis of a theoretic principle and is present in Shakespeare's use of liminal settings to subvert and invert autocratic boundaries, and it is to this ethos I refer within this book. The value of this philosophical stimulus in Shakespeare's works cannot be underestimated. As this analysis will explore, there are carnivalesque elements throughout the playwright's considerable oeuvre, the constant presence of which creates dramatic frictions. Furthermore, these elements very often manifest themselves in specific liminal settings that encourage resistance by means of their cultural significances – spaces where power is more easily negotiated or subverted.

For Bakhtin, carnival and the grotesque is a liminal state – 'its images present simultaneously the two poles of becoming: that which is receding and dying, and that which is being born; they show two bodies in one, the budding and the division of the living cell'.[39] From this somewhat cryptic definition we are led to understand that carnival is not static, but is rather mutable, constantly in flux, ambiguous. Shakespeare encapsulated this concept in the conversation between shepherd and clown in his *Winter's Tale*: 'thou met'st with things / dying, I with things newborn' (3.3.117–118). It is impossible to regulate properly or to censure, its nature being slippery and inconstant. In terms of understanding a structured early modern society, the carnival element upsets a circumscribed top-down hierarchical model and rather shows an element of resistance and subversion, even discontent and rebellion emerging from the margins of the community. By way of cultural output, carnival may be seen in the feast of fools where persons and offices of power are lampooned, and in the skimmington ride where patriarchal order is mocked and ridiculed in the streets. Within theatre the carnivalesque would open the way for linguistic ambiguities, parody and allegorical reference to contemporaneous persons or events, inversions of the natural order or parallels that accentuate flaws in the system. This is exactly what Bakhtin is afraid to commit to saying. Rather, he asserts that the Rabelaisian grotesque 'grand style' is understandable only within the contexts of its unique cultural and historical setting, a style that was increasingly misunderstood over the next centuries until Rabelais and his contemporaries were either lost or deemed odd idiosyncrasies.[40] For Bakhtin, early modern satire and parody has a different cultural meaning that would demand a re-examination of the works of Shakespeare and his contemporaries. However, as clichéd as overused idioms such as that found in Ben Jonson's eulogy to Shakespeare may be, the sense of his writings being 'not of an age, but for all time' is largely conveyed in the fact that much of the humour and carnivalesque spirit exists intact and relevant, both in early modern and modern contexts.[41] Clearly, early modern ideas of carnival were not as 'gay and bright' as Bakhtin imagines, but rather an ambivalent, in-between, sweet-and-sour, 'mirth in funeral and with dirge in marriage' (*Hamlet*, 1.2.12), that promoted the stage as a place of ritual subversive inversion. Certainly, when we consider the bleak winter imagery at the close of *Love's Labour's Lost*, where 'greasy Joan doth keel the pot' (5.2.904), or the unbridled threats of a jilted Malvolio in the final scene of *Twelfth Night*, there are distinctly dark and the open-ended conclusions to some of Shakespeare's more awkward comedies.

It is here that we return to Victor Turner's anthropological model of liminality, a perspective he redressed in the 1970s to look at processes that challenged the status quo, applying pressure on a society's prevailing ideological principles. He writes, 'human social groups tend to find their openness to the future in the variety of their metaphors for what may be the good life'.[42] The early modern stage became the platform for such metaphors, the play a 'micro-event' that explored possible futures, challenged orthodoxy and prevailing ideals, and drew on the fears, aspirations and grievances of the larger *communitas*. Turner's formula for understanding such social processes is strangely synonymous with the patterns Bradley and Tillyard identified within Shakespeare's plays:

> In previous studies I have used the notion of a social drama as a device for describing and analysing episodes that manifest social conflict. At its simplest, the drama consists of a four-stage model, proceeding from breach of some social relationship regarded as crucial in the relevant social group, which provides not only its setting but many of its goals, through a phase of rapidly mounting crisis in the direction of the group's major dichotomous cleavage, to the application of legal or ritual means of redress or reconciliation between the conflicting parties which compose the action set. The final stage is either the public and symbolic expression of reconciliation or else of irremediable schism. The first stage is often signalised by the overt, public breach of some norm or rule governing the key relationship, which has been transformed from amity to opposition.[43]

However, Turner's final stage provides an insight into a possible alternative reading of the ambiguous ends to several of Shakespeare's plays. The fluid conclusions to the aforementioned *Dream* and *Twelfth Night* see fools and fairies have the final say, morally detached forest denizens invade the court of humans and a pessimistic, clownish retainer intone 'the rain it raineth everyday'. Bradley discouraged looking for deeper meaning in Shakespeare's indefinite and apparently conflicting inclusions, warning the reader not to 'look for subtlety in the wrong places'.[44] He accounted for such anomalies as Shakespeare's 'want of care', the hurried writing of one who:

> wanted to get his work done and made a slip, or in using an old play adopted hastily something that would not square with his own conception, or even refused to trouble himself with minutiae which we notice only because we study him, but which nobody ever notices in a stage performance.[45]

Yet what Bradley put down to the writer's working to deadlines, and neglectful inability to finish works quickly enough, becomes a symbol of opposition and subversion in Turner's liminal world. As he puts it:

> The besetting quality of human society, seen processually, is the capacity of individuals to stand at times aside from the models, patterns, and paradigms for behaviour and thinking, which as

children they are conditioned into accepting, and, in rare cases, to innovate new patterns themselves or to assent to innovation.[46]

This idea of a culture of change and possible resistance to the status quo became the focus of a new form of literary criticism in the late 1970s that corresponded to international responses to the Vietnam conflict, the rise of feminism and black power movements. Founded on the writing of Raymond Williams who argued that literature and art do not stand apart from social practice, the lens through which Renaissance texts came to be examined became socio-political. No longer were artifice, style and humanist approaches the tools for extracting meaning from Shakespeare. Rather, new historicism and cultural materialism promised to open up a new and rich vein of understanding through considering historical, cultural and political backdrops. Rejecting Tillyardian concepts of a common ideal or 'the collective mind of the people', cultural materialists claimed that 'culture is not by any stretch of the imagination – not even the literary imagination – a unity'.[47]

Cultural and historical inundation began to open the potential for alternate readings, for possible subversion within the plays of early modern England. Instead of the structural, thematic or character-based analysis of the earlier part of the century, now there was a search for patterns of 'consolidation, subversion, and containment'. Jonathan Dollimore explains these terms thus:

> The first refers, typically, to the ideological means whereby a dominant order seeks to perpetuate itself; the second to the subversion of that order, the third to the containment of ostensibly subversive pressures.[48]

This political approach prompted focus on power, the challenge to and eventual containment of threats to the central body politic, and constituted an extension of the challenge to, or complication of, the Marxist cultural model Williams extended in the late 1970s. Williams proposed that there exist certain hegemonies within the superstructure that both reflect *and* challenge dominant ideologies and cannot always be reconciled with a single central worldview. He asserted, 'the complexity of a culture is to be found not only in its variable processes and their social definitions – traditions, institutions and formations – but also in the dynamic interrelations, at every point in the process, of historically varied and variable moments'.[49] This formulation hints at cultures within cultures, each affected not simply by economic factors but by broader historical influences. He goes on to posit the idea of differentiating between dominant, residual and emergent cultural elements. To some extent, early modern poetry, court masques and mayoral processions were part of a residual culture that was 'incorporated as a specific political and cultural function'.[50] Such forms were appropriated to establish the ideologies surrounding sound social frameworks. Yet as these forms became dominant cultural methods they were, through certain ambiguities of language, imagery and performance, open to manipulation or interpretation. It is the concept of emergent cultural hegemonies that encourages the idea of ambiguity, ambivalence, resistance and subversion. As Williams says, 'it is exceptionally difficult to distinguish between those [cultures] which are already elements of some new phase of the dominant culture and those which are substantially alternative or oppositional to it'.[51] For Williams, the emergent culture is a liminal zone, a place where ideas and identities are hazy, and a testing ground for new cultural positionalities and social possibilities. Where this methodology succeeded was in acknowledging drama and literature as the means by which social and political issues are dramatised.

However, the development of new historicism from Williams's concepts ultimately read any challenges to the status quo as contained, quelled and resolved within the text, the central social ideological structure overcoming subversion. As Stephen Greenblatt's landmark essay, 'Invisible Bullets: Renaissance Authority and its Subversion, *Henry IV* and *Henry V*', explained, 'Shakespeare's plays are centrally and repeatedly concerned with the production and containment of subversion and disorder'.[52] Famously concluding with Kafka's 'there is subversion, no end of subversion, only not for us', Greenblatt extinguishes any subversive sparks by the means of central social authority.[53] What he and other new historicists failed to identify was a crucial element to this two-step process – that of adaptation and change. Greenblatt himself acknowledges that there exist 'ironic reservations' at the end of certain plays that do not fit with constrictive ideas of containment.[54] Turner's 'processual structure of social action' is cursorily acknowledged in Greenblatt's words: 'it will eventually become apparent that some sacrifice of fundamental values has taken place'.[55] But there is no recognition that, in containing dissidence, what often occurs is, as Turner described, a shift of the centre, a compromise where the periphery has exerted a subversive challenge that, in spite of its containment, has resulted in what may be a scarcely perceptible move on the part of the established social norm.

New historicist top-down approaches to social structure have limited the development of this theory, with emphasis placed on the central seats of power in a pyramid hierarchy that has not progressed from the Tillyardian model. It is only in recent years that a revised historical-theoretical approach to early modern social structure and the function of theatre as a means of expressing dissent has emerged. Chris Fitter's *Shakespeare and the Politics of Commoners: Digesting the New Social History* (2017) re-evaluates and reframes the politics of Renaissance England. Not wishing to look solely at popular or dominant political and social contexts, as new historicists have before, Fitter privileges what he sees as the 'politics of commoners', a term he defines as the marginal yet populous social groups among which Shakespeare himself had grown up, and which comprised the bulk of the audience for which he wrote. By addressing the 'potentially adversarial politics of the wider commons', Fitter considers the tensions, revolts, rebellions and riots that emerged from within the commonality to challenge central government.[56] What results is a truly original and theoretically challenging set of perspectives that demonstrate Shakespeare's sensitivity to what Fitter terms 'plebeian culture' and situates a critical popular voice in dialogue with, and often in contention with, the ideologies of the state.

Fitter presents this view of early modern politics as far more complex and interactional, the hierarchies of power between government and people more fluid and interdependent than scholars have previously imagined. Where this plays out on Shakespeare's stage is in what Fitter sees as the dramatist's treatment of rumour and his 'recognition that commoners were both politically avid' and in possession of 'formidable agency'.[57] There is quite literal evidence of this in the disturbing presence of Rumour as the Prologue to *2 Henry IV*. Shakespeare's stage directions indicate that the anthropomorphic Rumour enters in a robe 'painted full of tongues' (stage direction), and when the incarnation of gossip opens its mouth it is as 'loud Rumour' (line 2), a democratising and pervasive presence that is not only impossible to contain but is welcomed by the 'discordant wav'ring multitude' (line 19).[58] Understanding the power exerted by public speculation and rumour, Shakespeare presents a very different picture of the passage of power in early modern society. Picking up on this, Fitter argues that the plays in performance represent a carnivalesque 'flanking action' that subverts hierarchic authority. In what is to date one of the more convincing challenges to new historicist theories on containment, Fitter contends that Stephen Greenblatt's model of political subordination under dominant early modern hegemony collapses when one takes into account the multifaceted relationship between crown and commoners. Within these complicated socio-political connections, theatre becomes not only a tool of the state but also a forum for social critique. Thus we might say there is *indeed* subversion; it is constantly present as the flux of power shifts back and forth within early modern plays. These subversive ideologies and challenges to authority often originate from liminal characters and in liminal spaces.

In the last few years literary theorists have revisited the idea of the liminal within literature. Hein Viljoen and Chris N. Van Der Merwe's *Beyond the Threshold: Explorations of Liminality in Literature* (2017) comprises a collection of essays focusing primarily on the literature to have emerged from postcolonial African nations. However, it does highlight the progressive understanding of literary liminality and hybridity. Viljoen describes 'narrative identities' as being interrupted by trauma, causing characters to refashion or reassimilate their identities with the dominant societal structure.[59] Within this process is Homi Bhabha's 'third space of enunciation', a zone that exists between communal and personal identities.[60] This space is the limen – the point between the centre and periphery. It is the place of social ritual, rites of passage, and moral and social responsibilities.

Both Bhabha and Bakhtin look at this in-between space as a home for hybridity that brings two or more languages into dialogue. Bakhtin's 'heteroglossia', or the interference of differing languages, voices and social discourses, is a realm of change, development and pushing or redefining boundaries. In short, it is a place of constant flux and play of power. Parody is one such example of this interface and interplay of consciousness. So too does Bhabha's 'third space' disrupt the narratives of identity – it is within this space that the meaning of culture is contained and *not* within the centre. In the space between translation and negotiation something new emerges, a challenge to the old hierarchies and precedents of power.

According to Viljoen, 'creativity comes from the margin', the border that is double, both boundary and hybrid space.[61] Margins represent both endings and beginnings, demarcating zones of meaning and opening them to ambiguity. The periphery is occupied by marginals, in-betweeners, outsiders, or 'liminars', who sometimes find themselves in such positions from which they become critics of social structure in the name of the *communitas* – the lower level – those who reside just within the border, confined by the strictures of society. These liminars lie halfway between separation and integration, midpoint between one social status and the next, in the unique position of seeing both sides of the border. As such, these individuals or groups, just as with the artist and man in the doorway of Velázquez's *Las Meninas*, are better able to see both margins and centre, in that their identities are more explicitly defined by their relationship to both margins and centre whereas someone operating within the centre alone does not.

Further divisions within society are developed in Michael J. Braddick and John Walter's collection of essays, *Negotiating Power in Early Modern Society: Order, Hierarchy and Subordination in Britain and Ireland* (2001). The idea of a societal hierarchy composed of high and low elements, the privileged and poor, is not a new concept. However, founding their theory on the work of sociologist James C. Scott, they observe that 'behind the public transcript of compliance and deference lies a more knowing and manipulative consciousness'.[62] One of the expressions of this 'manipulative consciousness' is carnival, attesting to the disaffection with order, as well as the need to subvert it. This negotiation takes place between the dominant and subordinate elements of society: 'the relatively weak could claim agency through the manipulation of the texts, languages and performances which were intended to explain, demonstrate and justify the power of their superiors'.[63]

Bakhtinian and new historicist ideas of containment and allowance have only extended our understanding of Shakespearean society, culture and politics so far. If society is fluid, with a constant dialogue and exchange of power between the high and low, the centre and periphery, then change, adaptation, even revolution, is inevitable – containment is only possible through compromise, assimilation or obliteration. The underlying principal motivation behind carnival is experimentation with new possibilities. Braddick and Walter understatedly summarise this idea: 'behavioural conformity, and the use of dominant discourses does not necessarily signal ideological commitment to the stated order of things'.[64] If we are to think of society as being static, the dominant hierarchies of Church, Court and patriarchy unchanging, magnanimously 'allowing' and 'containing' small transgressions, then we fail to acknowledge that they no longer occupy the central position they occupied *prior* to their 'compromise'. Their position, the centre, has been moved, at times imperceptibly, through the power exerted by those at the margins taking advantage of the interstices and loopholes within the structure and shifting it to their advantage.

Carnival might be seen as tentative millenarianism, the belief in an impending transformation, an imagining of other social orders. In a sense, theatre is a permanent state of carnival, a dissident space that enables experimentation with alternative hierarchies of power. So too does theatre, at times, serve as a reminder of the obligation the powerful have to protect the weak. As John Walter observes in his essay 'Public Transcripts, Popular Agency and the Politics of Subsistence in Early Modern England', the balladeer Thomas Deloney's song of 1598 that pointed out the obligations Elizabeth had towards her hungry populace was part of a 'transcript grounding legitimacy in the use of power to protect, *inter alia*, the subsistence of subordinate groups [and] underwrote a political culture which, paradoxically, could be read as emphasising the duties of the powerful and the rights of the weak'.[65] Walter lists grumbling, cursing, appeals, complaints, petitions, coercion and even violence as being in the arsenal of the lowly as the means to facilitate change and put pressure on the central societal structures. He also mentions the 'creative adaptation of plays and their texts' as a platform for protest. This appropriation of 'popular cultural forms' in popular theatre, performed in both the court and the streets, attests to the malleability of the original texts as well as the nuances within them that lent themselves to such interpretations and performances.

The deployment of *Richard II* in the Essex Rebellion is often cited as an example of the potential of theatre for expressing political dissent.[66] This is further illustrated in the events of 1621 when tenants in Westmorland staged a play in front of what was by then a castle fallen into disrepair but nevertheless a symbol of authority in the area, being in the possession of the Parrs (Catherine Parr was the last wife of Henry VIII). Their grumbling turning to cursing over the long-running disputes over borders in the region, their play staged a representation of hell where false landlords had been cast and therein were tormented.[67] Both the setting of the play as well as the material performed constituted an openly subversive political act, a reframing of accepted cultural expression as a means to apply pressure to the centrally held attitudes of society.

Whilst socio-political contexts and ideas of carnival have been clearly explored within early modern texts, an analysis of their association with the liminal has not been sufficiently undertaken. In recent years certain forays have been made into the liminal and its potential within theatre to negotiate and manipulate hierarchies. In 2004 Douglas Bruster and Robert Weimann considered the Elizabethan dramatic Prologue in its positioning 'outside' of the play.

> From this crucial position, prologues were able to function as interactive, liminal, boundary-breaking entities that negotiated charged thresholds between and among, variously, playwrights, actors, characters, audience members, playworlds, and the world outside the playhouse. The conventional nature of early modern prologues facilitated rather and diminished their ability to comment meaningfully on the complex relations of playing and the twin worlds implied by the phrase *theatrum mundi*.[68]

As far as liminal characters go the Prologue is pre-eminently positioned. Playing the role of go-between, the Prologue is positioned as a mediator betwixt audience and players, the reality of the literal world and the constructed reality of the theatre. As such 'both roles involve a paradoxical relationship to power: the usher and prologue found themselves vested with a kind of authority [...] that was neither permanent nor simply given'.[69]

Traversi described theatre as 'requiring the *participation* of the audience as a necessary element'.[70] Part of the unique nature and power of the Prologue's position is to introduce the idea of a mental, ideological or moral contract or transaction – to obtain the complicity of the audience in the events about to unfold. It is not simply an apologetic or obsequious segue that seeks to elicit the approval of the patrons but an invitation to cross the:

> Liminal space between the actual and the potential [...] It was over this threshold that the prologue invited the audience to move, to participate in and reflect upon a set of new, and newly-imagined, possible worlds that had at their base the conjunctures of authority characterising the larger social, cognitive, cartographic, and – politically – international spaces of early modern representation.[71]

Thus a prologue is endowed with a peculiar agency that lends authority to the production, charged with collecting the good will, or at the very least the complicity, of the audience through artful rhetoric. In this case we think of Marlowe's opprobrious and amoral Prologue, Machiavel, in *The Jew of Malta*, or Shakespeare's inspiring and charismatic prologue to *Henry V*. Kenneth Branagh's opening scene for his film adaption of *Henry V* sees Derek Jacobi appear in the in-between space of the set, a unique *mise en scène* that juxtaposes modern lighting and film equipment with the set props we will see used throughout the production. This seemingly innocuous anachronism is a challenge that parallels the prologue's invitation to the audience to suspend scepticism and commit their imaginations. His exit through the huge doors, yet another liminal threshold, invites the audience to enter and hence seal a contract of collusion, to buy into the fantasy, immerse themselves in the between-space of the fictional world and grant the players licence, authority.

Performance theory and liminality

In 1988 Stephen Greenblatt turned his back on dissident readings of Shakespeare's texts. There could be 'no subversion' when historical contexts pointed to the existence of a cultural containment at constant work to control and frame potentially unorthodox literature.[72] Fundamentally, theatre and the arts ultimately served to reinforce the status quo, with power circulated and controlled by immovable social structures. 'Doubleness', ambiguity and suggestively rebellious discourse could be folded into the dominant ethos prescribed by the English Renaissance hegemonies of Church and crown. As I have already posited, such a view does not consider that any move to contain, absorb, reject or accommodate cultural expression necessarily alters the position of the central administration. Internal frictions caused by incongruent social agendas and discordant hegemonies created interstices that could be taken advantage of by those at the periphery of society. These liminal zones became the places where alternative models of social order could be played out, generating subversive imaginings that challenged the overriding ideological and social frameworks.

Historical approaches to early modern theatre as a political tool have been largely limited to textual analysis supplemented by historical contexts. Until Robert Weimann's work on the sociological evolution of medieval and Renaissance theatre, the performative element of early modern theatre was largely overlooked. In 1978 Weimann published *Shakespeare and the Popular Tradition in the Theater*, bringing a refreshingly dense dimension of performance theory to Shakespeare's texts as well as the historical cultural and traditional elements that coalesced into the Elizabethan theatre. Looking at the dynamics of stage arrangements, in particular the textual clues to a play's physical staging and 'spatial differentiation', Weimann posited that the viewer would have to interpret a 'complex and sometimes quite rich and suggestive drama'.[73] Through his look at diverse texts and performances (mummers, morality, mystery and miracle plays), Weimann examined not only the development and translation of characters and tropes from late medieval to early modern theatres, but the way in which staging and the space of the stage could be used to create a performer-audience overlap. The spatial distinction between locus and platea highlights conceivable socio-political tensions apparent beyond the limitations of purely historical textual approaches.

The locus constitutes a 'fixed and focused scenic unit': the courtyard of Macbeth's castle, Henry's camp at Agincourt, Titania's arboreal midsummer fairy-court, the tempest-tossed deck of Alonzo's ship.[74] These loci form the upstage imagined world, a representation the audience is complicit in maintaining as observers or outsiders. However, the platea constitutes a blurring of the distinct worlds of representation and reality, of players and audience. Dissociated from the locus, the platea constitutes a liminal area that allows audience and actor to connect through 'an anachronistic form of semiritual burlesque and self-expression'.[75] The platea is the in-between world of the dramatic aside, the extemporaneous clown, the Chorus and, to some extent, the soliloquy with its confiding and engaging qualities. Richard Gloucester may be one of the most despicable of villains Shakespeare scripted – duplicitous and unscrupulous, he rarely speaks a word of truth within the *locus* of the stage settings. Yet in the downstage platea-like shared space between audience and actor his frequent candid asides constitute a temporary departure from, or suspension of, the locus. This phenomenon is encapsulated in Richard's frank confession at the end of the first scene:

> He cannot live, I hope; and must not die
> Till George be pack'd with post-horse up to heaven.
> I'll in, to urge his hatred more to Clarence,
> With lies well steel'd with weighty arguments;
> And, if I fall not in my deep intent,
> Clarence hath not another day to live:
> Which done, God take King Edward to his mercy,
> And leave the world for me to bustle in!
> For then I'll marry Warwick's youngest daughter.
> What though I kill'd her husband and her father?
> The readiest way to make the wench amends
> Is to become her husband and her father:
> The which will I; not all so much for love
> As for another secret close intent,
> By marrying her which I must reach unto.
> But yet I run before my horse to market:
> Clarence still breathes; Edward still lives and reigns:
> When they are gone, then must I count my gains.
> (*Richard III*, 1.1.145–162)

These words convey the self-conscious tyrant revealing himself in what Weimann has us understand is Shakespeare borrowing directly from the tradition of the medieval Vice in the morality plays.[76] As such, the eponymous despot is frequently positioned as a liminal character in the very play he leads. His deformity is not only physical but is also a deformity of character that lends itself to distorting and collapsing the space he occupies – opening up the stage and the inner workings of his mind to his audience in whom he confides, playfully outlining his plots and even addressing them with a rhetorical 'What though I kill'd her husband and her father?' (line 154).

Richard's Vice-like disclosure of his Machiavellian manoeuvring, covering everything from marriage to murder, is disarmingly divulged to his audience, a technique more often employed by the clown whose origins also lie with the medieval Vice, the sanctioned means to represent transgressive behaviour on the stage. David Wiles notes that, while 'the Vice exists in a moral/philosophical dimension, the clown exists in a social dimension'.[77] This dimension is physically represented by the downstage platea, where the representational quality of theatre is thinned and subverted. Richard, assuming the Vice/Clown position, engages his audience (in)directly, eliciting a response that effectively entices them to side with his morally repugnant yet dramatically seductive plots.

Problematising the Renaissance paradigms of verisimilitude and humanist rhetoric, this liminal space becomes the realm of subversion that questions the validity of that which it seeks to represent. The platea is where the inversions, quips, deliberate ribaldry and the foregrounding of actor over role occurs. For Shakespeare's early modern audiences this potential privileging of performance over text probably posed little problem, yet for those who concentrate on the text alone, the absence of such performativity diminishes the subversive undercurrents. This performative space is aware of its audience and burlesques more serious, elevated themes and ideologies. Whilst theatre itself was not directly in opposition to the orthodoxies of the day, neither was it any longer under the complete control of the traditional hegemonies that dictated the material it presented. Weimann advances the idea that in the late sixteenth century London's new theatrical culture, a culture that had borrowed from, not to mention corrupted, traditional performative tropes, was 'independent of the controlling influence of clergy and conservative guilds'.[78] The potential for ambiguity, not just within the text but also within its performance, meant that even those tasked with duties of censorship would not always identify references that could be politically or socially subversive. Richard Dutton observes that the Master of Revels, despite his duty to suppress seditious material, was actually 'a friend of the actors' and that his ' "allowance" made for a range and complexity of expression on the social, political and even religious issues of the day that was remarkable, given the pressures on all sides to enforce conformity or to repress comment altogether'.[79] Thus, the potential of textual ambiguities combined with the sheer scope of performative prospects opened the way for social commentary in a way that could engage the audience directly.

The use of in-between spaces is never more pronounced than when employed by Choruses and clowns. Prologues and epilogues, introductory and concluding commentaries, are often the remit of either a dedicated Chorus such as in *Henry V* or a comic character such as Puck in *A Midsummer Night's Dream* or Feste in *Twelfth Night*. The space between the locus of the action and the audience is where the imaginary and the real confront each other, and the audience is invited to be complicit in either the preceding or following action. Such a transaction takes place at the opening of *Henry V* with the Chorus, as with Richard, employing the rhetorical question to draw his audience into the play-world. However, the Chorus does more than appeal to his onlookers, he deliberately draws attention to the physical space of the theatre and its limitations:

> Can this cockpit hold
> The vasty fields of France? or may we cram
> Within this wooden O the very casques
> That did affright the air at Agincourt?
>
> (*Henry V*, Prologue. 11–14)

Here, the Globe is portrayed as a changeable, inconstant place that one day will serve as a 'cockpit' for bloody entertainment, and on the next will play host to imaginary worlds. It is a liminal space that subverts even the laws of time, 'turning th'accomplishment of many years into an hourglass' (lines 30–31). Within this space sumptuary laws and rules governing social station are broken, common men play the parts of nobles, and even history is subjected to the imaginative distortions of a writer or actor. Time and space are malleable and the events that unfold in this space are now negotiated by the Chorus, who bargains with the audience to create a pact that tips the balance of power in his favour. Imagination lies at the centre of this contract, as the Chorus attests: 'and let us ciphers to this great account, on your imaginary forces work'. Stephen Orgel insists:

> Imagination here is the real power: to rule, to control and order the world, to change or subdue other men, to create; and the source of power is imagination, the ability to make images, to project the workings of the mind outward in a physical, active form, to actualise ideas, to conceive actions.[80]

As can be seen from the liminal role of the Chorus, these negotiations of power are not necessarily restricted to the locus of textual representation; they also take place in the platea – from whence the authority of the drama can be transacted and established. As Bruster and Weimann posit, from this position, seemingly 'outside the world of the play', *Henry V*'s Prologue serves 'to legitimate the common stage as a public medium of historical understanding regardless of its imperfect iconography', that is, the limitations of physical representation.[81]

The use of such spaces was not always as direct or overt as the Prologue of *Henry V*. There is probably no finer example of liminal chicanery than in Francis Beaumont's *The Knight of the Burning Pestle* (1607) when the Prologue is interrupted by the appearance of two spectators within the audience, one of whom clambers onstage demanding a change of material. Breaking theatrical convention, the audience is suddenly as much a part of the play as they were observers. As the self-conscious meta-drama unfolds, the lines between fantasy and reality, locus and platea, and actor and audience, blur. The sophisticated tussle between Prologue and Actors-cum-Audience deconstructs and subverts the familiar shape of theatre, at the same time satirising the actual audience who become the butt of the joke.

Principles of performance, particularly the theories further developed by Robert Weimann's *Author's Pen and Actor's Voice* (2000) and Keir Elam's *The Semiotics of Theatre and Drama* (1979), on the dialectics of dramatic text and performance text, open the way for viewing Elizabethan and Jacobean theatre as an entity constantly developing, reimagining classical and historical characters and conventions, challenging and subverting even its own structure in such a way that the idea of containing it within socio-political norms, on a textual, let alone performative, level, becomes unrealistic.

Exploring these theories, particularly where they dwell on the liminal, and combining them with Victor Turner's anthropological model of societal structures and liminality proves to be a way to develop new historicist theories regarding the containment of power on the stage. The chapters that follow focus on how Shakespeare's use of particular liminal settings not only plays with social structures but repeatedly subverts them, positing alternative models and promoting dissident narratives.

Notes

1. Hugh Honour and John Fleming, *A World History of Art*, 7th ed. (London: Lawrence King Publishing, 2009), p. 588.
2. Michael Foucault, *The Order of Things* (London: Tavistock, 1970), p. 16.
3. Ibid., pp. 13, 14.
4. Ibid., p. 15.
5. Claude Lévi-Strauss, *Structural Anthropology*, trans. Claire Jacobson (London: Basic Books, 1963), p. 131.
6. Victor Turner, *Dramas, Fields, and Metaphors: Symbolic Action in Human Society* (Ithaca, NY: Cornell University Press, 1974), p. 237.
7. Victor Turner, *The Ritual Process: Structure and Anti-structure* (Chicago: Aldine Publishing Co., 1969), p. 112.
8. Ibid., p. 112.
9. Ibid., p. 128.
10. Ibid., p. 127.
11. For further reading on the debates and developments in this topic see Jeffery S. Siker, *Homosexuality in the Church: Both Sides of the Debate* (Westminster: John Knox Press, 2014).
12. Turner, *Ritual Process*, p. 125.
13. Ibid., p. 178.
14. Victor Turner, *Dramas, Fields, and Metaphors: Symbolic Action in Human Society* (Ithaca, NY: Cornell University Press, 1974), p. 14.
15. Ibid., p. 16.
16. Mikhail Bakhtin, *Rabelais and his World*, trans. Helene Iswolsky (Bloomington: Indiana University Press, 1984), p. 131.
17. A. C. Bradley, *Shakespearean Tragedy: Lectures on Hamlet, Othello, King Lear, Macbeth* (New York: St Martin's Press, 1978), p. 73.
18. Ibid., p. 75.

19 Ibid., p. 33.
20 E. M. W. Tillyard, *The Elizabethan World Picture* (London: Chatto & Windus, 1973), pp. 100, 102.
21 Sir John Davies, *Nosce Teipsum*, in *The Complete Poems of Sir John Davies*, ed. Alexander B. Grossart (London: Chatto & Windus, 1876), p. 9.
22 Tillyard, *Elizabethan World Picture*, p. 96.
23 Sir Thomas Elyot, *The Boke of the Governour*, ed. H. H. S. Croft (London: Kegan Paul, 1883), p. 238. https://archive.org/stream/bokenamedgouerno01elyouoft/bokenamedgouerno01elyouoft_djvu.txt [accessed 6 Dec. 2017].
24 Sarah Thesiger, 'The Orchestra of Sir John Davies and the Image of the Dance', *Journal of the Warburg and Courtauld Institutes*, 36 (1973), 277–304, p. 284.
25 David Underdown, *Revel, Riot and Rebellion: Popular Politics and Culture in England, 1603–1660* (Oxford: Clarendon Press, 1985), p. 9.
26 See Graham Holderness, *Shakespeare's History* (Dublin: Gill & MacMillan, 1985).
27 Derek Traversi, *An Approach to Shakespeare*, vol. 1 (London: Hollis & Carter, 1968), p. 10.
28 Ibid., p. 12.
29 Ibid., p. 16.
30 Derek Traversi, *Shakespeare: 'Richard II' to 'Henry V'* (London: Hollis & Carter, 1979), p. 1.
31 Ibid., p. 2.
32 Bakhtin, *Rabelais and his World*, p. 7.
33 Ibid., p. 9.
34 Ibid., p. 11.
35 Ibid., p. 47.
36 Ibid., p. 49.
37 For a more expansive exploration of carnival see Julius R. Ruff's *Violence in Early Modern Europe* (Cambridge: Cambridge University Press, 2001); François Laroque, *Shakespeare's Festive World: Elizabethan Seasonal Entertainment and the Professional Stage*, trans. Janet Lloyd (Cambridge: Cambridge University Press, 1991); and Michael D. Bristol's *Carnival and Theater: Plebeian Culture and the Structure of Authority in Renaissance England* (New York: Methuen, 1985).
38 Bakhtin, *Rabelais and his World*, p. 7.
39 Ibid., p. 52.

40 Ibid., p. 62.
41 Ben Jonson, 'To the Memory of My Beloved. The Author Mr. William Shakespeare', *The Norton Anthology of Poetry*, 5th ed., ed. Margaret Ferguson, Mary Jo Salter and Jon Stallworthy (New York: W. W. Norton & Co., 2005), p. 343.
42 Turner, *Dramas, Fields, and Metaphors*, p. 14.
43 Ibid., pp. 78, 79.
44 Bradley, *Shakespearean Tragedy*, p. 77.
45 Ibid., p. 78.
46 Turner, *Dramas, Fields, and Metaphors*, p. 15.
47 Jonathan Dollimore and Alan Sinfield (eds), *Political Shakespeare: Essays in Cultural Materialism* (Manchester: Manchester University Press, 1996), p. 6.
48 Ibid., p. 10.
49 Raymond Williams, *Marxism and Literature* (Oxford: Oxford University Press, 1977), p. 121.
50 Ibid., p. 123.
51 Ibid.
52 Stephen Greenblatt, 'Invisible Bullets: Renaissance Authority and its Subversion, *Henry IV* and *Henry V*', in *Political Shakespeare: Essays in Cultural Materialism,* ed. Jonathan Dollimore and Alan Sinfield (Manchester: Manchester University Press, 1996), p. 29.
53 Ibid., p. 45.
54 Ibid., p. 29.
55 Ibid., p. 27.
56 Chris Fitter (ed.), *Shakespeare and the Politics of Commoners: Digesting the New Social History* (Oxford: Oxford University Press, 2017), p. 1.
57 Ibid., p. 8.
58 For all directions and quotations see William Shakespeare, *The Oxford Shakespeare: The Complete Works*, 2nd ed., ed. John Jowett, William Montgomery, Gary Taylor and Stanley Wells (Oxford: Clarendon Press, 2005).
59 Hein Viljoen and Chris N. Van Der Merwe, *Beyond the Threshold: Explorations of Liminality in Literature* (New York: Peter Lang, 2017), p. 10.
60 Homi Bhabha, *The Location of Culture* (Abingdon: Routledge, 2005). p. 55.
61 Viljoen and Van Der Merwe, *Beyond the Threshold*, p. 10.
62 Michael J. Braddick and John Walter (eds), *Negotiating Power in Early Modern Society: Order, Hierarchy and Subordination in Britain and Ireland* (Cambridge: Cambridge University Press, 2001), p. 5.
63 Ibid., p. 5.

64 Ibid., p. 6.
65 Ibid., p. 128.
66 See Paul E. J. Hammer, *The Polarisation of Elizabethan Politics: The Political Career of Robert Devereux, 2nd Earl of Essex, 1585–1597* (Cambridge: Cambridge University Press, 1999), and Alexandra Gajda, *The Earl of Essex and Late Elizabethan Political Culture* (Oxford: Oxford University Press, 2012).
67 Braddick and Walter, *Negotiating Power*, p. 130.
68 Douglas Bruster and Robert Weimann, *Prologues to Shakespeare's Theatre: Performance and Liminality in Early Modern Drama* (Abingdon: Routledge, 2004), p. 2.
69 Ibid., p. 32.
70 Traversi, *An Approach to Shakespeare*, p. 1.
71 Bruster and Weimann, *Prologues to Shakespeare's Theatre*, p. 37.
72 Stephen Greenblatt, *Shakespearean Negotiations* (Oxford: Oxford University Press, 1999), p. 65.
73 Robert Weimann, *Shakespeare and the Popular Tradition in the Theater* (Baltimore: Johns Hopkins University Press, 1978), p. 79.
74 Ibid., p. 79.
75 Ibid., p. 80.
76 Ibid., p. 70.
77 David Wiles, *Shakespeare's Clown: Actor and Text in the Elizabethan Playhouse* (Cambridge: Cambridge University Press, 1987), p. 23.
78 Weimann, *Shakespeare and Popular Tradition*, p. 171.
79 Richard Dutton, *Mastering the Revels: The Regulation and Censorship of English Renaissance Drama* (London: Macmillan, 1991), p. 248.
80 Stephen Orgel, *The Illusion of Power: Political Theater in the English Renaissance* (Berkeley, CA: University of California Press, 1975), p. 47.
81 Bruster and Weimann, *Prologues to Shakespeare's Theatre*, pp. 2, 134.

2

Between ocean and land: 'The guiled shore to a most dangerous sea'

Between 1490 and 1492, whilst Columbus sailed the oceans, the textile merchant and cartographer Martin Behain and the artist George Glockendon constructed from paper, linen and wood what remains the oldest extant terrestrial globe – the *Erdapfel*, or 'Earth Apple'. Today, this three-dimensional representation of the planet, with its vast bodies of water and delineated landmasses, can be seen in Nuremberg's Germanisches Nationalmuseum. By the time it was finished it was already obsolete. At the time that Shakespeare was writing, terrestrial globes and maps were becoming increasingly common as England went through what Chris Barrett describes as a 'cartographic revolution' that saw maps on the backs of playing cards and globes gracing the interiors of wealthier homes.[1] The early modern period saw a sharp rise in popularity for detailed spheres of reference and maps. Early cartographic references that imaginatively noted everything from the boundaries of civilisation, such as *'Hic Sunt Dracones'* on the Hunt–Lenox Globe (1504), gave way to the exhaustive navigational charts of the Age of Exploration, and even to John Leake's *Prospect of London* (1667), the original *London A-Z*.

Yet it was not simply scientific discovery that changed the methods of mapping and mapmaking or that sparked public interest in cartography and possession of artistic representations of the world. It was also humankind's attempt to grasp the enormity of the physical world they inhabited, an insatiable curiosity to note one's own place, position and identity, that called for the proliferation of maps, globes and charts. For centuries the Church had explained the spiritual geographies a human being would pass through beyond their brief presence on the earth, and Dante's *Divine*

Comedy stands foremost in representing such spaces in verse. Yet such models failed to satisfy the inherent need to clarify, qualify and quantify the bounds of corporeal existence. The Renaissance saw a surge in science and art, exploration and conquest, that in many ways sought to chart and cement understanding of the cosmos and its varied topographies and inhabitants.

When the Burbages' theatre in Shoreditch was dismantled in the winter of 1598, its timbers were transported south, across the Thames, and reassembled to make what would become Shakespeare's 'wooden O'. Yet the new edifice did not retain its previous name of The Theatre. We do not know who chose the fresh appellation for the building on the banks at Southwark but the name certainly reflected the developments in the world at large. Where universities and royally commissioned explorers plotted the laws and limits of the physical spheres, and churches and seminaries attempted to ascertain moral regulations for the divine, Shakespeare's theatre, The Globe, became a metaphor and container for the affairs of men, charting both the familiar territories and the frontiers of human behaviour and experience. As the oft-quoted melancholic Jaques expressed, 'all the world's a stage' (*As You Like It*, 2.7.139), and Shakespeare's new theatre was the very place in which to explore the world's allegorical geographies and boundaries. John Gillies notes the roundness of Shakespeare's theatre as a reflection not only of the round Earth, the *theatrum mundi*, but also the celestial spheres of cosmic order.[2]

Shakespeare's concept of the globe/Globe representing the order of things is articulated in the expression of concern by Ulysses over the breakdown of command in the Greek camp that uses the imagery of terrestrial and cosmic spheres to illustrate the consequences of destabilising authority:

> The heavens themselves, the planets and this centre
> Observe degree, priority and place,
> Insisture, course, proportion, season, form,
> Office and custom, in all line of order;
> And therefore is the glorious planet Sol
> In noble eminence enthroned and sphered
> Amidst the other; whose medicinable eye
> Corrects the ill aspects of planets evil,
> And posts, like the commandment of a king,

> Sans cheque to good and bad: but when the planets
> In evil mixture to disorder wander,
> What plagues and what portents! what mutiny!
> What raging of the sea! shaking of earth!
> Commotion in the winds! frights, changes, horrors,
> Divert and crack, rend and deracinate
> The unity and married calm of states
> Quite from their fixure! O, when degree is shaked,
> Which is the ladder to all high designs,
> Then enterprise is sick! How could communities,
> Degrees in schools and brotherhoods in cities,
> Peaceful commerce from dividable shores,
> The primogenitive and due of birth,
> Prerogative of age, crowns, sceptres, laurels,
> But by degree, stand in authentic place?
> Take but degree away, untune that string,
> And, hark, what discord follows! each thing meets
> In mere oppugnancy: the bounded waters
> Should lift their bosoms higher than the shores
> And make a sop of all this solid globe:
> Strength should be lord of imbecility,
> And the rude son should strike his father dead:
> Force should be right; or rather, right and wrong,
> Between whose endless jar justice resides,
> Should lose their names, and so should justice too.
> Then every thing includes itself in power,
> Power into will, will into appetite;
> And appetite, an universal wolf,
> So doubly seconded with will and power,
> Must make perforce an universal prey,
> And last eat up himself.
>
> (*Troilus and Cressida*, 1.3.85–124)

The Ithacan monarch's heliocentric model of governance parallels that of the heavenly spheres. He avers that, should the planets move independently of the direction set by the sun, then chaos would ensue and 'this solid globe' would be swallowed by its oceans. The message is clear: the Grecians must observe the same universal order beheld in the movement of the planets or risk descending into anarchy and witness the ultimate failure of their seven-year siege of Troy. It is of interest that the 'dividable shores' here represent the binaries of order and disorder – the lands symbolic of stability whilst the 'bounded waters' signify the means by which hierarchies of power are overthrown. Hence, the globe, and by extension, The Globe Theatre, becomes a dramatic metaphor for human systems of power and social governance – notably, endangered by the elements at their edges, the liminal threat at their shores, the unruly sea of humanity. Furthermore, as one cannot look at a terrestrial globe's landmasses without considering the oceanic expanses that both divide and connect them, Shakespeare's sea-settings can never be looked at in isolation or disconnection from the land, these two literal and theatrical geographies coexisting and in constant dialogue.

This chapter develops the notion that Shakespeare was repeatedly drawn to the dynamic and dramatic potential of a literary geography that placed the sea and city in close proximity. I argue that when these two physical entities come into contact, both on the page and the stage, they create a unique and liminal space that naturally promotes conflict, ambiguity, rebellion and the opportunity to invert the status quo. Bassanio describes this peculiarly unstable relationship to Portia when he muses that 'ornament is but the guiled shore / To a most dangerous sea' (*The Merchant of Venice*, 3.2.97–98). For the amorous supplicant, exterior embellishment is as deceiving as the shore – there one minute and gone the next at the whim of treacherous tides and the hazardous waves. The shorelines, harbours and islands are not just where the untamed oceans break upon the established and unyielding land, they are also rhetorical images of the social pressure from the margins breaking upon or slowly eroding the centralised and seemingly solid structures that, like the man-made piers below Venice, may eventually lose to the pressures from beneath the surface.

Both as a setting and as a metaphor the oceans offered the playwright a rich semantic and cultural paradigm that spoke to the anxieties over national identity, the uncertainties of the future and the inevitability of change. In this regard, the pelagic expanses form a backdrop for an age of discovery, of conquest in the New World, of establishing colonies and trade routes that furthered England's interests overseas.[3] However, I would argue that Shakespeare's seas also represent a power struggle on a more personal level. Caroline Spurgeon highlighted Shakespearean sea-imagery as synonymous with the 'passions and emotions of men', the untamed, intractable and raging oceans a reflection of the internal conflict that exists when human appetite meets the limits of censure.[4]

In this regard, a close examination of the playwright's dramatic seas yields an abundant insight into the contestation of the pillars of society with its rules, decorum and reasoning. Shakespeare's diverse depictions of the limitless sea as ungovernable, mad, angry, destructive and as catalyst for change are always in relation to the affairs of humankind. This necessitates a consideration of what happens when the sea and all it represents touches the shores of civilisation. The sea and shore dichotomy is explored in one of the playwright's earliest works, *The Comedy of Errors*. Using this play as a case study reveals Shakespeare's fascination with the way in which the status quo could be upset through this exceptional liminal topography.

Shakespeare and the sea of Dee

One does not need to delve too deeply into Shakespeare's works before getting a taste of brine. The seas and oceans make appearances in many of his plays and poems. *A Comedy of Errors, Twelfth Night, Pericles, The Winter's Tale* and *The Tempest* each feature the violence of the stormy seas and its force in the fate of Shakespeare's protagonists, Ariel's 'never-surfeited sea' (3.3.55) the very personification of fate. Hamlet's destiny is altered at sea when he comes in contact with the pirates. *Timon of Athens* concludes with the eponymous hero's retreat to the shore of the sea, as far as is humanly possible to live away from the society he has come to shun. *The Merchant of Venice* and *Othello*'s island settings are reflected in the language of the text, with the sea as the source of some of Shakespeare's more esoteric language, Othello's 'bloody thoughts' likened to the violent sea (*Othello*, 3.3.460), and Antonio's troubled mind 'tossing on the ocean' (*The Merchant of Venice*, 1.1.8). In fact, maritime metaphors and motifs salt not just these but many more of his plays, revealing the writer's deep attraction to all things oceanic. A. F. Falconer's compendium, *Shakespeare and the Sea* (1964), contains an extensive list of nautical references, though his arguments also attempt to convince the reader that Shakespeare had been a mariner first and writer second, the 'lost years' spent on the waves.

In more recent times Shakespeare's fascination with the sea has been the focus of literary theorists such as Steve Mentz and Dan Brayton. *At The Bottom of Shakespeare's Ocean* (2009) sees Mentz push the ideas of 'new thalassalogy', or a historiographic approach to Shakespeare's sea-settings. Using Renaissance concepts and beliefs of the sea and oceanic trade and travel, Mentz looks forward to more contemporary literature and ecological thought concerning the planet's watery expanses. In a similar vein, Dan Brayton's *Shakespeare's Ocean: An Ecocritical Exploration* (2012) seeks to rectify modern critical bias towards the terrestrial over the aqueous and employs examples throughout Shakespeare's plays to push modern environmental agendas. However, despite Brayton and Mentz's imaginative readings of the plays, and at times insightful historical contextualisation, the significance of the sea in its political, social and performative elements is often overlooked. Since the publication of these two maritime texts there has been an increased interest in how contemporaneous attitudes shaped dramatic geographies.[5] Laurence Publicover acknowledges the need to look not only at the 'locational complexities' of Shakespeare's settings but the 'cultural circumstances' that moulded them.[6] Thus, it is important to establish what the sea meant to Shakespeare and his audiences, and consideration of the visual representations of sea and shore in the maps and terrestrial globes of the day provides a vision of these spaces that the playwright harnessed within his plays.

In 1577, just eleven years before the Spanish Armada sailed through the Channel, the mathematician, cartographer and astronomer John Dee wrote his *General and Rare Memorials Pertayning to the Perfect Arte of Navigation*, a treatise on the advantages of expanding England's empire through the development of an Imperial Navy. The title page is replete with symbolic inference, Elizabeth at the helm of a ship under the rays of divine blessing depicted by the Hebrew tetragrammaton (YHWH or YAHWEH) at the top right corner (Figure 2.1). Following the archangel Michael, who bears a sword and a shield emblazoned with St George's cross, the monarch's ship of state glides with full sails on serene seas towards a benighted foreign fleet. Auspiciously, the figure of *Occasio* (Opportunity), with her single lock of hair

Figure 2.1 Title page from John Dee's *The General and Rare Memorials pertayning to the Perfect Arte of Navigation* (1577).

on an otherwise bald head, beckons Elizabeth, extending a laurel wreath that promises success in her imperial conquest.[7] Kneeling on the shore is Britannia, whom Leslie B. Cormack describes as 'beholden to this monarch, rather than in any way defining her', looking to Elizabeth as saviour and agent for expansion.[8]

The imaginative title page to Dee's *General and Rare Memorials* provides us with a glimpse of how some in early modern England may have viewed the sea, as the source of potential power and colonial expansion. During the latter part of the sixteenth century Richard Hakylut's *Divers Voyages Touching the Discoverie* of America (1582) and *The Principall Navigations, Voiages, Traffiques and Discoueries of the English Nation* (1589) endorsed the annexation of North America as political and economic acumen. Walter Raleigh's *The discovery of the large, rich, and beautiful Empire of Guiana, with a relation of the great and golden city of Manoa (which the Spaniards call El Dorado)* (1596), spoke of the incomparable wealth free to those who would brave the seas – a tempting prospect for a nation competing with the rapidly expanding affluence and influence of the Spanish Empire.[9] Shakespeare certainly was aware of such views as *The Tempest* explores the ideology of colonisation.[10] Indeed, the similarities between Prospero and John Dee, who was both bibliophile and occultist, have led some to identify the latter as an inspiration for the Shakespearean character.[11] The dynamics of territorial power are laid open by the playwright as both the conquerors and the conquered, the colonisers and the dispossessed, engage in a tug-of-war over a tiny island. The seas opening the way to wealth through trade is the backdrop to *The Merchant of Venice*, where the fates of Antonio's small fleet of merchant vessels provide the groundwork for the dramatic events that result from their loss.

Shakespeare also touches on the opportunities the seas open to would-be colonisers in *Pericles*. Mentz boldly proclaims, 'Pericles is a coloniser', the fishing metaphors within the text a 'way to extract value from the water' and Pentapolis a 'new model for deriving sustenance from the sea'.[12] Further to this, Stuart Elden observes that in *Pericles* the description of the fishermen as having a 'watery empire' (2.1.49) suggests the sea is more than a means of travel but 'a place to be controlled in its own right'.[13] What can be ascertained from this play as well as contemporaneous texts is that the sea offered the island nation of England an opportunity to expand its empire in terms of political and economic sway in a time when the scientific development of navigational and cartographic techniques and the discovery of new lands had created frontiers over which European kingdoms sought to exert their control.

It is noteworthy that in Dee's illustration, semi-obscured by the right margin, sits a skull. This seemingly innocuous *memento mori* nevertheless serves as an ominous reminder of the consequence of any human endeavour, and its placement on such a grand vision of England's future suggests that, even with the backing of God and the welcoming arms of Fortune, conquest inevitably results in human sacrifice. Dee's prophecy of England's naval successes cannot eliminate the realities associated with sea-going endeavours – the unruly waters, temperamental currents, wild weather, uncharted reefs and the rigours of warfare that in only a few short years would see the wreck of no fewer than thirty vessels of the Spanish Armada.

This is the sea that Shakespeare describes in his plays, the oceanic expanses translating to spaces of uncontrollable elements and capricious fates. The 'angered ocean' (*Antony and Cleopatra*, 2.6.21) is a fearful place with the potential to overthrow the will of great men. As the soldier warns Antony, 'do not fight by sea; / Trust not to rotten planks' (3.7.61, 62), and this theme of trusting the unknown recurs throughout the plays as a means of expediting conflict and change. Antonio declares that 'all my fortunes are at sea' (*Merchant of Venice*, 1.1.177), the mercurial fortune and fate of the waters relied on to bring his literal fortune home. As Salarino observes, 'the pageants of the sea – / Do overpeer the petty traffickers / That curtsy to them' (1.1.11–13). It is the sea's fellowship with a capricious fate that Shakespeare draws on more than any of its other emblematic significances. The peace between France and England in *1 Henry VI* rests on both the safe passage of Henry's gift and the arrival of Princess Margaret; and the king somewhat fatalistically remarks, 'Commit them to the fortune of the sea' (*1 Henry VI*, 5.1.50). Seeming to subscribe to this curious philosophy, Margaret later remarks that 'the pretty-vaulting sea refused to drown me' (*2 Henry VI*, 3.2.94). Ariel instructs the shipwrecked nobility of *The Tempest* that Destiny's instrument is 'the never-surfeited sea' (3.3.55), and that the elemental spirits are 'ministers of fate' (line 61). What is interesting in this exchange is that the powers of humans are subjected to and shaped by higher determinations, the 'incensed seas and shores' (line 74) subverting the position and purposes even of kings – Alonso's authority trumped by the forces of nature and the vagaries of fortune. It is a sentiment repeated in Shakespeare's sixty-fourth sonnet where the poet declares, 'I have seen the hungry ocean gain / Advantage on the kingdom of the shore' (lines 5, 6), the inevitability of changing fortunes and time laying waste to the seemingly impermeable. This anthropomorphic sea acts as the catalyst for change in the fortunes of many of Shakespeare's protagonists, their destinies altered by unruly and unmanageable fates.

The sea also acts as a symbol, a metaphoric signpost, for the state of mind of an individual or the situation they find themself in. Lear is described by Cordelia as 'mad as the vexed sea' (*King Lear*, 4.3.2), and Gertrude laments Hamlet's behaviour as 'mad as the sea and wind when both contend / Which is the mightier' (*Hamlet*, 4.6.6, 7). The benighted Prince of Denmark likens his predicament to an unforgiving and uncontrollable 'sea of troubles' (3.1.61), man's 'enterprises of great pith and moment' (line 88) subject to 'currents turning awry' (line 89). Both Falstaff and Henry play with oceanic imagery in *1 Henry IV*, the fat knight proposing they form a merry band of shady gentlemen who are 'governed, as the sea is, by our noble and chaste mistress the moon' (1.2.28, 29), to which the prince replies that such men who 'ebb and flow like the sea' (lines 31,32) inevitably 'flow' to an unsavoury end at 'the ridge of the gallows' (line 38). Here Shakespeare introduces the sea as a reflection of the side of humanity that rebels against order and the pillars of society. Othello describes these impulses as 'like to the Pontic sea, / Whose icy current and compulsive course' (*Othello*, 3.3.456, 457) mirror his own 'bloody thoughts' (line 460).[14] Unsurprisingly, anger too is a common Shakespearean association with the sea, Pericles proclaiming, 'I could rage and roar / As doth the sea' (*Pericles*, 3.3.10, 11). So too are the infidelities of man sung by Balthazar in *Much Ado About Nothing*, 'Sigh no more, ladies, sigh no more, / Men were deceivers ever, / One foot in sea and one on shore, / To one thing constant never' (2.3.61–64). As such the sea is not simply a force of nature but, as Henry VIII expresses it, 'the wild sea of my conscience' (*Henry VIII*, 2.4.197) represents the force and power of (human) nature. Interiority and concepts of the self are closely affiliated with identity, both individual and social. As such, a particular web of associations connects the sea to ideas of 'The Other'.

The other: issues of identity

It is significant that in each of Shakespeare's plays set in island locations, such as Cyprus in *Othello*, Venice in *The Merchant of Venice* and the nameless and ambiguous island in *The Tempest*, the playwright foregrounds yet another culturally important issue – that of the 'other'.[15] John of Gaunt may have described England as 'This precious stone set in the silver sea / Which serves it in the office of a wall / Or as a moat defensive to a house / Against the envy of less happier lands' (*Richard II*, 2.1.46–49), yet as the voyages of discovery became more frequent, the travelogues of explorers and navigators more accessible, England's watery defences could not withhold the influx of more exotic materials and foodstuffs. The *Oxford English Dictionary* lists one of the earliest occurrences of 'potato' as coming from Sir John Hawkins's notes on his voyage to Florida in 1565, where he describes it as an edible root that surpasses the parsnip and carrot. Yet by the turn of the century Falstaff loudly declares, 'let the sky rain potatoes' (*The Merry Wives of Windsor*, 5.5.18, 19). Around the same time that the humble potato breached England's 'moat defensive', tobacco leaf made the trip across the Atlantic. The remains of 400-year-old clay pipes dug up from Shakespeare's garden suggest that even the playwright smoked the foreign leaf.[16]

The sea did not just bring exotic foods and plant-based stimulants to England's shores; it also brought tales of strange foreign peoples and customs. Shakespeare's Caliban stands foremost in this representation of the 'other', what Alden T. Vaughan and Virginia Mason Vaughan describe as 'an opposing force [...] onto whom the dominant culture projects its fears of disorder' and 'a powerful symbol of resistance and transgression'.[17] The popular medieval work *The Travels of Sir John Mandeville* (c.1357) provided fantastical descriptions of a world beyond the quotidian European experience, including mythical beasts and men whose heads grew from their chests. Othello's exploits and travails include descriptions lifted directly from *Mandeville*: 'And of the Cannibals that each other eat, / The Anthropophagi and men whose heads / Do grow beneath their shoulders' (*Othello*, 1.3.142–144). Ironically, it is the Moorish general himself who becomes the victim of his 'otherness', his racial origin and appearance singling him out as barbaric.[18] Margo Hendricks notes that the Renaissance understanding and depiction of race

> is envisioned as something fundamental, something immutable, knowable and recognizable, yet it can only be 'seen' when its boundaries are violated, and thus race is also, paradoxically, mysterious, illusory and mutable. As a classificatory category the

Renaissance concept of race, it turns out, was rife with fault-lines, which human beings proved quite adept at exploiting.[19]

Shakespeare harnesses this paradoxical 'boundary' of otherness in *Othello*, not just as a means to draw attention to preconceptions of racial difference, but also to focus on the other side of this conceptual coin – that of national identity. Bruce Lenman notes that, although by the end of Elizabeth's reign there was still 'no significant overseas imperial development', what did exist was a 'violent conflict of different English identities'.[20] This theory of multiple national characteristics and values is played out on Shakespeare's stage. The figures of Shylock, Othello and Caliban are not simply representations of repellent otherness, fuel for xenophobia. Rather, Shakespeare's centring of these characters, often with conflicting depictions, complicates any hard-and-fast social protocols around the way foreigners should be viewed. Alan Sinfield warns against more modern, overtly sympathetic readings of Shakespeare's foreigners, stating, 'this need not mean that recognition of common humanity is always a false move, but that it affords no advantage where it is only a token'.[21] However, what Shakespeare does in foregrounding 'the other' is not simply to reinforce entrenched imperialist ideals but instead to sow the seeds of doubt – not only that the foreigner on the shore may have more in common with the European, but that the European, and by extension the Englishman, may not be the shining example of Christian charity, moral purity and intellectual superiority. Effectively, and to reiterate Lenman's assertion, Shakespeare highlights the 'conflict of different English identities', and these liminal island settings are a means to throw together disparate cultures and peoples in an attempt not only to contrast but expose flaws and subvert the orthodox superlatives associated with concrete identity.

The island setting of *The Tempest* offers a glimpse of a problematised 'other' in the shape of its indigenous occupant. Caliban's humanity, or at least physical human shape and ability to speak, is buried beneath Prospero's scorn for the creature he sees as fit only for servitude: 'He does make our fire, / Fetch our wood, and serves in offices / That profit us' (1.2.311–313). Alden and Virginia Vaughan note that '"Monster" is Caliban's most frequent sobriquet [...] [and] appears in the text some forty times, usually with the pejorative adjective: "shallow," "weak," "credulous," "most perfidious and drunken," "puppy-headed," "scurvy," "abominable," "ridiculous," "howling," "ignorant," and "lost." '[22] This descriptive grotesquery would seem to reinforce imperialist ideologies of superiority over the Africans or Native Americans described in the accounts of contemporaneous voyages.[23] Furthermore, as Paul Brown argues, the binaries of Miranda and Caliban, virgin and rapist, cultured maid and covetous savage, seek to legitimise the colonial appropriation of power.[24] Yet, as Vaughan and Vaughan observe, there is an ambiguity about Shakespeare's depiction of the island inhabitant: 'Caliban is human but has beastly qualities; he is savage but potentially redeemable, he resists European efforts at education and "civilitie" but – despite Prospero's insistence that nurture will never stick to him – he learns a European language and is remarkably articulate in it'.[25] The dispossessed and abused native is more victim than villain, engaged in a power struggle over control of his island that pits him against overwhelming numbers and bewildering social etiquettes. Yet by the play's close, the Europeans leave the island to Caliban who admits he will be 'wise hereafter' (5.1.295), an equivocal comment that suggests either the native will emulate the civility of the invaders or be wary of any who would seek to take his homeland from him again. As Brown articulates, *The Tempest* is 'no all-embracing triumph for colonialism', rather, it is a text of 'contradiction and disruption', the island a site of 'radical ambivalence'.[26] I would argue that identity, that of the so-called civilised European, and by extension the Englishman, is subverted by depictions of incivility, cruelty and slavery. As such, the setting of the island surrounded by its tempestuous waters constitutes a container in which sits a miniaturisation of structured society, its elements easily identified owing to its few occupants.

Othello presents yet another indefinite view of otherness in its titular hero and island setting divided by war. Both Moor and Christian, Othello cannot be pigeon-holed as a Muslim agent of Satan, as John Fox proclaims all Turks to be in his *Second Volume of the Ecclesiastical History Containing the Acts and Monuments of Martyrs* (1563).[27] Ironically, Othello is the defender of a Christian state against the threat of the Turkish Empire. Ania Loomba notes that early modern accounts of the East depict Turks as jealous and unnaturally sensuous.[28] Yet Othello is far from this stereotype, his own servant admitting that 'The Moor – howbe't that I endure him not – / Is of a constant, loving, noble nature' (2.1.287–288). Rather than some sort of racially inherent jealousy, it is the jealousy and discrimination of the Venetians that eventually drives a wedge between Othello and Desdemona. Despite the Moorish general's false modesty in declaring 'rude I am in my speech' (1.3.81), his eloquence in self-expression and reasoning shows him to be an artful rhetorician. Coupled with his feats of arms, his social graces and his articulate manner, Othello has earned the respect of the Venetian Duke and Brabanzio, the father of Desdemona, who both 'loved' and 'oft invited' the Moor to his house. It is only when the subject of miscegenation arises that underlying prejudices emerge. After the clandestine marriage of Othello and Desdemona, Iago baits Brabanzio with animalistic analogies such as 'an old black ram is tupping your white ewe' (1.1.88, 89) and 'you'll have your daughter covered with a Barbary horse, you'll have nephews neigh to you, you'll have coursers for cousins and jennets for germans' (lines 113–115). The gross racial slurs that liken Brabanzio's new in-laws to farm animals, his daughter effectively mounted by a horse, invoke the fear that comes with a threat to identity. The point that Iago makes is not simply a means to goad Brabanzio but goes straight to the root of the issue – what happens to identity when the culturally and racially dissimilar mix? What does the world look like when apparently disparate elements combine? Black and white, human and animal, Christian and Muslim, East and West – Iago implies that the synthesis of two cultural incongruences produces nothing less than an aberration. Magnifying his otherness is Othello's station as Governor of Cyprus, a role that would see Europeans as inferior in position. E. A. J. Honigmann wryly observes, 'that a black man lords it over Europeans, let alone marries an upper-class white wife, upsets all contemporary notions of decorum'.[29] Yet despite Honigmann's acknowledgement that Shakespeare seems to employ the Moor as a means to challenge racial stereotypes he does not link this to the concept of identity.

Since the emergence of critical race studies at the turn of the twenty-first century, *Othello*, both in terms of historical context and performance, has witnessed something of a radical revision. In 2016, Honigmann's edition of The Arden Shakespeare's *Othello* was reissued with an introduction by Ayanna Thompson that reflected these new approaches. Ben Okri's *A Way of Being Free* (1997) presents *Othello* as a white construction that centres on Black masculinity, whilst Dympna Callaghan also asserts that within the play 'there are indeed no authentic "others" – raced or gendered – of any kind, only their representations'.[30] Whilst this volume does not develop these lines of argument, it does engage with the depiction of otherness, 'authentic' or otherwise. Lisa Hopkins pointedly connects otherness and identity with *Othello*'s liminal island geographies when she notes:

> In this overall context of uncertainty about boundaries both physical and political, the city of Venice, with its many constituent islands, and the war-torn island of Cyprus provide a diptych which offers a richly suitable setting for a play which images both the insularity and the fluidity of human identity, and which suggests, above all, that identity is collectively rather than individually constituted, and that it is subject to forces which may change and shape it in unpredictable and unwelcome ways which are themselves conditioned by and dependent on both time and place.[31]

The next logical step in confronting ideas of what constitutes the other in terms of ethnic typecasting is for Shakespeare's contemporary audience to re-evaluate itself in relation to previously held concepts. As Stephen Greenblatt observes, the literary works appearing at the time Shakespeare wrote point to what Greenblatt describes as 'anxious awareness' resulting from 'the great "unmooring" that men were experiencing, their sense that fixed positions had somehow become unstuck'.[32] Indeed, Shakespeare 'Unmoors' his Moor by destabilising formerly entrenched ideas of what constitutes the 'other' and in doing so fuels anxieties over identity.

Shylock is yet another figure that Shakespeare uses to bring the issue of identity to the fore. Whilst there is a tendency to read Shylock in a more compassionate, post-Holocaust light, he is ultimately a Renaissance caricature of the Jew. John Drakakis firmly asserts *Merchant* to be a 'racist text', despite his acknowledgement that Shakespeare appears to give Shylock 'a more perplexing gloss' than ethnic difference alone.[33] The seemingly humanised Shylock remonstrates, 'Hath not a Jew hands, organs, dimensions, senses, affections, passions? Fed with the same food, hurt with the same weapons, subject to the same diseases, healed by the same means, warmed and cooled by the same winter and summer, as a Christian is? If you prick us, do we not bleed?' (3.1.53–58). Yet, ultimately, despite physical and emotional commonalities, Shylock conforms to the distorted archetype of Jewishness and is punished for it.[34] Terry Eagleton notes that the play presents a contrast of archaic Old Testament juridical observance with New Testament ideals of love, forgiveness and tolerance.[35] However, Drakakis goes on to describe *Merchant* as a 'challenge to identity politics' that 'confront[s] western Christian culture with its own discomforting limitations'.[36] Furthermore, John Gillies observes that, within the diverse island community, disparity between Christian and Jew is 'undercut by the fact that all the Venetian characters have recourse to a common commercial vocabulary'.[37] These factors coalesce within the play to complicate ideas of otherness. There may not have been a recognised, open Jewish community in England when Shakespeare wrote *Merchant*, but there *was* a religiously fractured society. Catholic recusants and radical Puritans represented the extremes of a number of faiths that had either endured or resulted from violent changes all of which took place within living memory. The scene-dominating Shylock served as a reminder of the ongoing crisis of identity that England was experiencing as a result of entrenched religious difference.

What each of these plays does in using the setting of sea and shore, the liminal edge of worlds where cultures and customs, experience and ideology, collide, is to play with, even destabilise, concepts of identity. Whether through challenging predominant preconceptions of the foreigner, or using the anxieties and prejudices synonymous with religious and racial distinction to expose and satirise issues closer to home, Shakespeare's island-plays centralise pertinent contemporary conflicts of identity. Gillies describes this particular phenomenon as 'poetic geography', that is, 'any geography which differentiates between an "us" and a "them"'.[38] Yet Shakespeare goes further than simply differentiating between disparate cultures and systems of belief; his poetic island geographies destabilise the very idea of 'us', by (con)fusing the concept of 'them'. This returns us to the anthropological dilemmas Victor W. Turner expressed in *The Ritual Process: Structure and Anti-Structure* (1969) that sought to ascertain the societal processes 'centralism and decentralization', 'idea and reality'.[39] The challenge to centralised ideology through the exposition of what may at times amount to uncomfortable realities ultimately exerts pressure and decentralises previously held notions. In reference to Shakespeare's oceanic settings and the ideology of national identity, depictions of otherness have the potential to decentre previously distinct concepts. As Gillies notes,

> Unlike the ruler, who characteristically controls the centre, the voyager controls the boundaries. It is the voyager's function to manage the exotic: which may mean either bringing it safely within the pale or excluding it entirely. [...] Shakespeare's voyagers tend to form deeply compromising relationships with the exotic, to the point where the two types sometimes merge in the same character.[40]

However, the liminal seashore does not simply serve to deconstruct identity, but rather is employed to challenge the very structures of authority, something Shakespeare does in one of his earliest plays.

Komisarjevsky's bollards: the boundaries of conflict

Theodore Komisarjevsky's 1938 production of *The Comedy of Errors* in Stratford-upon-Avon has been cited as the last century's most famous production of the play in terms of imagination, staging and costume.[41] Gaudy get-up that fused modern and historical fashions, and a 'toytown set', created a surreal and carnivalesque atmosphere that brought new interest to the play.[42] What is perhaps overlooked in this staging is the deliberate division of upstage and downstage by what appear to be three quayside bollards connected by a chain. The upstage houses representing the city of Ephesus are conspicuously foregrounded by three white marine mooring posts that delineate the limits of the city from the sea (Figure 2.2). Whilst these stage-dressings may initially seem innocuous inclusions in a play set entirely on land they create a liminal space, a threshold that serves not only as a reminder of the historical backdrop that has led to the play's events, but also as a metaphor for the themes and conflicts addressed in Shakespeare's shortest play.

This foregrounding of the sea is significant in *Errors* as it is in many ways the source of the friction, confusion and instability experienced by the play's cast. Ralph Berry observes 'that sense of the sea – waiting, pulling, imperious – is strong in *The Comedy of Errors* [...] a reminder, in its ebb and flow, of the mysterious forces that govern the individual'.[43] Ephesus may be the setting of the play but the plot begins at sea with the separation of both sets of twins and

Figure 2.2 'The Abbess Appears' Act 5, Scene 1 in Theodore Komisarjevsky's 1938 production of *The Comedy of Errors* in Stratford-upon-Avon.

the division of a family, all caused by the chaos of the deep. This is underscored in the tragic tale Egeon tells of his family's sundering: 'A league from Epidamnum had we sail'd, / Before the always wind-obeying deep / Gave any tragic instance of our harm' (1.1.62–64). Here the sea is given an identity, a mercurial and volatile entity that answers to the elements and is impervious to the will of human beings. Dan Brayton observes that the sea is the source of all-encompassing 'aesthetic possibilities', a metaphor that embodies the trials and tribulations of human existence, and 'a seemingly measureless and ungovernable entity which, like the imagination and the self, contains hidden depths'.[44] Egeon, his name itself a corruption of the Aegean on which his family were sundered, comes from the sea, driven not by mercantile enterprise, secular undertaking or civic duty, but by deeper, inner urgings to unite his household. As Egeon's account begins he declares that 'the world may witness that my end was wrought by nature, not by vile offence' (1.1.33, 34). The aged merchant does not qualify what this nature is – his account includes both the caprices of the force and fury of the natural elements as well as his inward 'natural' desire to find his lost sons.

As previously discussed, Shakespeare's sea is often the symbol of, or precursor to, change and social reorganisation. The tension and action of *Twelfth Night* originates in the sea, a shipwreck that puts three souls and those whose lives they touch on very different courses. For the twins, Viola and Sebastian, it is the catalyst for separation, chaos and the removal of personal security, prompting a radical reimagining and remodelling of selfhood on the part of Viola. For Antonio, the sea reverses his social situation, reducing him from captain to fugitive. Sebastian lashes himself to a mast, submitting himself to the vicissitudes and caprices of a force of nature that does not bow to the will of men. Yet this force is not portrayed as sinister; rather, Sebastian is described as last being seen holding 'acquaintance with the waves' (1.2.16), almost tender imagery. Much of this imagery is borrowed from *Errors*, including Egeon and Emilia's fastening themselves and their family to a mast, the two sets of twins' confusion of identity, and the inversion of fortune for Egeon who goes from merchant to criminal. Even Egeon refuses to attribute his family's misadventures to the sea, rather blaming 'fortune' (1.1.105). Mentz notes the power of the sea 'as both a nearly inconceivable reality and a mind-twisting force for change and instability'.[45] Clarence's dream in *Richard III* is one of prolonged drowning in 'the tumbling billows of the main' (1.4.20), a vision that precedes the radical change in fortunes of the Duke who is equally unable to stave off his very real and precipitate death. In the case of Egeon, this 'mind-twisting force' has caused him to devalue his life and break, like the waves of the Aegean, on the shores, like so much detritus that is only a fragment of his Syracusan heritage and values, a man tossed about and at the mercy of elemental and primal forces.

Yet at the edge of the sea Egeon is confronted with a different authority, the city-state of Ephesus – a jurisdiction whose man-made laws push against the nature of Egeon's mission. Once again we are presented with terms of jurisdiction, influence and control – in this case it is not the forces of nature that dictate the movement and fates of men but civic powers. Dispensing with a prologue, Shakespeare tasks Duke Solinus with setting the geographical and political backdrop of the play.

> Merchant of Syracuse, plead no more;
> I am not partial to infringe our laws:
> The enmity and discord which of late

> Sprung from the rancorous outrage of your duke
> To merchants, our well-dealing countrymen,
> Who wanting guilders to redeem their lives
> Have seal'd his rigorous statutes with their bloods,
> Excludes all pity from our threatening looks.
> For, since the mortal and intestine jars
> 'Twixt thy seditious countrymen and us,
> It hath in solemn synods been decreed
> Both by the Syracusans and ourselves,
> To admit no traffic to our adverse towns Nay, more,
> If any born at Ephesus be seen
> At any Syracusan marts and fairs;
> Again: if any Syracusan born
> Come to the bay of Ephesus, he dies,
> His goods confiscate to the duke's dispose,
> Unless a thousand marks be levied,
> To quit the penalty and to ransom him.
>
> (1.1.3–22)

In just twenty lines we are made aware of the enmity the two Greek states bear each other. It is an antagonism born, not from differences in ideology, religious beliefs or customs, but from trade disputes that have escalated to result not only in an embargo but also in the death penalty. The Syracusan Egeon, doubly damned by his prior occupation as merchant as well as his city of origin, has crossed both mercantile and geographic boundaries. Here, on the Ephesian shores of the Aegean, the influence of distant Syracuse expires. Interestingly, these borders are, as Julie Sanders observes, only 'notionally fixed', adding that shorelines are 'permanently evolving boundaries, fluid frontiers, a contact zone between land and water that raises a pertinent set of issues relating to change, mutability and drift'.[46] When Shakespeare later writes of 'the varying shore o' the world' (*Antony and Cleopatra*, 4.16.11), he does so not just in terms of tidal movement but also the shifting states of humankind. In *Errors*, the political and economic conflict between the two cities is a recent phenomenon, yet the shoreline represents not only the Ephesian social identity, but its central authority over the lives of any who venture within its bounds – one that is set apart from their sister-state in the west with whom it was once part of a whole. The sea represents these shifts, and Egeon's appearance is a symbol of its presence, both at the beginning and conclusion of the play, marking the potential for change in the relationship between these two cities.

What is of particular note in the Duke's decree is his inclusion of the Bay of Ephesus within the physical limits or jurisdictions of the city, a body of water that has no natural confine or clearly delineated margin other than the land it touches. In what may at first appear to be a somewhat ridiculous attempt to control the uncontrollable, the Ephesian law of the *land* is imposed on the *sea*. Yet this idea of laying claim to both dominion and sovereignty over coastal waters was becoming more of a reality by the late sixteenth and early seventeenth centuries. As England began to establish itself not only as a maritime power but also in terms of empire, there was an increasing need to distinguish dominions beyond the land's edge that might be contested by rival commercial powers, namely the Dutch, French and Spanish. As John Dee's map demonstrates, there were those within the Elizabethan court who advocated naval domination of the waters beyond England's immediate shores. Bradin Cormack notes that the cartographic documentation of the early years of James's reign often displays the lines of the compass rose extending to the imagined limens of dominion and notes that such a concept manifests itself in many of Shakespeare's works.[47] This topographic appropriation of the seas, though impossible at the time to police, let alone enforce, points to the inherently human desire to control and contain the uncontainable – to impose the will of man over the unknown or unknowable. As Cormack observes, 'to move out beyond national borders was necessarily to move [...] into alternative jurisdictions, or into spaces like the sea in which direct containment was *de facto* impossible'.[48]

However, the implication of the state stretching its authority to manage the unmanageable, to enclose the limens of nature within its power, goes beyond mere geographic conceits. As with the intrinsic inference in Egeon's name, Solinus represents the divinely ordered, heliocentric world, with its clearly defined hierarchies, laws, rights and responsibilities. Egeon's opening speech prefigures the Duke's assertion when he explains:

> At length the sun, gazing upon the earth,
> Dispersed those vapours that offended us;
> And by the benefit of his wished light,
> The seas wax'd calm. (1.1.88–91)

In laying claim to the waters beyond the limits of the city, Solinus metaphorically attempts to extend his control to the invisible forces of nature, to bring order to chaos.[49] Together, Egeon and Solinus introduce the age-old themes of man versus god; of human will over the elements; of the resilience of the bonds of earthly sovereignty, marriage, family and social protocol against the inward, irrepressible nature of humankind. On the one hand the Duke, representing centralised authority and power, seeks to extend that power over the ambiguous and ungovernable seas, extending this to the familial drive of the merchant to find his lost sons, whilst the Merchant argues that such regulations are simply implausible in the face of that which is 'wrought by nature' (1.1.34) – both elemental and human.

It is here that we return to Komisarjevsky's bollards, the seemingly innocuous set that demarcated upstage and downstage. These fixing points represent the attempt to control nature, to halt the effects of tides and the temperamental sea. Symbolically, they divide the two states of the human condition – one ruled by social strictures and centralised monarchical and religious structures, and the other a more elemental, unmanageable, changeable and primal set of internal directives that at times override the status quo. Solinus and Egeon embody these two states, one attempting to control the movements and behaviours of his citizenry, the other coming from the sea to contest the censures of the Ephesian province.

A closer look at Shakespeare's plays gives us an idea as to further meaning in such a setting, one that would have had significance to the Globe's audience. Berry notes that the stage forms a promontory that juts out into the audience.[50] In *3 Henry VI*, Richard soliloquises 'I do dream of sovereignty, / Like one that stands upon a promontory / And spies a far-off shore where he would tread' (3.2.134–136). Here, the actor stands, probably at the edge of the stage and facing the audience – an ambitious, soon-to-be-king contemplating power and his desire to wield it over England's populace. So too in *The Tempest*, Prospero vows to give up the source of his power on 'the strong-based promontory' (5.1.46) by throwing his magic book into the sea. In each of these cases Shakespeare appears to reference the physical stage that divides the world of the play from that of the audience, an audience who comes to represent the sea itself. In *Pericles*, the stage direction, 'Enter Pericles on shipboard' (3.1.0) follows Gower's prompt to the audience that 'this stage the ship, upon whose deck / The sea-tossed Pericles appears to speak' (3.0.59,60), once again placing the audience as the riotous sea. The playwright's implication that the elemental and uncontrollable watery expanses are in fact synonymous with the crowd is not simply fanciful artistic flair. The aforementioned associations of the sea with transgressive power and authority that stands in defiance of collective control implies a friction between the inner socio-political structures and the limens of society. This imagery speaks to a fundamentally fluid society that is both unstable and uncontrollable; any attempt on the part of centralised power to regulate and lay claim to such 'elements' as impossible as controlling the sea and the physical elements.

In attempting to shore up new historicist theories of the containment of power, Neema Parvini dismisses the cultural materialist approach to Shakespeare as a 'metacritical exercise' to 'shift focus from the plays themselves to what people have made of them'.[51] It is precisely this thinking that a re-evaluation of these texts seeks to overturn, rather concentrating on the staging and cultural contexts in which they were performed to establish a base for resistance and subversion. Parvini correctly claims that new historicists see power everywhere, yet I would aver that this is also true of cultural materialists. What is critical in taking both movements to the next developmental stage is not simply acknowledging the presence of power but also its constant flux and the pressures the edges of society exert on the centre in subtly shifting the positions of power. This relationship between inner and outer, central power and liminal influence, is exactly the kind of dialogue Shakespeare sets up in his staging of the sea and shore. Further consideration of *The Comedy of Errors* and the historical and geographic contexts of its staging highlight early modern power-plays of which his audience would have been more than aware.

The liberties of sin: between the city and the sea

Our first introduction to Antipholus of Syracuse is in Ephesus's mart, a fair or market. These hubs of trade funnelled society into a centralised precinct that saw locals and foreigners, buyers and sellers, aristocrats and lowborn, merchants, entertainers and beggars pushed into close proximity. As such it becomes more than simply a geographic location such as a church or a house, but relies on its identity and definition by interaction and exchange, both verbal and commercial. What is of note in *Errors* is that, apart from the three scenes inside the Phoenix, the home of Antipholus of Ephesus and Adriana (2.1, 3.2, 4.2), the settings for the remaining eight scenes are either satisfyingly ambiguous or else take place in public spaces such as the mart and its adjacent streets, with the most fluid and liminal of such spaces that of the 'lockout scene' taking place either side of the door to the Phoenix. The appeal of including these open spaces is in their ubiquity, their sense of movement with the passage of people from all social strata. Theatrically, these spaces make possible all manner of unlikely exchanges and chance encounters, also opening the way for clashes of class and ideology. Markets were a place of spectacle, of bartering and haggling over worth or value, of arrangements and promises. In short they constituted a fluid environment that was open to all. The observers' familiarity with such spaces opened the way for an intellectual exchange between stage and audience, where the stage interactions, judgements and skirmishes prompt personal connection with one side or another.

Antipholus of Syracuse is in the streets and market of Ephesus for less than an hour before he has just such an encounter with his slave's twin, whose enigmatic replies leave the foreigner confused and in fear of his safety. As *persona non grata*, the Syracusan is only too aware that the streets, despite their distractions, are also a dangerous place and that his only insurance against death is the thousand marks his slave has borne to the Centaur. Now that this money is gone the city takes on an altogether more sinister aspect.

> They say this town is full of cozenage,
> As, nimble jugglers that deceive the eye,
> Dark-working sorcerers that change the mind,
> Soul-killing witches that deform the body,
> Disguised cheaters, prating mountebanks,
> And many such-like liberties of sin:
> If it prove so, I will be gone the sooner.
> I'll to the Centaur, to go seek this slave:
> I greatly fear my money is not safe.
>
> (1.2.97–105)

It is the pattern of thought Antipholus follows after his exchange with the Ephesian Dromio that is important here. Feeling threatened he immediately retreats to a place that no longer reflects his earlier sentiments of wonder and curiosity – 'I'll view the manners of the town, / Peruse the traders, gaze upon the buildings' (1.2.12,13). For the unnerved tourist, Ephesus now takes on more menacing characteristics. As discussed earlier, John Gillies notes that the 'other' or the 'unnatural' is a deeply 'ideological construction' that is often alluded to in terms of geography.[52] The irony here of course is that both Syracuse and Ephesus are very much mirror cities, sharing language, customs and trade (not to mention two pairs of twins) – their respective citizens indistinguishable in terms of speech, dress and deportment. In his 1984 production for the BBC James Cellan-Jones's set focused on the centralised market, its cosmopolitan and international feel underscored by the stage space being an enormous map of the Greek principalities throughout the eastern Mediterranean, a visual referent to the homogenised society throughout the empire. However, it is the Syracusan's ingrained ideological map that now associates deception, vice and the occult with Ephesus, referencing the Pauline burning of magic books in Ephesus (Acts 19). Travellers' tales and home prejudices that have fed the Westerner's conceptualisation of Ephesus loom larger than life and the 'other' becomes a threat and no longer a curiosity, prompting a hasty retreat to the sea.

Yet it is Antipholus' comment on the 'liberties of sin' (line 102) that most likely had the greatest impact on an early modern theatregoer. For some of Shakespeare's audience the liberties of sin may have brought to mind Paul's admonition to his Galatian brethren: 'ye have been called unto liberty; only use not your liberty as an occasion unto the flesh' (Galatians 5:13). Misuse of Christian liberty was a theme developed by anti-theatrical writers such as Stephen Gosson and Philip Stubbs, and the jumpy Syracusan's line may well have parodied the rhetoric of such puritan pamphleteers. Yet for most of those in attendance this line was a direct reference to locations just outside London's walls, the very locale in which they were watching Shakespeare's plays – the Liberties.

The Liberties of London constituted the outlying conurbations, external to the city proper. Outside the auspices of Surrey and London City, the Liberty of Southwark ostensibly fell under the authority of the Bishop of Winchester whose impressive twelfth-century palace dominated the south bank of the Thames, and the populace was granted certain 'liberties' to engage in activities otherwise prohibited in the City of London or the outlying counties. By the late sixteenth century, the Liberty of the Clink, in which The Globe theatre would be built, was famous for its theatres, gambling establishments, bear-baiting pits, 'Winchester Geese' or prostitutes, and those who plied trades either morally dubious or socially censured, all of which were forbidden inside the city walls.[53] Gamini Salgado notes that these suburbs

> signified the haunts of pleasure and vice – well organised, well protected and highly profitable – where the sober citizenry as well as their less sober brethren could amuse themselves with playgoing, bear-baiting and whoring before they crossed the water back to the comfort of their walled and gated city.[54]

As such, the Liberties represented both a geographic and socio-political threshold defined not only by the edge of the Thames but also by the promotion of a divergent culture and moral direction. Steven Mullaney describes these suburbs as a 'transitional zone between the city and the country, various powers and their limits', and 'as a culturally maintained domain of ideological ambivalence and contradiction'.[55] This description of an alternative, in-between space, where subversive acts and attitudes prevailed, where the status quo was challenged and where normative behaviours and practice were confronted and inverted by the privileging of bodily cravings and the darker side of humanity, constitutes Antipholus's 'liberties of sin'. Even in the midday sun the Ephesian streets take on a sinister and dark hue, with their courtesans, cozeners, thieves and occultists, and the newcomer's speech betrays, more than simply a fear for his money, a concern for his eternal soul.

However, there is a greater significance in Antipholus's comment on the liberties of sin. In such an obvious geographic referent Shakespeare places the action in dual worlds – Ephesus and London. The significance is greater, though, than simply a familiar topographical prompt. London was itself a maritime city, one of the largest in Europe at the time. Falconer notes that the tracts of Admiral Monson, compiled between 1585 and 1603, speak of the stretch of the Thames up to London Bridge as being full of ships, and London's streets inundated with mariners.[56] The Thames's northern banks formed the natural defences of the city, with the imposingly arched and crowded London Bridge to the east, blocking larger vessels from heading further up river. On the south side of the estuary the Liberties of Southwark would have provided a welcome distraction for sailors and citizenry alike, lured by the promise of all manner of worldly entertainments.[57] Yet the congested bridge, with its requirement for those crossing it to carry a passport before negotiating the span, would have encouraged most visitors and locals to pay a penny to the myriad boatmen who plied their trade ferrying between London's two halves.[58] For the most part, those who attended the theatres on the southern bank would have crossed the watery barrier between England's mercantile, religious, juridical and monarchical hub and the off-centre lewd and lascivious Liberties, flush with cosmopolitan crews and local populace.

Duncan Salkeld's *Shakespeare and London* (2018) is a fascinating look at not only the geographical but the political, religious and cultural environs in which the playwright wrote and performed. Southwark's Liberties, Salkeld maintains, had 'a reputation for scandal and licentiousness' associated with its diverse entertainments that catered to the gamut of human interests.[59] For Antipholus of Syracuse, the crossing of water symbolised the departure from order, morality and the familiar into the almost supernatural world of the 'other' with its debauchery, corruption and duplicity. Thus, the parallel Anglo-Mediterranean geographies Shakespeare created reflected contemporaneous socio-cultural structures. The idea of twin cities is cultivated – Syracuse and Ephesus, central London and the Liberties – regions divided only by a stretch of water. Yet the watery expanses, whether they are the width of the Thames or the breadth of the Aegean, represent a sea change in those who traverse them – a metamorphosis from insider to other, from resident to tourist, and all that this entails. Dramatically, it becomes the source of conflict, tension and confusion as cultures clash and prejudices come to the fore.

Constructing literary landscapes: betwixt the supernatural and the Church

The Comedy of Errors is positioned as a perfect example of Shakespeare's recycling of classical motifs and using them as a palimpsest on which to construct or refashion familiar cultural geographies. It is not simply his use of antithetical sea and shore imagery that stands out within this play, but rather his use of opposing ideologies and practices that are embodied in their settings and place names. As previously shown, a consideration of the juxtaposition of a seemingly immovable state, represented by the Ephesian city, and the pressures of human nature, exemplified in the movements of the elements, speaks to subversive social undercurrents. Yet there are also problematic conflicts between ideological and social perspectives that are reflected in the literary geographies Shakespeare creates within the play.

A feature of the map or of the terrestrial globe is that of nomenclature. No cartographic reference is complete without its key signposts – the names that demarcate specific locations. What is of particular significance in a discussion of the construction of literary geographies within *Errors* is Shakespeare's deliberate inclusion or invention of specific names for locations within Ephesus, names that were not present in the material he sourced for his play. In doing so, we do not so much move away from the central emphasis on the liminal geographies of sea and shore as concentrate our focus on particular points of friction that exist within the aforementioned spaces. As discussed in Shakespeare's parallels between the maritime cities of London and Ephesus, these are sites of division, particular areas within them forming the loci of contestation.

There has been considerable study into the origins of Shakespeare's plots and their origins. The reuse, reconditioning or plagiarism of Greek, Roman, Italian and contemporary plays was a perfectly acceptable means of generating new theatrical material. In this tradition, *Errors* draws heavily on the characters, plot and geography of Plautus's *Menaechmi*. William Hazlitt famously wrote that 'this comedy is taken very much from the *Menaechmi* of Plautus, and is not an improvement on it', a judgement that seems overly harsh given that it is in the *differences* between the plays, their subtle shifts in location, storyline and the smallest of details, that we often derive a sense of how contemporaneous social concerns emerge on the early modern stage and how Shakespeare constructed geographies that reflected these concerns.[60] This is particularly evident in the way religion is both intrinsically in dialogue with classical mythologies and oral tradition – a phenomenon that is expressed in the way Shakespeare's characters move through the spaces he creates – spaces that, for his audiences, would have contained meaningful cultural associations.

First, it is important to consider the way in which names serve to promote certain associations. Plautus's protagonists are the twin brothers Menaechmus and Sosicles, the latter renamed Menaechmus, like his sibling, during the play. Rather than use the same names or a variation on them, as he at times did in other plays that were lifted from previous fictions, Shakespeare changes the names of his twins to Antipholus. Ben Jonson's high praise for Shakespeare's literary genius also famously contained what appeared to be a barely veiled slur, 'thou hadst small Latin and less Greek'.[61] Yet here Shakespeare demonstrates his grasp not only of Greek legend and language, but also of his reaching a certain educated part of his audience at Gray's Inn where *Errors* is believed to have first been performed.[62] Antipholus is not a Greek name but is rather a composite of Greek origins – 'Anti', or opposite, and Pholus, the name of a wise centaur in Greek mythology. Certainly, when we witness the prejudices of Antipholus of Syracuse or the presumptions of his Ephesian twin, their lack of wisdom is apparent. Those young revellers who in the Christmas celebrations of 1594 witnessed the first performance of *Errors* would have been the students and barristers of Gray's Inn, an establishment that prided itself in producing some of the finest minds of the day and whose patron was none other than Elizabeth. It may be surmised that those who witnessed the play's performance were familiar with Plautus, whose works were used to instruct Latin at much earlier ages than at the Inns of Court and who would have recognised the cultural and linguistic playfulness intrinsic in the leads' names. Furthermore, centaurs were mythical creatures composed of both human and animal elements, the head, torso and arms of a man, and the body of a horse. This physical duality, hinted at in the names of the twins, is reflected in their unstable identities. Once again conjuring imagery and associations with the sea, the Syracusan Antipholus laments:

> He that commends me to mine own content
> Commends me to the thing I cannot get.
> I to the world am like a drop of water
> That in the ocean seeks another drop,
> Who, falling there to find his fellow forth,

Unseen, inquisitive, confounds himself:
So I, to find a mother and a brother,
In quest of them, unhappy, lose myself.

(1.2.33–40)

Kent Cartwright notes that in this personal confession of the psychological ramifications of familial separation, Antipholus 'forfeits his selfhood [that] the family both gives and denies'.[63] Thus Shakespeare's cultural associations potentially carry far more weight than may at first be apparent. It may be easy to dismiss Juliet's pondering over the significance of a name from her balcony as a juvenile flight of fancy, yet it would seem that in plagiarising Plautus, Shakespeare did just that – bringing together ideas of conflict in the very names of his protagonists.

Yet there is a greater significance to the nomenclature within *Errors*. The Centaur, the Phoenix and the Porpentine are all names of buildings in Shakespeare's play, names that do not appear in the Plautine original and are immediately associated with strange, even mythical creatures. The centaur, with its composite features, is a creature caught between worlds, liminal, torn between the elevated and the bestial, the Bakhtinian embodiment of the dichotomy of human reasoning and animal instinct. In *The Book of Beasts*, T. H. White's translation of a twelfth-century bestiary, it notes certain psychological and physiological similarities between horses and men, particularly their emotional responses to grief and loss, and asserts, 'hence in Centaurs the nature of men and horses can be mixed'.[64] The phoenix is another mythically liminal creature that represents a state of renewal, rebirth and perfection – a transitional beast that epitomises paradoxical states – life and decay, birth and death. So too is the porpentine or porcupine an interesting inclusion in these place names. The Geneva translation of the Bible, with which Shakespeare would have been familiar, substitutes the three instances of porcupine with the more recognisable hedgehog. Used infrequently and obscurely as a heraldic device, the porcupine, native to the Levant and armoured in a coat of quills, conjures imagery of the exotic, bizarre and mysterious. According to certain classical beliefs the porcupine could both defend itself with its quills but also shoot them from its body like arrows that would pierce predators.[65] What Shakespeare does in the simple inclusion of these names of buildings is conjure imagery of the fantastic, the folkloric, and a culture in which the mythic is associated with the mundane, interwoven in the social fabric as household names.

Using these fabled referents, Shakespeare brings to the fore a significant cultural tension – that of the clash between oral traditions and the newly minted religious pragmatism that stood at the core of Protestant dogma. The miraculous feats of Catholic saints married closely with potent 'old wives' tales' of mysterious fay and the unseen realms of demons and devils had the potential to increase the power of prejudice as a filter through which one might erroneously look at the world. Such cultural strains become the theme of the Syracusan Antipholus's journey. Shakespeare plays on these fears, anxieties no doubt shared by some of those present at the early productions of *Errors*, that liminal spaces are where the strength of one's convictions and the veracity of one's deep-seated personal beliefs and superstitions are tried and tested. Interestingly, the language used by the Syracusans throughout the play reflects their preconceptions of Ephesus as a place of magic and sorcery, with Dromio at one point exclaiming:

> O, for my beads! I cross me for a sinner,
> This is the fairy land; O, spite of spites,
> We talk with goblins, owls and sprites!
> If we obey them not, this will ensue:
> They'll suck our breath or pinch us black and blue.
>
> (2.2.194–198)

This fairy realm, so often portrayed as an ambivalent world filled not only with malevolence but also mirth, is paralleled with Ephesus, or by extension, as previously shown, a representation of the Liberties of Southwark. Dromio's fear humorously mirrors his master's in that his reaction betrays a religious reflex to reach for his rosary 'beads' and to make the sign of the 'cross' to ward off evil (line 194). Playing on superstitions surrounding fairy predispositions to 'pinch' their victims, it is no coincidence Shakespeare introduces the exorcist, Dr Pinch, to cure the Ephesian Antipholus of his madness. Furthermore, responding to the courtesan's request for the return of her ring, both Antipholus and Dromio label her 'Satan', 'devil', 'Mistress Satan', 'devil's dam', 'fiend', 'sorceress' and 'witch' (4.3.49–80). Yet Shakespeare artfully dispels these prejudicial notions and reveals them as ridiculous preconceptions, the play's conclusion heralding a 'gossips' feast' (5.1.405) whereby the Syracusans would be united with the Ephesians in familial *communitas*, the 'errors' of deleterious racial and religious slurring banished as unfounded fear and foolishness. Keith Thomas observes that a belief in fairies was not necessarily in direct opposition to Christian belief systems, a fact attested to by Dromio's exclamation being preceded with 'O, for my beads! I cross me for a sinner' (line 194). Thomas notes: 'one striking aspect of fairy-beliefs was their self-confirming character. The man who believed in fairies could, like the astrologer or the magician, accept every setback and disappointment without losing his faith'.[66] Dromio's fairy comments are directly in relation to the unfathomable Ephesian world in which he and his master find themselves – an inverted world where two strange women entertain his master and he finds himself doorman in a foreign house. To make sense of this peculiar environment, and even more peculiar turn of events, Dromio resorts to deep-rooted oral traditions. This powerful cultural landscape had been present as long as Christianity in the British Isles. Despite some of the more forward thinking of Shakespeare's contemporaries dismissing such beliefs as 'erroneous and superstitious rubbish that needed to be stripped away from the essence of truth', these traditions proved harder to root out from the more rural communities.[67] When set upon by children dressed as fairies, even the worldly-wise Sir John Falstaff is caught out by his culturally received belief structures:

> And these are not fairies? By the Lord, I was three or four times in the thought they were not fairies, and yet the guiltiness of my mind, the sudden surprise of my powers, drove the grossness of the foppery into a *received belief* – in despite of the teeth of all rhyme and reason – that they were fairies.
> (*The Merry Wives of Windsor*, 5.5.120–125, emphasis mine)

An understanding of the cultural diversity that existed in England in the late sixteenth century helps contextualise this melange of myths and seemingly disparate dogmas. This was a time when the Renaissance with all its concomitant classical imagery had captured the imaginations of the nation's playwrights, poets and artists. Ecclesiastically, it was a world of change composed of a society whose faith had been radically refashioned within living memory and where religious persecution was rife. It was also a time when factors such as lower literacy in isolated communities provided the ideal conditions for oral traditions to continue to exert an influence on the quotidian.

To this supernatural blend Shakespeare adds an abbess, a female head of a Catholic order of nuns. Egeon's wife, separated in the wreck and unaware of the existence of her family both dwelling in and visiting Ephesus, has turned to the life monastic. Preceding Pericles's wife Thaisa, who coincidentally also assumes a devout existence when separated from her family, the hitherto absent abbess appears in the final scene to rectify the catalogue of errors, miscommunications, prejudices and imbalances of power to seemingly restore order. The *deus ex machina* was often a key figure in classical drama yet is strangely absent in Plautus's *Menaechmi*, the issues arising from mixed identities being resolved simply by bringing both brothers on stage at the same time and realisation dawning through their exchange. Yet Shakespeare departs from this obvious solution to complicate his resolution with the most controversial of twists.

We have no doubt as to the setting of the final scene in *Errors*. Pressing his master to cross the protective threshold, Dromio urges 'this is some priory; in or we are spoiled!' (5.1.37). This religious geography carried with it considerable cultural resonance, not least as a place of sanctuary for the condemned. Though an imaginary setting, the connotations are real. Henri Lefebvre noted the unique production of space relating to religious loci when he stated that there is

> a sense in which the existence of absolute space is purely mental, and hence 'imaginary'. In another sense, however, it also has a social existence, and hence a specific and powerful 'reality' [...] In the temple, in the city, in monuments and palaces, the imaginary is transformed into the real [...] a mental space into which the lethal abstraction of signs inserts itself.[68]

Harnessing these inferences, just as he did with Egeon's entrance from the sea, Shakespeare translates this site of contestation onto the stage as a means to challenge the authority of the Ephesian state. On the surface it may appear that the status quo is balanced beautifully by the intervention of the Abbess. Patriarchal order is restored, social and familial rifts are healed, and there is a satisfying equilibrium as the 'happily-ever-after' is reached. However, there is considerable significance in first a woman and second a Catholic not only mediating the mess created in the confusion over identity, but also standing in direct opposition to the state, facilitating the pardon of Egeon, and potentially changing the governor's stance on Syracuse. Patriarchy may be restored but only via its temporary subversion. Adriana and Antipholus may indeed have their marriage reinforced through the intervention of the Abbess, but not before she has exercised her power to overrule the wishes of Adriana to gain entry and see the man she believes to be her husband. The holy woman's last words to Adriana before walking away and thereby concluding further argument are 'Be quiet and depart: thou shalt not have him' (5.1.112), not only appropriating the language of the ten Mosaic statutes but then overruling divinely consecrated unions of marriage. Wielding her deific powers yet again, from the steps of her priory the Abbess directly counters the Governor's judgement upon Egeon, boldly declaring, 'whoever bound him, I will loose his bonds / and gain a husband by his liberty' (lines 339, 340). Obliged to capitulate to the powers of the ageing anchorite, the Governor is swept along by this strangely unstoppable woman in a setting that weakens his power, even refusing the proffered ransom money. The Ephesian state may return to a stable and composed condition, with preconceptions over difference and 'otherness' ironed out, but only after it has been destabilised and had to submit to the intervention of a woman on the stairs of a church.

Whilst it would be unwise to label *Errors* as a pro-Catholic play that looks wistfully back at pre-Protestant tradition and order, the mock exorcisms of Pinch and the clownish Dromio reaching for his rosaries aside, the inclusion of the level-headed, commanding and upright figure of Emilia and the setting of the priory does introduce a certain element of ambivalence over religious authority and doctrine. Considering the religious climate in which Shakespeare wrote his dramas, such theatrical manoeuvring and subversive play at work in the Abbess stands out as a contrast to prevailing sentiment. Ephesus, like London, is a jumble of conflicting ideologies, cultural heritage and faiths and *Errors* reflects this in its polyvalent literary geography.

The lockout: transgressing the master/slave dichotomy

Perhaps the most obvious of liminal settings about which conflict is created in *Errors* is the lockout scene (3.1). On returning to his home, the Phoenix, for his midday meal, the Ephesian Antipholus, accompanied by Dromio of Ephesus, Balthazar the merchant and Angelo the goldsmith, finds his door bolted. What ensues is a comedic interchange between the doorkeeper, Dromio of Syracuse, the occupants of the house, and an increasingly confused, embarrassed and irate householder who is unable, either through forceful words or physical exertion, to gain entry to his home.

The dearth of stage directions in the folio edition of *Errors* has led to conjecture as to how this scene was actually staged. However, Cartwright mentions that modern productions have recreated this threshold to either display the occupants of the house on one side of a makeshift partition containing a door or else invisible to the audience and speaking from within, either through a grate or the boards of one of the stage doors.[69] By whatever means such staging is managed, what is created is an exceedingly familiar liminal space, one that Velázquez depicted in *Las Meninas*: a doorway that draws attention to its potential to generate friction through ambiguity and disorientation, not dissimilar to that of the drunken Porter in *Macbeth* who sees himself as the gatekeeper of Hell.

The Phoenix's doorway also offers a meaningful theatrical function. It represents a threshold between the public and the private, the street and the domicile, civic authority and familial or domestic control. In and of itself it is not a place of authority but of the meeting of two worlds, a literal gateway through which the function or responsibility of the individual changes on entry or exit. On one side of the threshold a servant or slave is given the ability to speak in insults towards his social betters, whilst on the other side a figure of authority is reduced to a supplicant, a beggar. The doorway is the limen in which traditional power structures become fluid.

Antipholus of Ephesus opens the scene in conversation with two of the city's respected merchants and artisans before the doors of his house. The appearance of his slave results in him insulting Dromio, and labelling him an ass. Yet, on being refused entry, it is Antipholus who is pronounced a 'hind' by his servant's twin, reversing the master–slave dichotomy. Despite Balthazar's pretensions at elevated philosophical reasoning with his often-ridiculous and ponderously aphoristic speech, the scene is dragged downwards into the lower bodily stratum rife with bum-jokes. The obvious pleasure at seeing his master reduced to a mendicant as well as to cunningly usurp his own name and position moves the Ephesian Dromio to play further with such puerile imagery – 'a man may break his word with you, sir, and words are but wind; Ay, and break it in your face, so he break it not behind' (3.1.75, 76). For Antipholus, a man's house is no longer his castle in which he reigns supreme but a privy in which he is a toothless petitioner; so too are his secrets no longer sacred but irreverently broadcast on his doorstep. Power, the patriarchal order, the agency of a master over slave and the socio-religious conventions of dignity and decorum over wrath and lewdness are inverted in this liminal space. The master and slave dichotomy referenced in the 'lockout' scene of *Errors* is not to be confused with the Hegelian Master–Slave Dialectic in which two self-conscious entities within a hierarchy become conscious of the other thus defining their relationships and roles.[70] Nor is Jacques Lacan's Discourse of the Master the rubric through which this scene takes on significance, whereby subordination is masked by a kind of familial submission.[71] Though there is traction for such theories within this scene, the resistance to and subversion of class-based hierarchies carries with it more Marxist overtones. Yet what is significant here is that it is not the character of the individuals in this scene that is responsible for the destabilising of power relationships but rather the very nature of the liminal space in which they interact that allows, even promotes, subversion. This reorientation of the natural order is a dramatic derivative of such in-between spaces and is used for more than simply the means to complicate plot, develop character or provoke laughter. Rather, this space is about the contestation of power, the destabilisation of authority and the possibility of differing social agency.

Peter Stallybrass and Allon White developed the concept of low and high oppositions within hierarchies, what they call the 'four symbolic domains – psychic forms, the human body, geographical space and the social order'.[72] They go on to explain that 'transgressing the rules of hierarchy and order in any one of the domains may have major consequences in the others', a concept that is evident in other Shakespearean plays.[73] The opening to *A Midsummer Night's Dream* is a description of a world upside down, the inversion of patriarchal order and the discord between Titania and Oberon being reflected in wild weather patterns and cosmic portents.

> Therefore the winds, piping to us in vain,
> As in revenge, have suck'd up from the sea
> Contagious fogs; which falling in the land
> Have every pelting river made so proud
> That they have overborne their continents...
> ...And this same progeny of evils comes
> From our debate, from our dissension;
> We are their parents and original.
>
> (2.1.89–117)

For the Athenian court and surrounding kingdom the dissention between the fairy monarchs has caused considerable damage and upheaval. It is noteworthy that, once again, references to the sea and shore are used to express the inversions of hierarchies and destabilisation of models of power. In *Hamlet*, the transgression of natural order and the killing of a king result in the dead breaking their bounds and haunting the night, as well as the invasion led by Fortinbras. Hamlet declares: 'the time is out of joint' (1.5.188), Denmark's times and events following the murder of its rightful king likened to a dislocated limb, the whole body politic off balance and in distress as a result of a single injury. The physical, geographical, moral, spiritual and social orders are never isolated or contained but are subverted and destabilised through an all-pervasive, interlinking, cosmic knock-on or butterfly effect. Thus, the lockout scene demonstrates the dramatic capital that can be applied in liminal settings – spaces where power and place change, inverting high and low, outside and inside, confusing established models of power.

Conclusion

What is evident from Shakespeare's geographies is that they are constructed using cross-cultural layers that in turn create worlds both surreal and yet strangely familiar. His Anglo-Ephesus is a liminal landscape that is ideally situated close enough to the public consciousness as to address authority and societal power structures and subvert them. As shown, the playwright here references two liminal places defined by their physical and symbolic tendency toward pushing together the great assembly of humanity and creating division, friction, imbalances and disruptions of power, as well as the occasion and opportunity for change. Whether they are the streets and markets of Ephesus or the Liberties of London, such places challenge dominant or received ideologies, and central to this is the juxtaposition of sea and shore. The shorelines of Ephesus and Southwark represent the threat to order. Their respective 'liberties' are a reflection of what happens when power is contested at the limens of society.

As Shakespeare reminds us, more so than the forests and gardens that will be discussed later on, the sea is furthest from civilisation, representing the frontier or extent of human jurisdiction, the space in which human endeavour confronts a power beyond its control and a realm of possibility existing within the imagination as that which is to be conquered. Shakespeare's shores are thus often a metaphor for the limens of society, the wilder side of humanity removed from the centre. Such spaces house denizens of duality, difference and dissidence and these areas become theatrical and cultural currency in representing ideologies at odds with the status quo.

In this regard *A Comedy of Errors* stands out as a play wherein the sea is ever-present, even when much of the action takes place in the streets and structures of a Mediterranean city. The literary geographies and liminal spaces Shakespeare created through contrasting the city and sea not only reflect contemporary anxieties over national identity, what constituted the 'other', frictions between religious standpoints and the systems of patriarchy and class, but crucially present a distinct resistance to the containment of power. The shifting geographic threshold of sea and shore is where authority is in constant flux and thus is open to contestation. Yet this slippage and negotiation of power is not a characteristic of this setting alone. As the following chapters demonstrate, Shakespeare's consistent use of other liminal settings maintains pressure on systems of authority that repel attempts to manage or contain subversion.

Notes

1 Chris Barrett, *Early Modern English Literature and the Poetics of Cartographic Anxiety* (Oxford: Oxford University Press, 2018), p. 4.
2 John Gillies, *Shakespeare and the Geography of Difference* (Cambridge: Cambridge University Press, 1994), pp. 75–77.
3 For further reading on England's colonial expansion see Bruce Lenman, *England's Colonial Wars 1550–1688: Conflicts, Empire and National Identity* (Harlow: Pearson Education, 2001), and Stuart Elden, *Shakespearean Territories* (Chicago: University of Chicago Press, 2018).
4 Caroline Spurgeon, *Shakespeare's Imagery* (Cambridge: Cambridge University Press, 1952), p. 24.
5 See David McInnis, *Mind-Travelling and Voyage Drama in Early Modern England* (London: Palgrave Macmillan, 2012), and Claire Jowitt, Craig Lambert and Steve Mentz (eds), *The Routledge Companion to Marine and Maritime Worlds 1400–1800* (Abingdon: Routledge, 2020).
6 Laurence Publicover, *Dramatic Geography: Romance, Intertheatricality, and Cultural Encounter in Early Modern Mediterranean Drama* (Oxford: Oxford University Press, 2017), pp. 2, 3.
7 Peter J. Forshaw, 'The Hermetic Frontispiece: Contextualising John Dee's Hieroglyphic Monad', *Ambix*, 64(2) (2017), 115–139, p. 118.
8 Leslie B. Cormack, 'Britannia Rules the Waves?: Images of Empire in Elizabethan England', in *Literature, Mapping and the Politics of Space in Early Modern England*, ed. Andrew Gordon and Bernard Klein (Cambridge: Cambridge University Press, 2001), p. 50.
9 Ania Loomba notes the expansion of overseas trade not only of the Spanish but the Portuguese and of the 'fast expanding Turkish Empire', *Shakespeare, Race and Colonialism* (Oxford: Oxford University Press, 2002), pp. 13, 14.
10 For further reading see Alden T. Vaughan and Virginia Mason Vaughan's *Shakespeare's Caliban: A Cultural History* (Cambridge: Cambridge University Press, 1991) as well as Ania Loomba's *Shakespeare, Race and Colonialism* (Oxford: Oxford University Press, 2002).
11 Peter J. French, *John Dee: The World of the Elizabethan Magus* (Abingdon: Routledge, 2002), p. 19.
12 Steve Mentz, *At the Bottom of Shakespeare's Ocean* (London: Continuum, 2009), pp. 71, 72.
13 Stuart Elden, *Shakespearean Territories* (Chicago: University of Chicago Press, 2018), p. 152.

14 It is of note that when Othello later attempts to justify the murder of his wife, he describes Desdemona as 'false as water' (5.2.143), a simile that plays on the tidal theme of changeable humanity.
15 Though Venice is actually built on nearly 120 small and, for the most part, submerged islands of silt, its reputation as a man-made 'floating city' lends it even greater liminal significance as a civilisation established within the bounds of the Adriatic Sea, both geographically defiant yet ultimately more sensitive to the impact of its watery environs.
16 In 2015, a group of scientists in South Africa examined disinterred pipe-fragments from Shakespeare's garden, discovering traces of cannabis on four of the pieces. The ensuing sensational media-speculation headlined the question of whether Shakespeare was 'high when he penned his plays?' (*The Independent,* 9 Aug. 2015), and another assigned the playwright the more lurid appellation of 'Breaking Bard' (*The Sun,* 10 Aug. 2015). Regardless of the supposition, what is evident is that, by the time Shakespeare was writing, the availability and consumption of imported goods from the New World was widespread.
17 Vaughan and Vaughan, *Shakespeare's Caliban*, p. xv.
18 Iago refers to Othello as 'an erring barbarian' (1.3.356), whilst Rodrigo uses the pejorative term 'the thicklips' (1.1.66). The latter may indicate a physical trait playgoers would have associated with Moors, but may also be a corrupted, lisping-homophone for 'cyclops', yet another of *Mandeville*'s monstrous aliens.
19 Margo Hendricks, 'Race: A Renaissance Category?' in *A Companion to English Renaissance Literature and Culture*, ed. Michael Hattaway (Oxford: Blackwells, 2003), p. 696.
20 Lenman, *England's Colonial Wars 1550–1688*, p. 9.
21 Alan Sinfield, *Faultlines: Cultural Materialism and the Politics of Dissident Reading* (Oxford: Clarendon Press, 1992), p. 300.
22 Vaughan and Vaughan, *Shakespeare's Caliban*, p. 14.
23 Though this analysis does not engage with the debates over whether Caliban was a dramatic product of early modern accounts of the exploration and colonisation either Africa or the New World, Vaughan and Vaughan's *Shakespeare's Caliban* (1991) offers a thorough analysis of the arguments.
24 Paul Brown, ' "This Thing of Darkness I Acknowledge Mine": *The Tempest* and the Discourse of Colonialism', in *Political Shakespeare: Essays in Cultural Materialism*, ed. Jonathan Dollimore and Alan Sinfield (Manchester: Manchester University Press, 1996), p. 62.

25 Vaughan and Vaughan, *Shakespeare's Caliban*, p. 50.
26 Brown, 'This Thing of Darkness', p. 68.
27 Whilst Othello is not a 'Turk' per se, this term is synonymous with both those of oriental extraction as well as the Muslim faith. To this end Debra Johanyak notes that in *Othello*, Shakespeare expresses 'a deep fascination not only with issues of race but also with Christian-Muslim tensions shaping Europe's relationship with the Ottoman Empire'. ' "Turning Turk," Early Modern English Orientalism, and Shakespeare's *Othello*', in *The English Renaissance, Orientalism, and the Idea of Asia*, ed. Debra Johanyak and Walter S. H. Lim (New York: Palgrave Macmillan, 2009), p. 78.
28 Loomba, *Shakespeare, Race and Colonialism*, pp. 93, 94.
29 William Shakespeare, *Othello*, ed. E. A. J. Honigmann (Walton-on-Thames: Thomas Nelson & Sons, 1997), p. 29.
30 Dympna Callaghan, *Shakespeare without Women: Representing Gender and Race on the Renaissance Stage* (London: Routledge, 2000), p. 75.
31 Lisa Hopkins, *Shakespeare on the Edge* (Aldershot: Ashgate Publishing, 2005), p. 94.
32 Stephen Greenblatt, *Renaissance Self-Fashioning: From More to Shakespeare* (Chicago: University of Chicago Press, 1980), p. 88.
33 William Shakespeare, *The Merchant of Venice*, ed. John Drakakis (London: Bloomsbury, 2010), p. 30.
34 For Renaissance attitudes towards the Jews one need look no further than Martin Luther's vitriolic text, *On the Jews and their Lies* (1543). A fascinating visual representation of the Jewish experience can be found in Rebecca Abrams, *The Jewish Journey: 4000 Years in 22 Objects from the Ashmolean Museum* (Oxford: Ashmolean Museum Press, 2017).

In terms of prevailing attitudes towards Jews in early modern England see James Shapiro's *Shakespeare and the Jews* (New York: Columbia University Press, 1996) and Lucien Wolf's 'Jews in Elizabethan England', *Transactions of the Jewish Historical Society of England*, 11 (1928). What is historically pertinent, however, is that on 18 July 1290 Edward I issued a royal edict to expel all Jews from England by November of that year. The Crusades, the perceived commercial acumen of Jews in England, extortionate tax rates and the eventual legalisation of usury for Christians had fuelled an increased vilification and persecution of England's Jews, leading to their eventual demonisation and expulsion. Four hundred years later, at the time Shakespeare wrote *The Merchant of Venice*, Edward's law was still in place and Jews were still an object of otherness, exaggerated through the passage of time.

35 Terry Eagleton, *Sweet Violence: The Idea of the Tragic* (Oxford: Blackwell, 2003), p. 165.
36 William Shakespeare, *The Merchant of Venice*, ed. Drakakis, p. 28.
37 John Gillies, *Shakespeare and the Geography of Difference* (Cambridge: Cambridge University Press, 1994), p. 133.
38 Ibid., p. 6.
39 Victor W. Turner, *The Ritual Process: Structure and Anti-Structure* (Bungay: Chaucer Press, 1969), pp. 130, 131.
40 Gillies, *Shakespeare and Geography of Difference*, p. 101.
41 William Shakespeare, *The Comedy of Errors*, ed. Kent Cartwright (London: Bloomsbury, 2016), p. 119.
42 Ralph Berry, 'Komisarjevsky at Stratford-upon-Avon', *Shakespeare Survey*, 36 (1983), 73–84, p. 81.
43 Ralph Berry, *Shakespeare and the Awareness of the Audience* (London: Macmillan, 1985), p. 34.
44 Dan Brayton, 'Sounding the Deep: *Shakespeare and the Sea* Revisited', *Forum for Modern Language Studies* 46(2) (2010), 189–206, p. 190.
45 Mentz, *At the Bottom of Shakespeare's Ocean*, p. x.
46 Julie Sanders, *The Cultural Geography of Early Modern Drama, 1620–1650* (Cambridge: Cambridge University Press, 2011), p. 55.
47 Bradin Cormack, 'Marginal Waters: *Pericles* and the Idea of Jurisdiction', in *Literature, Mapping and the Politics of Space in Early Modern Britain,* ed. Andrew Gordon and Bernhard Klein (Cambridge: Cambridge University Press, 2001), p. 167.
48 Ibid., p. 174.
49 Ironically, it is the moon and not the sun that ultimately controls the tides and movements of the sea. In Solinus extending his powers over the sea he effectively upsets rather than reinforces visions of divine order.
50 Berry, *Shakespeare and the Awareness of the Audience*, p. 7.
51 Neema Parvini, *Shakespeare and New Historicist Theory* (London: Bloomsbury Arden, 2017), p. 120.
52 Gillies, *Shakespeare and Geography of Difference*, p. 15.
53 *Errors* composition predates the erection of The Globe, with its first recorded performance at the Gray's Inn on 28 December 1594 as part of the Holy Innocents' Day festivities. There is evidence that the play may have been revived in 1597–8, in which case it is likely to have been performed in one of the theatres situated in London's Liberties. See Shakespeare, *A Comedy of Errors*, ed. Cartwright, p. 110.
54 Gamini Salgado, *The Elizabethan Underworld* (London: Book Club Associates, 1977), p. 49.

55 Steven Mullaney, *The Place of the Stage: License, Play, and Power in Renaissance England* (Chicago: University of Chicago Press, 2000), p. ix.
56 A. F. Falconer, *Shakespeare and the Sea* (London: Constable & Co., 1964), p. xi.
57 The Admiral's Men, operating first from The Rose until taking up residence in the newly built Fortune theatre in 1605, sported a suitably nautical name. Changed from Lord Howard's Men following the appointment of their benefactor, the Earl of Nottingham, to the position of Lord High Admiral in 1585, the Admiral's Men's prominence rivalled that of Shakespeare's own Lord Chamberlain's Men. For more on this company see Andrew Gurr, *The Shakespearean Stage 1574–1642* (Cambridge: Cambridge University Press, 1992).
58 Duncan Salkeld, *Shakespeare and London* (Oxford: Oxford University Press, 2018), p. 45.
59 Ibid.
60 William Hazlitt, *Characters of Shakespeare's Plays* (London, Oxford University Press, 1966), p. 260.
61 Ben Jonson, 'To the Memory of My Beloved the Author, Mr. William Shakespeare and What He Hath Left Us', in *The Norton Anthology of Poetry* (5th ed.), ed. Margaret Ferguson, Mary Jo Salter and Jon Stallworthy (New York: W. W. Norton & Co., 2005), p. 342.
62 Alan H. Nelson and John R. Elliott, Jr., *Inns of Court Records of Early English Drama*, vol. 2 (Cambridge: Cambridge University Press, 2011), p. 364.
63 Shakespeare, *The Comedy of Errors*, ed. Cartwright, p. 15.
64 T. H. White, *The Book of Beasts* (London: Jonathan Cape, 1969), p. 86.
65 Beryl Rowland, *Animals with Human Faces: A Guide to Animal Symbolism* (Knoxville, TN: University of Tennessee Press, 1973), p. 133.
66 Keith Thomas, *Religion and the Decline of Magic* (London: Penguin, 1991), p. 733.
67 Adam Fox, *Oral Tradition and Literate Culture in England, 1500–1700* (Oxford: Clarendon Press, 2000), p. 1.
68 Henri Lefebvre, *The Production of Space*, trans. Donald Nicholson-Smith (Oxford: Blackwell Publishers, 1991), p. 251.
69 Shakespeare, *A Comedy of Errors*, ed. Cartwright, pp. 96, 97.
70 For a greater understanding of George Hegel's Master/Slave Dialectic, or more accurately, lordship and bondage, see G. W. F. Hegel, *Phenomenology of Spirit*, trans. A. V. Miller (Oxford: Clarendon Press, 1977).

71 For a more detailed breakdown of Lacan's Discourse of the Master see Mark Bracher's, 'On the Psychological and Social Functions of Language: Lacan's Theory of the Four Discourses', in *Lacanian Theory of Discourse: Subject, Structure and Society*, ed. Mark Bracher (New York: New York University Press, 1994), pp. 107–128.
72 Peter Stallybrass and Allon White, *The Politics and Poetics of Transgression* (Cambridge: Cambridge University Press, 1986), p. 3.
73 Ibid.

3

Subversive sylvan settings: Dark humours and the theatrical forest

Elizabeth Nott, widow and resident of Stratford-upon-Avon, died in 1595. What little we can piece together of the life of one of Shakespeare's fellow Stratfordians comes from the inventory made of the possessions she left behind. Among those items considered worthy of inclusion due to their fiscal value are a sieve, a small table and a pillow. The very last items included in the inventory consist of a small pile of 'tymbir & wod', a curious inclusion by today's standards due to its seeming insignificance.[1] Yet the presence of Mrs Nott's wood stack on the inventory points to the economic importance that wood and, by extension, England's woodland played in the late sixteenth and early seventeenth centuries.

Vin Nardizzi's *Wooden Os: Shakespeare's Theatres and England's Trees* (2013) notes that 'price indices for the sixteenth and seventeenth centuries confirm that wood products were some of the most expensive items a consumer purchased' and that the inflation on everything from wood consumed for cooking fires to timber used to build England's navy saw prices triple between 1501 and 1601.[2] Clearly, the value of Elizabeth Nott's woodpile is reflected in a growing national concern over the future of England's natural resources, a fact attested to by John Manwood, a judge and gamekeeper, in his 1592 *Treatise of the Laws of the Forest* where he laments that 'so many do daily so contemptuously commit such heinous spoils and trespasses therein, that the greater part of them are spoiled and decayed'.[3] Robert Pogue Harrison summarises Manwood's exposition as an attempt to reassert the royal forest as 'granting wildlife the same sort of asylum that the Church granted criminals or fugitives who entered its precincts'.[4] England's shrinking woods and forests were not only the concern of those that policed their borders. Want of woodland prompted petitions to Parliament to implement a regime of reforestation such as the impassioned pamphlet of Arthur Standish entitled *The Commons Complaint* (1611) that warns: 'no wood no kingdom'.[5] Standish's rhetoric includes a recommendation for husbandmen and farmers to replant trees that have been felled and dedicate a portion of acreage to planting woods that must be left for up to eighty years to allow the trees to reach maturity, whilst setting aside a portion for firewood. What is significant to the modern historian is the important link between the natural world, in this case the forest, and the idea of 'kingdom', sovereignty and civilisation. Two distinct environs, yet the latter is economically dependent on the existence of the former.[6]

However, more than just economic significance, the early modern forest also carried with it certain cultural resonances in legends and oral traditions. The Arthurian tales of Thomas Mallory, the *Pearl* Poet's epic, *Sir Gawain and the Green Knight*, the legendary heroic figure of Robin Hood and the folkloric fairy realms all bore close ties to England's sylvan sanctuaries. Wild men, maleficent sprites and political fugitives similarly populate Shakespeare's wild woods. Robert Pogue Harrison notes that, for an outlaw or wild man:

> The forest represents his locus of concealment [...] the place of cover which symbolically governs the comic absurdity that defines the relation between reality and appearance, or the institutional order and its own shadow. Forests represent an inverted world, or the shadow of irony itself [...] deception serves ultimately to unmask the deceptive veneers of the ordinary.[7]

Harrison here touches on the function of forests in embodying not so much a binary of civilisation and social order but rather their shadowy representation – at once recognisable yet embellished, corrupted and even inverted. It is this paradoxical space that conceals those who enter from the judgemental eyes of society and serves to expose their true nature. It is precisely these shadowy functions that drew Shakespeare and his contemporaries towards their deployment as both settings for action and metaphors for the concerns of early modern plays. In employing this setting within early modern theatre playwrights could potentially open the way for dramatic manipulation and play on the advantage of locating contemporary realities, traditions and organisations in a contrasting yet familiar environment. I would argue that the cultural connotations of the sylvan setting being a place of 'inversion' effectively offered the dramatist a means to comment on, satirise and subvert the institutions upon which social, religious and juridical authority were maintained. As a liminal space, both geographically and within the collective cultural consciousness, the forest becomes a testing ground for alternative models of power.

In venturing into Shakespeare's sylvan settings this chapter seeks to re-evaluate the meanings and dramatic functions of this recurrent topography. Through consideration of the historical and social attitudes towards woods and forests and the critical approaches to Shakespeare's use of them, I will challenge the popularly held conceptions of this space as being the locus of benign transformation. Rather, through attention to gendered readings, and psychoanalytical approaches to behaviours and language within such spaces, the forest becomes a place of carnivalesque inversion and a setting that augments or amplifies the inner person. Effectively, whoever enters its shelter has his or her humours amplified for good or ill – confronted with a mirror of their inner character free of the constraints of social, moral, legal and religious boundaries. As such the forest is potentially violent, dangerous and a threat to order – a liminal landscape that constitutes aggressive change, resistance, and even revolution.

The sylvan divide – forest and wood

One of the keys to understanding this recurrent terrain and its significance on the Shakespearean stage is the language in which it is described. Anne Barton makes the observation that the sylvan nomenclature found in *As You Like It* and *A Midsummer Night's Dream* is quite different. Shakespeare favours 'forest' in *As You Like It*, the word appearing thirty-one times throughout the play with only three references to 'wood'. Yet in *Dream*, 'forest' is only mentioned three times. The first two references are to forests outside of the Athenian woods, the 'forests wild' (2.1.25) in which Oberon travels; and as one of many temporary courts established by the fairy queen, 'on hill, in dale, forest, or mead' (2.1.83). The third reference to a forest is in Puck's song as he anoints the eyes of Lysander with the love potion, its use as the means of maintaining the metre of the ditty – 'Through the forest have I gone / But Athenian found I none' (2.2.72, 73). What seems to emerge from the use of these terms in certain instances is that there is a specific and deliberate demarcation between types of forest and wood. Though the application of a general rule for specific meanings associated with the two terms is injudicious, what is apparent is that there are multiple cultural significances associated with sylvan settings. To comprehend how Shakespeare employs these complex implications we must first look at the early modern understandings of these terms.

Britain, like much of Europe before the great prehistoric migrations of humans, had been heavily wooded. For civilisation to develop and prosper, great tracts of land were cleared, not only to make way for pastures and arable land but also to remove the threat of predators whose natural haunts were beneath the canopy of the wild woods. Throughout the Middle Ages these predators – wolves, bears and lynx – were hunted to extinction throughout the isles, removing the immediate threats posed by the forested lands. Late medieval economic expansion, in the form of the production of iron and agriculture, as well as increased population that required building materials, saw the deforestation of swathes of virgin forests until, as Keith Thomas notes, by early modern times much of Britain's woodland had disappeared.[8] However, it was not simply economic motivations or controlling public safety that saw the reduction of Britain's wilderness. The untamed trees and undergrowth did not just harbour wild beasts but were also the source of entrenched superstitions and fears. Thomas writes that the woods were synonymous with the animalistic, 'hence the assumption that any men who lived in the woods must be rough and barbarous'.[9] The woods thus represented a world apart from civilisation, an ancient world from the shadows of a darker age.

Yet Britain's sylvan landscapes also offered those with the means and opportunity to pursue the sport of hunting. To ensure the future of these pastimes required the conservation of large wooded environs – the managed forest preserves. William the Conqueror established the convention of afforestation, the conversion of land within certain boundaries into Royal Forests, subject to a set of laws 'outside' (Latin: *foris*) the law of the land. The Latin term *foresta* implies not only a wilderness but also a juridical expression pertaining to 'land that had been placed off limits by a royal decree'.[10] Thus royally delineated forests, as opposed to the wilder woodlands and wealds, became peculiar geographies in as much as their purpose and designation changed from savage, wild, even fearful places, to that of a glorified playground for the nobility. This renaming or repurposing is noteworthy for several reasons. First, the forests were now the sole property of the king, a single individual who was responsible for their upkeep, policing and protection. However, appropriating the wild was also an act of hubris as the claiming of enormous swathes of land required policing, yet officials were hard-pressed to enforce the law. The forest canopy still sheltered outlaws, and the king's land offered a wealth of natural resources, in both its flora and fauna, that was too great a temptation for commoner and aristocrat alike.

The second reason why afforestation is of interest is to do with the cultural significance of such spaces. Chivalric tales such as Edmund Spenser's *Faerie Queene* (1590) are full of references to knights venturing into forests to seek adventure through the slaying of its ferocious denizens. Anne Barton observes that forests have a

> grip on the human imagination; they can occasion deep-seated anxiety, which the rational mind cannot dismiss out of hand. The giants, wild men and outlaws that lie in wait there can claim a very extensive English and European mythology as mysterious woodland inhabitants and hazards.[11]

Yet such folktales often involve a far more interesting event – the metamorphosis of a civilised man to a beast, or wild man. From medieval myth come those who, upon entering the forest, are transformed and regress into a bestial state, forced to confront their own monstrous natures. Lancelot, rebuked by Guinevere, flees to the woods 'and was wild wood as ever was man'.[12] Following the news of Angelica's marriage to a Moor, Ariosto's Orlando is discovered 'running frantic' (*Orlando Furioso*, Canto 24, LVI) through the forest, one observer exclaiming, 'the wretch's fury; how he shed / His arms about the forest, tore his clothes, / Slew hinds, and caused a thousand other woes' (LI).[13] Geoffrey of Monmouth's *Vita Merlini* (c.1150) explicitly describes Merlin's descent into wildness and madness as he retreats into the forest. Thus the forest is a place of ambiguity – it is outside the law of the land in that it falls under the auspices and care of the crown, yet it still retains its more ancient identity of a wild place where men and beasts retreat beyond the reach of the law, a place of obscurity and shadow that represents the pre-civilised, Mesolithic humans who lived both in the forest and off it.[14]

What emerges from this foray into medieval and early modern sylvan semantics and reference is that there are two forests, the ancient and wild woods and the royally demarcated and protected forest preserves. Each of these spaces brings with it a certain cultural significance, the former conjuring images of the mysterious, bestial, uncivilised, untamed and threatening wildernesses that preceded humanity's attempts to conquer the countryside. The latter is a geography governed by law, bearing the impression of man, a place of privilege, directly under the auspices of the monarchy. Thus, when Shakespeare references the woods and forests he does so with a clearly established understanding of their differences and socio-cultural significance. In *Timon of Athens* the protagonist's disgust with the civilised world brings on a stream of invective:

> Breath infect breath,
> That their society, as their friendship, may
> Be merely poison!
> [*He tears off his clothes*]
>   Nothing I'll bear from thee,
> But nakedness, thou detestable town;
> Take thou that too, with multiplying bans.
> Timon will to the woods; where he shall find
> Th'unkindest beast more kinder than mankind.
>
> (4.1.30–36)[15]

The eponymous misanthrope's bile is directed at the society in which he had previously so unwisely invested. Shedding the last vestiges of his ties to humanity and the civilised Athens, he tears his clothes off and flees the city for the woods. Of note is that it is not the forest he retreats to, as he would be dwelling in a place still associated with the society he so despises. Rather, it is a place of savagery and unkind beasts, a place where Timon can immerse himself in the bestial, the wild – figuratively and literally going back to nature.[16] There is only one reference to the forest in *Timon* of *Athens* and it serves to reinforce the idea of social imposition and appropriation of the wild. Apemantus the cynic visits Timon in his cave in the woods. The half-naked troglodyte engages in a bitter exchange with the sceptic whose sour views of Athenian society he now shares. Bewailing the dog-eat-dog world in which they live, Timon asks, 'what beast couldst thou be that were not subject to a beast?' (4.3.345–346). It is Apemantus's reply that uses the peculiar meaning of the forest that is significant – 'the commonwealth of Athens is become a forest of beasts' (4.3.349–350). Echoing Timon's earlier railing against Athens's parasitic establishment, with its 'affable wolves' and 'meek bears' (3.7.94), Apemantus reduces the city, and more notably its government and what it represents on social, cultural and juridical levels, to a forest – a managed sanctuary of wild beasts. Shakespeare's deliberate use of these two words and their respective inferences evokes culturally familiar geographies – in this case establishing contrasts between wood and forest, the natural world with its primitive yet comprehensible hierarchies of predator and prey, and the civilised world which is in so many ways a reflection of the bestial, unsophisticated woods but with the addition of one thing – the imposition of human law.

Barton observes that at times 'the two locales [city and forest] can merge, even seem to exchange identities', and Apemantus's metaphor certainly establishes a similarity between forest and city.[17] However, as with his treatment of the sea, Shakespeare more often than not contrasts his sylvan landscapes with those of the city. Timon's antipathy towards Athenian society motivates his move into the isolation of the woods, though even here the city's dignitaries and social set seek him out – his move a political one, an act of rebellion and protest, a vote of no confidence in the social structures embodied in the city. In *A Midsummer Night's Dream* the lovers flee the constraints of the city with its patriarchal strictures and gravitate towards the shelter and obscurity of the wood.

It is in yet another Athenian wood that Palamon takes refuge in *The Two Noble Kinsmen*, and in which he and Arcite arrange their duel away from the eyes of Theseus. Valentine becomes a Robin Hood figure as the leader of a band of forest outlaws outside the city of Milan. The suitably named Silvia (also the name of the Roman goddess of the forest) escapes the city and the constraints of her father, the Duke, to find her Valentine, only to be waylaid by a predatory Proteus in the forest of *Two Gentlemen of Verona*. Rather than suffering his exile in another country or city, Duke Senior chooses to take up residence in the forest and set up his alternative court under a leafy canopy in *As You Like It*. In each of these plays the woods and forests serve as inversions of the city, the centralised and established seat of power. These liminal spaces not only open the way for the exploration of alternative social models but also of the darker side of human nature – an arena in which ideologies and social structures can be subverted.

An individual who ventures into the woods effectively moves into a place outside of society, assuming the role of a cultural exile or pariah. This is not simply a medieval trope, taken from the chivalric tales of knights wandering into forests and woods, seeking either a proving-ground for feats of valour or acts of devotion, or else isolation and refuge from the strictures of court, only to be transformed into beasts for a time. Rather, these images run throughout classical mythology, and are even present in the Bible. Though the biblical characters do not specifically live in woods, Palestine and the Middle East having more deserts than forests, their retreat from society into wild and ungoverned spaces aptly prefigure European arboreal expanses. The New Testament contains the prophet-in-the-wilderness story of John the Baptist who lived off locusts and wild honey whilst communing with God, and the Old Testament describes the Babylonian King Nebuchadnezzar as a king-turned-beast. The latter legend, recorded in the Book of Daniel, contains a description of the chain of events that precipitated the King's metamorphosis from man to beast.

> The kingdom is departed from thee ... The same hour was the thing fulfilled upon Nebuchadnezzar: and he was driven from men, and did eat grass as oxen, and his body was wet with the dew of heaven, till his hairs were grown like eagles' feathers, and his nails like birds' claws.
> (Daniel 4:31–33)

These accounts illustrate that movement into the wilderness or forest can depict a departure from 'kingdom', or established society with its rules, statutes, hierarchies and protection, and that such a move triggers transformation. Shakespeare utilises these well-known concepts of social withdrawal in his sylvan topographies.

Whether such an exile is self-imposed, such as in the case of Timon of Athens, or enforced through necessity as in the case of Valentine in *Two Gentlemen of Verona*, it empowers the sylvan traveller to engage in the reinvention of the self outside of the strictures of a regulated society. Nebuchadnezzar's physical and mental state is altered by his stint in the wilderness, reduced to a primal and desperate creature – a motif that recurs in Bottom's transformation into a beast and the savagery conducted in the forest in *Titus Andronicus*.

The 'Wildman' trope is embodied in the Shakespearean characters of Oliver in *As You Like It* and the eponymous Timon, figures that are transformed either voluntarily or by accident through their interaction with the woods. Barton highlighted the significance of the classical Greek *hyle*, a word used simultaneously for forest and chaos, in an attempt to rethink the meaning of the forest in Renaissance drama.[18] The Wodewose or Wildman appears throughout the period, variously depicted as hairy, primitive and animalistic. Yet Barton does not draw any sort of meaningful cultural significance from this figure – hinting at, but never joining the dots to possibilities of alienation from God, or from corrupted society or even the thought of internal struggle between humankind's visceral nature and the higher ideological and socially laudable ethic to which they aspire. Abigail Scherer comes closest to understanding the dramatic purpose of the Wildman in her assertion that such a character presents 'a living challenge to reason and its emerging restraints during the early modern period in England'.[19] This internal conflict between man's attempts to control his nature and his desire to be freed of all social constraints is enacted within Shakespeare's sylvan settings. Timon's wildness is synonymous with his geographic environ. His servant describes him as a lost creature that 'walks like contempt alone' (4.2.15). This 'contempt' takes the form of Timon's riling against the hypocrisy and corruption of the so-called democratic and civilised city of Athens. In this instance the Wildman is neither primitive nor animalistic, nor is he a chaotic, disordered or mad figure. Rather, Shakespeare inverts city and forest, Wildman and citizen, to critique, satirise and subvert an image of civilisation upon which his own early modern society was modelled.

Realising the forest – dramatic representations of green space

Polly Findlay's *As You Like It*, for the National Theatre in 2015, is probably one of the most imaginative and thought-provoking visual stagings of the play as she merged and mirrored aspects of the urban and its concomitant ideologies within her innovative Forest of Arden. The court was presented as the office floor of a modern corporation, the courtiers replaced with executives, the lavish furnishings of a palace substituted with uniform rows of ubiquitous grey desks and tables that were subsequently hoisted skywards to become the chaotic wintery, skeletal tangle of the forest's bare canopy (Figure 3.1). Critics labelled the spectacular transformation as everything from 'an ingenious visual coup'[20] to an 'anti-Edenic Dismaland'.[21] Alice Saville hinted at the significance of the translation that takes place in staging forest and city when

Figure 3.1 Polly Findlay's *As You Like It*, for the National Theatre in 2015.

she claimed it to be a 'visual transition from repressive order to wild wood chaos with the most spectacular scene change the National has housed in years'.[22] However, these visual signifiers of the forest as a reflection or reorganisation of the urban social scene into a parody was for the most part missed in critical responses to Lizzie Clachan's extraordinary set. The understanding of the forest as society inverted, a geography that is at once familiar yet strange, a liminal setting that reflects certain aspects of society but displays them as skewed, even ugly, follows Anne Barton's previously noted observations of forest and city merging or inverting their identities. In this respect we may come to understand the significance and social process of staging and reception of the forest in early modern theatres.

It is this kind of image that Shakespeare cultivates and teases out in his contrasting the forest with the city in his plays. From the recurring Athenian woods to the forest of Arden, Shakespeare situates the action of many of his plays in what Northrop Frye labelled the 'green world', a conceptual social space or virtual geography that served to contrast civilisation with the natural world.[23] Frye describes this green world as central to comic plots that move from city to forest and back again, exploring 'the ritual theme of the triumph of life and love over the waste land'.[24] Linking this ideal to the 'dream world that we create with our own desires', he claims that Shakespearean comedies illustrate 'the archetypal function of literature in visualising the world of desire, not as an escape from "reality," but as the genuine form of the world that human life tries to imitate'.[25] The green worlds of the forests, woods, moors and the like here come to represent an alternative reality, a world free of the constraints of social practice with its moral strictures and oppressive etiquette.

In his contrast of city and country, Raymond Williams amalgamated forest and pastoral under the heading of 'country' or 'nature', describing it 'as a retreat and solace from human society and ordinary human consciousness'.[26] When viewed in this light, the forest becomes a realm that allows the visitor to explore another side of his or her humanity, to challenge and change their social circumstance as they see fit. Whilst it is true that many of Shakespeare's comic plays follow this formula of correcting or altering the realities of a structured society only after a jaunt into the wild where other options are explored, Frye's critical approach to the forest and wilderness is somewhat reductive and confining. In this light the green world of the forest is Arcadian, benign and harmonious. Yet this image can hardly be justified in the woods of *A Midsummer Night's Dream*, a far from idyllic setting with fey tricksters and spiteful fairies. Frye's image of the comic greenwood bears an affinity to the Victorian notions of petite and temperate fairies and quaint gentle woods and a happily-ever-after resolution to a temporary social setback – a far cry from Puck's ominous first epilogue describing a world filled with portentous occurrences, ravenous and savage beasts, open graves and vivid nightmares. This latter world is closer to Frye's idea of tragic drama with its focus on loss of the 'green and golden world', synonymous with Edenic 'loss of innocence'.[27] Rather, Shakespeare's forests are more akin to the Spenserian 'woods and wanton wilderness' into which moral and social cultivation does not reach.[28]

Eight years after the publication of Northrop Frye's *Anatomy of Criticism*, which outlined the principles of his green world, Jan Kott countered Frye's Arcadian ideals when he described Shakespeare's midsummer comedy as 'this cruel dream' and a 'brutal and violent play'.[29] For Kott, the forest represents a departure from the constrictions of normative sexual relationships, Bottom's transformation into an ass synonymous with 'abundant sexual potency' rather than folly.[30] So too is the forest which is the lovers' retreat from the strictures of Athenian law and patriarchal control.[31] In response to Kott's reimagining of the forest was Peter Brook's landmark production of *Dream* in 1970. The set comprised an unadorned, glaringly white box in which both the forest and the court were staged. Alan Howard and Sara Kestelman, doubling their roles as Theseus and Hippolyta, transformed into Oberon and Titania, effectively revealed the alter egos of the rulers, reinforcing this ambiguity of setting. Brook's use of doubling saw courtiers as fairies who, instead of the Victorian images of innocent children, were intimidating adult men.[32] The translation of Bottom from man to monster carried with it the most blatant sexual overtones and the deliberate mortification of Titania by her husband, the mechanical carried from the stage with an enormous erect phallus (an actor's arm thrust between Bottom's legs), and Mendelssohn's Wedding March ironically playing over the top of it all.[33] Far from the humour and family-friendly productions most commonly staged,

Brook's *Dream* emphasised the disturbingly skewed relationship between Titania and Oberon, and by extension that of Theseus and Hippolyta. For Brook as for Kott, *Dream* may have been set within the woods, but these woods were far from Frye's green world, rather a grotesque perversion of sexuality that challenged homogeneous social ideals. That the woods were indiscernible from the Athenian court blurred and challenged the parameters of these spaces along with their socio-culturally defined meanings and authority – the entire space becoming a liminal and blank canvas on which Brook could impose new visions of the play, contesting modern tendencies towards romanticising *Dream*'s woodland setting and its denizens.

So too does the sentimentalising of the Shakespearean forests fail to consider the contemporary attitudes towards England's forest preserves. Edward Berry notes that

> throughout the Elizabethan and Jacobean periods, the forests of England were sites of social, economic, and political conflict. Both the forests and the purlieus around them were often inhabited by poor people, vagabonds and squatters driven off farms elsewhere by the conversion of agricultural land to sheep-grazing.[34]

This idea of the forest as a haven for those citizens who were forced from their land occurs in *As You Like It*, giving extra weight to the Duke's metaphor for the forest as a city and the activities of the hunt representing the human predilection for tyranny and violence particularly towards one's fellow man:

> Come, shall we go and kill us venison?
> And yet it irks me the poor dappled fools,
> Being native burghers of this desert city,
> Should in their own confines with forkèd heads
> Have their round haunches gored
>
> (2.1.21–25)

This passage also places the forest as a uniquely liminal space, a 'desert city' in which socio-political conflict is staged – a place of ambiguity in which the politically disaffected, the socially displaced and the downtrodden are pitted against the establishment. We may call this space ambiguous because despite it being a preserve of the privileged it also constitutes a vast, dense space impossible to police effectively, that is out of the public eye and easy to lose oneself in. It is the place to which the Duke retreats, a political exile, setting up a court in opposition to his brother. Here the court is not a new forest-city in the sense of the forest metamorphosing into a city as with Findlay's production, but a representation of governing structures of civilisation experienced within the city, specifically an attempt at constructing a more liberal society in contrast to that of Duke Frederick. That Duke Senior and his entourage are likened to 'the old Robin Hood of England' (1.1.111) reinforces this image of political opposition and protest. Furthermore, Orlando's first impression of the forest reflects contemporary attitudes of the forest as being a place of political refuge but also barbarity and lawlessness: 'I thought that all things had been savage here' (2.7.107).

What Orlando's surprised observation highlights is that the forest is more than simply a leafy locale but that social and cultural expectations and individual epistemological experience and understanding turn a physical geographic space into a conceptual one. In his *L'Archéologie du savoir* (1969) Michel Foucault emphatically argued that assigning meaning was a process that passed 'through the authority of an individual or collective consciousness in order to grasp the place of articulation'.[35] In an attempt to qualify the transition from practical to epistemological, between the social space and the mental space, Henri Lefebvre posited that space is 'produced', the effect of knowledge and ideology.[36] Thus the significance of Shakespeare's forests and woods cannot be firmly fixed as either green worlds or realms of savagery but change according to individual and collective experience, or as Lefebvre posits, 'mental and social activity impose their own meshwork upon nature's space, [...] upon that chaos which precedes the advent of the body'.[37] The importance of the forest's ambiguity and fluidity is in its chameleonic adaptability to reflect or project the needs or urges of those 'bodies' who enter its borders, offering protection, a space of protest, a place of perversion and sexual appetite, but always maintaining its complex meanings in the individual or social consciousness. Thus, when used as a dramatic setting, the arboreal expanse becomes a space of friction and contestation in which individuals are forced to confront their deeper motivations and ideologies that may run counter to the socially established norms.

Possibly in an attempt to amalgamate the disparate theoretical and symbolic aspects of the dramatic forest, Jeffrey S. Theis proposes an entirely new way of identifying sylvan settings. Theis sees Shakespeare's representation of the forest 'as a theatrical stage where characters try out and test individual identities'.[38] Yet he complicates this setting with his definition of a new genre or, more precisely, sub-genre of drama – the sylvan pastoral. Defining this as 'pastoral moments set in wood', Theis seeks to move elements of the open countryside and cultivated fields under the boughs of the forest in a way that engages with 'forest-related issues', dominant socio-cultural concerns in respect to English forests and woodland, and the ideological inference of these spaces with their concomitant cultural meanings.[39] The forest becomes the centre not simply for anti-authoritarian 'Robin Hood' figures but also a haven for landless migrants who could stake a claim and eke out an existence in the woods in an increasingly enclosed land. Thus, the forest's bounds are problematised and its laws ambiguous in its economic, social and political significance in the building of ships and housing, hunting of game and preservation of natural reserves. In this way the forest is both wild and fragile, a bountiful haven of beasts and yet a limited resource, a monarchical jurisdiction yet easily appropriated by those who would settle under its canopy. What Theis suggests is that early modern 'sylvan pastoral' drama and poetry redefined the space of the forest. He avers that the Spenserian and Dantean allegorical portrayals of sinister woods that foster all the worst human qualities and that represent divine alienation are dismissed. Instead he proposes the sylvan pastoral be seen as a new space that is 'intelligible and habitable', a place where meeting a 'pastoral character whose knowledge of sylvan place, alleviates (or promises to alleviate) the migrants' fears'.[40] However, in this reclassification Theis forces further division and complication of the function of the forest, its ambiguities, its shared function in both comedic and tragic dramatic works, and the ever present moral, physical and ideological threat posed once a character enters its bounds.

Thus, significant complications arise in attempting to qualify the purpose of the wooded fringes of the civilised centres of Shakespeare's dramatic worlds. Are they benign or sinister, do they represent alienation or liberation, do they represent a challenge to social order and if so do they facilitate change not just in the individual who enters their depths but in the society from which he has been separated? What's more, how might early modern as well as contemporary staging of Shakespeare's sylvan settings complicate or reinforce such tropes?

In regards to the latter question, before a more thorough look at the dramatic forest can be undertaken, consideration must first be given to the physical representation or imaginative recreation of Shakespeare's wooded environs on the stage. Peter Brook's provocative 'white box' staging is actually less controversial than it may at first appear, as it looks back towards the limitations of the early modern stage. One might argue that the very space of the Globe's stage was dominated by two mighty oak pillars that could easily fill both the function of pillars within a court or the trunks of trees within a forest – tying social setting with liminal wilderness. In reference to these stage pillars, Tim Fitzpatrick concludes that the vertical stage posts could often signify trees and, by extension, the forest.[41] Though Shakespeare's stage directions are somewhat sparse, there are indications that these posts may have been used to represent trees in *As You Like It*, when Orlando hangs his verses on trees and is later castigated for it by Rosalind. Fitzpatrick also draws attention to the yew trees mentioned in *Romeo and Juliet* as being 'explicitly visual' and that the physical geography of the stage – its vertical posts – lends itself to actors using these permanent onstage resources as trees.[42]

That is not to say that there would not have been the odd visual aid in the form of stage properties employed to aid the audience's imagination. The debate over whether actual stage properties of trees were used in early modern theatres is not important here. However, there are certain arguments made on each side of the historical debate that are worthy of consideration when it comes to understanding the theatrical impact of forests and how an audience may have perceived them. Michael Hattaway presents the physical environs of the early modern theatre from its construction to its props or properties.[43] He argues that the elaborate props employed in court performances would likely have seen use on the public stages, a means to test or rehearse their use for enactments before a more genteel audience. This idea of visual aids and representations of forests, woods and trees to heighten the imagination of the observer, just as smaller props such as a crown, wig, sword or pig's blood would enhance the appearance of reality, is not implausible.

That such properties would be consistently reused for subsequent performances and even different plays fits in with the idea of theatre recycling everything from building materials, in the reconstruction of The Theatre as The Globe, clothing, in the hand-me-down finery used by actors, and even plots in the reworking of popular plays. However, what this also shows is that staging the forest was more than simply a prologue's job to embellish an 'unworthy scaffold' (*Henry V*, Prologue, 10) through words alone, beseeching an audience to 'eke out our performance with your mind' (Act 3, Prologue, 45). Rather, a physical representation could be conjured onto the stage not only to boost the imagination but also call to mind the cultural and social significance of forests and woods.[44]

In a radical extension of the debate over how forests and woods were represented in early modern theatre, Vin Nardizzi situates London's outdoor theatres (Globe, Fortune, Hope, Swan, Red Lion, Curtain, Red Bull, Rose, Newington Butts and Boar's Head) in an environmental and economic setting. Nardizzi sees these theatres as 'new woodlands' or 'virtual woods' in an urban location – playing on the significance of the very materials used in their construction.[45] Using references throughout Shakespeare's plays Nardizzi attempts to demonstrate that the playwright worked 'on and in concert with the audience's "thoughts"', to 'revitalize woodlands during performance', not through analogy or simile, but through fusing the sylvan space with the theatrical space in referencing the very materials that the theatre was built with – effectively 'enchanting dead wood'.[46] Nardizzi's thesis centres on the premise that 'England's trees – represented as theatre – were virtually brought back to life whenever a character entered the woods'.[47] Admittedly, this claim appears somewhat tenuous, as Nardizzi acknowledges it is impossible to determine how early modern theatregoers perceived the space of the theatre in woodland scenes. However, he does call on the ubiquitous playgoer and diarist Simon Forman's recollections of *Macbeth*, *The Winter's Tale* and *Cymbeline*, shown at The Globe in 1611, in each case making references to 'wod' and 'wodes' where there is either no stage direction in the text to suggest such specific settings.[48] It is implied that Forman filled in such a backdrop with the visual reminders of the theatre-that-once-was-wood embellishing his already vivid imagination. Nardizzi supplements Forman's reviews with John Norden and J. C. Visscher's respective visions of London and the early seventeenth century that each depict The Globe surrounded by trees and woodland, arguing that the theatre's geographic setting as well as its material structure heightened the audience's imagination in scenes that were set in woodland.

Nardizzi's work on uncovering dramatic references to the space of the theatre representing the forest through its very building materials may at the outset appear something of a leap, particularly from his ecocritical, socio-economic standpoint that attempts to take the value and significance of timber to a conscious place within theatre. Yet he addresses the performative space as important as the text itself in conveying and representing Shakespeare's wooded scenes.

Hence, what early modern and contemporary stagings of Shakespeare's wooded worlds highlight is that such spaces are heavy with cultural and social significance. As liminal spaces beyond the reach of centralised structures of authority, Shakespeare's forests and woods come to represent the dramatic setting of resistance to such systems of power. That it is a locale synonymous with inversion, transformation and defiance of collective control, represented by the city, makes the forest a semantically complicated and theatrically attractive space in which to present possibilities, even radical alternatives, to challenge the socio-political status quo.

The Freudian forest

The dramatic purpose of the forest reflecting the inner state of a character is carried through into Shakespeare's first foray into tragedy. The shadows of the woodland outside Rome in *Titus Andronicus* provide the opportunity for the wild abandon of Tamora and Aaron, followed by the murder of Bassianus, a gruesome foreplay to the violent rape and mutilation of Lavinia. In this, the forest is a reflection of the inner or repressed individual, free of the constraints of moral order, taking on the hue of their internal temperament and outlook. Indeed, as Berry notes, the forest is 'a projection of the forces that lie within the characters'.[49] In this regard, the forest becomes a metaphoric mind-space for the relationship between the conscious and unconscious, something Sigmund Freud's theory on the ego and the id aptly describes.

> The ego has the task of bringing the influence of the external world to bear upon the id and its tendencies, and endeavours to substitute the reality-principle for the pleasure-principle which reigns supreme in the id. In the ego, perception plays the part which in the id devolves upon instinct. The ego represents what we call reason and sanity, in contrast to the id, which contains the passions.[50]

We can see this theoretical mental power-dynamic in *Titus* where the forest's darkness and distance from the socially subscribed spaces of control allows for the emergence of the hedonistic Freudian id, unfettered from the ego's moral limitations. For Tamora, eager for a clandestine tryst with her lover, the forest is beauteous: 'everything doth make a gleeful boast' (2.3.11). Enchanted with birdsong and harmony in the elements and nature, Tamora's forest is a sensuous and pleasing environment, suited to her purpose – a repetition of the poetic wilds of *Venus and Adonis*. Yet for Aaron the forest is a much darker place that reflects his dreadful determination – 'Madam, though Venus govern your desires / Saturn is dominator over mine' (lines 30, 31). Aaron's aggression and murderous designs soon reshape Tamora's perception of the forest, which she now describes as 'a barren detested vale' (line 93), its vegetation appearing 'forlorn', 'lean' and 'baleful' (lines 94, 95). The Queen's abrupt shift in humour and her resultant representation of the surroundings reflects her murkier, suppressed state of mind and not only parallels, but is released by, the gloomy shelter of the forest.

A similar effect of the forest reflecting the true motivations and moral leanings of those who enter its canopy later occurs in *As You Like It*:

> Now, my co-mates and brothers in exile,
> Hath not old custom made this life more sweet
> Than that of painted pomp? Are not these woods
> More free from peril than the envious court?
>
> (2.1.1–4)

Despite Duke Senior's ignominious exile, his optimism and inner virtues are reflected in his expressions towards the new life in the forests of Arden. For the Duke, woodland life is 'more sweet', freed of the intrigues and savagery of the court; his relief takes on a philosophical bent that even the adverse elements are unable to dampen – 'these are counsellors / that feelingly persuade me what

I am' (2.1.10, 11). Perhaps it is this comment alone that defines the purpose of the Shakespearean forest – to hold a mirror up to unbridled desire, human nature and frailty. Free of the structures and strictures society attempts to place on the way its citizens behave and think, the woodland realms are on the edge of civilisation and allow Shakespeare to flesh out his characters, presenting his audience with the opportunity to witness the more unsettling sides of human behaviour. As Freud hypothesises, 'the ego constantly carries into action the wishes of the id as if they were its own'; and the forest is the setting in which these actions play out.[51] Within these liminal spaces are the fires of temptation, the lure of freedom, the space to challenge and invert the status quo, the occasion to confront humanity with all its corruption and virtue, and to 'persuade' the individual as to their true nature. The demons and devils within the forest are not pre-existing but are brought there within the minds of those who enter it, and from there they are figuratively given space either to flourish or be conquered.

That the Shakespearean forest serves to mirror the internal flaws and secret designs of characters who enter its shelter is further emphasised in Aaron's description of the forest as a cover for carnal excess:

> The forest walks are wide and spacious;
> And many unfrequented plots there are
> Fitted by kind for rape and villany:
> Single you thither then this dainty doe,
> And strike her home by force
>
> (2.1.115–119)

Once again it is violent and animal images of the hunt used to plot the misdeed against the Roman general's daughter. Contrasting the court with the wilderness, Aaron continues, driving home the image of the primal woods with forceful alliterative verse:

> To your wishes' height advance you both.
> The Emperor's court is like the house of Fame,
> The palace full of tongues, of eyes and ears,
> The woods are ruthless, dreadful, deaf, and dull.
> There speak and strike, brave boys, and take your turns.
> There serve your lust, shadowed from heaven's eye,
> And revel in Lavinia's treasury
>
> (2.1.126–132)

Here the woods are again shown to be in stark contrast to the city – cruel, lawless, a haven for violence and sordid action, conveniently sheltering the felons from both the eyes of the Court and the moral management of the Church. Robert Harrison describes the Church's hostility towards the 'impassive frontier of unhumanized nature' and a Christian mythology that built up around forests as being associated with 'bestiality, fallenness, errancy, [and] perdition'.[52] This forest of divine alienation shadows the Dantean progress into the abyss:

> When I had journeyed half of our life's way,
> I found myself within a shadowed forest,
> for I had lost the path that does not stray.
> Ah, it is hard to speak of what it was,
> that savage forest, dense and difficult,
> which even in recall renews my fear.
>
> (*The Divine Comedy*, Canto 1. 1–6)[53]

For Dante, as for Demetrius and Chiron, the forest is physically and morally outside of God's grace, a place of savagery, Shakespeare appropriating both language and metaphor from the Italian epic. A move into the forest thus represents the medieval worldview; a challenge to the heavenly order, the Church, the divinely appointed monarchy and the social organisation built around Christian ideals.

Shakespeare borrows the Chaucerian imagery of a house filled with eyes, ears and mouths in which the secrets of the inner person must be tamped down to avoid exposure, and contrasts it with the wildness of the woods in which such secrets could be released without fear of public censure. However, the allusion to Chaucer's *House of Fame* (1379), and the changed behaviours of Demetrius and Chiron once inside the woods opens the way for both a psychoanalytical and a feminist critique of what Shakespeare is doing within this liminal space. Aaron's winsome persuasion notably references Chaucer's fourteenth-century poetry, which lists a host of mythical Greek women deceived and mistreated by their lovers, prefiguring Lavinia's own unfortunate outcome. Chaucer drew from the same sources as Shakespeare, using the writings of Ovid, Boccaccio and Virgil, and bringing their women together in a dream-scape that paints the male protagonists as far from heroic, but rather as beasts whose lack of decorum and animalistic drives leave a host of broken women in their wake. What Shakespeare does, however, is take Ovid's Philomel and place her firmly in a forest setting where the imagery of the hunt marries violent masculine activity with sexual savagery towards Lavinia.[54] Roberts posits that the woods in *Titus Andronicus* represent the 'arena of the power struggle' between men and women.[55] As with Shakespeare's *Venus and Adonis*, the forest or hunting preserve becomes a place where women pursue love and men pursue fierce pleasure. However, in the case of Demetrius and Chiron, these violent sports are exercised on the female body. Freudian ideas of psychic impotence, later known as the whore-madonna complex or virgin-whore complex, play out in the seemingly contradictory speech patterns the brothers use.[56] Chiron's chivalric assertions of love for Lavinia begin with overly flowery and romantic proclamations of his worthiness for his 'mistress' grace' (2.1.34), his 'passions for Lavinia's love' (line 36), and that he 'love[s] Lavinia more than the whole world' (line 72).[57] His elder brother takes the line of patriarchal privilege, using anaphora to emphatically state 'she is a woman, therefore may be wooed / she is a woman, therefore may be won / she is Lavinia therefore must be loved' (lines 82–84). Though Lavinia may already be married, we are still presented with two prevailing contemporaneous attitudes towards women expressed by the brothers, namely romantic desire and protective ownership. Yet how quickly these ideals give way in the shadow world of the woods, acknowledged in Demetrius's closing Dante-esque line, *'per Styga, per manes vehor'* (line 136), 'through Stygian realms (the world of the dead) I am conveyed'. Darker thoughts lead to inevitable transgression but not before the language describing Lavinia undergoes a radical reshaping; the mistress becomes a 'minion' (2.3.124), the woman a 'wasp' (line 132) and the virtuous lady is now a 'trull' or prostitute (line 191). Here we see the Freudian notion of the virgin-whore dichotomy, revealed in the way Lavinia is fetishised, now synonymous with a piece of meat, a 'dainty doe' (2.2.24) to be brought to ground and butchered. Richard Tuch explains that the whore-madonna complex manifests as a tendency for men to view women one-dimensionally as either adorable or screwable, but not both. Women are categorized into one of two classes: ideal and pure women who are to be loved in a wholly tender, affectionate even worshipful way and harlot-like women who want nothing more than to screw and, accordingly, are viewed by these men as debased on account of their thirst for sex.[58]

He goes on to state that this complex, in Freudian psychoanalysis, manifests itself where the relationship between child and mother has been damaged and that, in order to elevate his mother to the madonna figure, the child must debase other women, displacing his 'hatred and sadism'.[59] Tamora certainly wields considerable power over her sons, demanding their loyalty and love to achieve her ends. Her demand to be revenged, 'as you love your mother's life / or be ye not henceforward called my children' (2.3.114, 115), is met with instant acquiescent displays of devotion as Bassianus is unceremoniously slain. Lavinia herself notes the toxic foundations of the relationship between the barbarian mother and her brutal offspring when she says, 'o, do not learn her wrath! She taught it thee / the milk thou sucked'st from her did turn to marble / even at thy teat thou hadst thy tyranny' (2.3.143–145). Perhaps most telling in this whore-madonna complex that reveals itself within the forest is Tamora's command to her sons regarding Lavinia's immediate future: 'away with her, and use her as you will / the worse to her, the better loved of me' (lines 166, 167).

What the forest opens up to Shakespeare is the opportunity to explore new models and dynamics of power, in this case, an Oedipal aberration of the mother/son relationship that turns socially acceptable behaviours towards women into stark and violent contrast. Jeanne Addison Roberts states that in *Titus Andronicus* 'the struggle is between men, but the necessary pawns are women, and the arena of power struggle is the forest'.[60] This assertion is not strictly true. As Tamora proves, it is *her* will that governs the behaviour of her sons, *her* barbaric blessing that ultimately condones their savagery and *her* need for revenge behind the grisly actions of her sons. If anything, it is Demetrius and Chiron who are pawns. However, the forest does indeed represent the 'arena of power struggle', a space in which resistance to patriarchal convention opens the way to new power dynamics. Here, on the edge of civilisation, in the dark and leafy margins, power is contested and what is deemed socially and morally true is inverted.

The gendered forest

Whilst Shakespeare uses the forest as a space to explore the deeper recesses of the human psyche and as the locus of transformation, it is also a landscape physically embodied in the boundaries of the body. In *Venus and Adonis*, the images of Venus as a forest in which her young lover can find all the primal and carnal pleasures of the hunt initially seems to express the patriarchal ideas of male dominion over the female body. Here we see a shift from the forest explicitly as an actual place with trees and animals to the understanding of the forest as an image or metaphor. As such the forest becomes a virtual geography, with symbolic topographies relating specifically to aspects of the human condition and experience. The poem is situated entirely in natural environs, shunning the city altogether with no other characters but the lovers. Parallels and euphemism between beast and man run throughout. Venus cites the 'law of nature', or the call to propagate and increase, as the reason the youthful Adonis should take her as his lover (line 171). Anatomising the geography of the forest and the imagery of the hunt she woos the handsome hunter with artful rhetoric:

> 'Fondling', she saith, 'Since I have hemmed thee here
> Within the circuit of this ivory pale,
> I'll be a park, and thou shalt be my deer:
> Feed where thou wilt, on mountain, or in dale;
> Graze on my lips, and if those hills be dry,
> Stray lower where the pleasant fountains lie.
>
> 'Within this limit is relief enough,
> Sweet bottom grass, and high delightful plain,
> Round rising hillocks, brakes obscure and rough,
> To shelter thee from tempest, and from rain:
> Then be my deer, for I am such a park.
> No dog shall rouse thee, though a thousand bark'.
>
> (lines 231–240)

Not only does the lustful goddess invert the patriarchal protocols of courtship in her headlong pursuit of the young man, she also reframes or reclaims the masculine domain of the forest, alluding to the enclosed limits of royal hunting preserves in the circumference of her 'ivory pale' arms. Here, the forest is described as a 'park', the term used by aristocrats for the land enclosed for hunting, not only to play on the idea of wild spaces reserved for manly pleasure and pursuits, but also as a means of softening and feminising the wild.[61] Elsewhere in the poem the setting is described as a 'wood' (line 323); hence Shakespeare's choice of nomenclature is a deliberate refashioning of the wild wood as a metaphor for possession; the ownership and privilege extended over the wilderness akin to that within the patriarchal bounds of marriage. This is not the only instance of this reframing of the woods in terms of a park in Shakespeare's works. In *Titus Andronicus* the mutilated Lavinia is found 'straying in the park' (3.1.88), likened to a wounded deer, the setting softened to hint both at parallels between the ritual nature of her ordeal and a hunt, and by extension as the property of Titus. In *Venus and Adonis* however, the feminine forest imagery is taken even further. The eroticised, gendered geography borders on the bawdy with both obvious and obscure references to breasts ('mountain', 'pleasant fountains'), buttocks ('round rising hillocks'), the sexual organs ('dale') and pubic hair ('sweet bottom grass', 'brakes obscure').[62] Jeanne Addison Roberts describes the two conflicting attitudes to the wilds of the forest as intersecting gender binaries. Adonis is preoccupied with the male vision of the forest, a proving ground for his masculinity; matched against the wild beasts he seeks only the company of his male peers and the thrill of the chase. However, as Roberts notes, 'Venus offers a feminised wild with an erotic prize', her euphemistic descriptions of the wilderness and the hunt challenging cultural stereotypes.[63]

Yet it is not only patriarchal privilege and gender binaries that are subverted in Shakespeare's tragic poem. Love itself is affected by the wild environs, and rather than courtly, romantic or dignified, is an impassioned, lustful craving on the part of Venus who is aggressively animalistic in her pursuit of Adonis. Their kiss is described not as an innocent or tender union but as sensual savagery; Venus is now the hunter and ravages her prey, who is once again described in terms of game brought down in the forest.

> Now quick desire hath caught the yielding prey,
> And glutton-like she feeds, yet never filleth;
> Her lips are conquerors, his lips obey,
> Paying what ransom the insulter willeth;
> Whose vulture thought doth pitch the price so high,
> That she will draw his lips' rich treasure dry,

And having felt the sweetness of the spoil,
With blindfold fury she begins to forage;
Her face doth reek and smoke, her blood doth boil,
And careless lust stirs up a desperate courage,
Planting oblivion, beating reason back,
Forgetting shame's pure blush and honour's wrack.

(lines 547–558)

The violence of Venus's assault on Adonis is styled in shocking language; the hapless youth overcome by the deity's visceral, lustful fury – here depicted as a vulture tearing flesh from a carcass. Not even the death of Adonis is portrayed in such terms of eroticised violence – if anything, the opposite is true, the boar described as 'the loving swine' who in 'nuzzling his flank' accidentally 'sheathed unaware the tusk in his soft groin' (lines 1115, 1116). Peter J. Smith describes Shakespeare's version of Venus as 'both a standard comic caricature and a threat', and goes on to add that her 'predatory appetite threatens to invert the patterns of male supremacy and female submission upon which a society like that of early modern England is predicated'.[64] Animal eroticism bound up with the imagery of the forest and hunt is not just a theme explored in this poem, but recurs in Shakespeare's association of predatory, potentially violent sexual craving with wild boars. Smith observes that both *Titus Andronicus* and *Cymbeline* use the boar as symbols of 'sexual malevolence'.[65] However, these other instances refer to masculine sexual power and not to the rapacious female sexual appetite displayed by Venus. Several years after the publication of *Venus and Adonis* Shakespeare revisited the perversion of sexual hierarchies in *A Midsummer Night's Dream*. This time it was another immortal in the woods, fawning over the inhuman form of an ass-headed clown – an inversion not only of sexual dynamics and patriarchal principle, but also of the classical myths surrounding the Cretan Minotaur.

What is noteworthy in the sylvan setting of Shakespeare's earliest narrative poem is that it complicates the 'green world' ideal set forth by Frye that the forest is a place of affirmative transformation and the triumph of love. Other than Shakespeare's 'transforming' or inverting gender stereotypes, the only metamorphosis it contains is the Ovidian conclusion to the tale of Adonis's change into a flower, forever a part of the wilderness he died in – ironically, not a symbol of masculinity, but the very thing he fought against: love. What Shakespeare does here is to play with conventional themes and twist them until they become absurd, grotesque and ambiguous. The forest setting is the locus for violence, the more sordid side to love, its canopy a shelter for the primal and visceral. Harrison, noted earlier, observes that the forest represents 'the shadow of the sexual impulse, where the benevolence of love gives way to dramas of violence'.[66] Rather than transforming per se, the forest allows an exploration of the darker side of the human condition, the desire for the forbidden and the corruption and subversion of laws, particularly those governing sexuality.

'A solemn hunting is in hand'

Shakespeare's hunt analogies run throughout the plays and constitute the need to prove oneself against nature – in the forests it is human nature that is the quarry, either being overcome and brought to heel or running loose to wreak havoc. Indeed, 'havoc' occurs nine times, both as a noun and a verb, in Shakespeare's plays and in each case it is used as a metaphor drawn from the hunt to imply recklessness, wildness and abandon – a departure from the civilised, chivalric and social ideal. Anne Barton observes that havocking was the term used for the practice of breaking into the grounds or park belonging to someone else and 'systematically slaughter[ing] everything in sight', effectively a bloody and uncontrolled destruction of life not for the necessity of food but the sheer thrill of unrestrained killing.[67] Menenius pleads, 'do not cry havoc where you should but hunt / with modest warrant' (*Coriolanus*, 3.1.274–275), a desperate attempt to curb the simmering aggression of Brutus and the agitated rabble and restore civic peace in *Coriolanus*. In *Henry V* the King is advised by one of his lords against leaving England's lands unguarded for Scotland, 'playing the mouse in absence of the cat / to tear and havoc more than she can eat' (*Henry V*, 1.2.172–173). King John's speech at the gates of Angers condemns the actions of the French who have 'wide havoc made / for bloody power to rush upon your peace' (*King John*, 2.1.221–222). Edward Berry notes the connection between the sport and more martial pursuits when he observes that the hunt was a 'training ground in the arts of war'.[68] The fact that the forest is the preserve of the hunt, itself a violent sport, points to the human predilection towards violence. He goes on to say that most of Shakespeare's metaphoric hunt-references emphasise 'unfettered violence and murderous bloodlust' rather than any sort of chivalric ideal.[69] In *As You Like It*, it is noteworthy that the verb Shakespeare uses is 'kill' and not 'hunt' when Duke Senior asks of Amiens, 'come, shall we go and kill us venison' (2.1.21). 'Hunt' would have maintained the iambic rhythm but also softened the idea of the activity, elevating it to the aristocratic sport. 'Kill' reduces the deed to an unmitigated act of violence, underscored when the Duke anthropomorphises the deer as 'native burghers of this desert city' (line 23) who are slain in their homes. The moralising and melancholic Jaques takes this imagery further, applying it to the nature of men whom he sees as 'usurpers' and 'tyrants' (line 61). The implication here is that the nature of man is to usurp his power, to take a position for which he is not entitled and to tyrannise those whom he should be viewing as his equal. The forest setting is what makes this observation all the more poignant as it suggests that, even outside the hierarchies of state-imposed authority and governance, man's inherent nature is to dominate and subjugate through violence.

This image of Shakespeare's Forest of Arden does not sit easily with previous romantic views of an idyllic leafy retreat in which William Hazlitt avers 'stern necessity is banished to the court' and in which 'the very air of the place seems to breathe a spirit of philosophical poetry'.[70] Even in more recent years have the quixotic notions of Arden persisted. In her chapter titled 'Another Eden, Another Arden', Katherine Duncan-Jones references *As You Like It* and the work of one of Shakespeare's contemporaries, Michael Drayon's *Poly-Olbion* (1612), as having the actual Forest of Arden in Warwickshire as both source and inspiration for their settings, imbued with nostalgia for a leafy heart of England.[71] She asserts that the literary pedigree of Warwickshire and its neighbouring counties, that each produced notable early modern poets, playwrights and writers, is seen as an 'Eden' of sorts, the mild political and religious climate in the 1570s and 1580s nurturing the creative arts. This is something of a misconception as she fails to consider the socio-political climate of London, a city that nurtured the creative talents of Dekker, Milton, Jonson, Hall, Middleton and countless other successful writers in this period. However, she asserts that Shakespeare's local wooded environs are represented in the Duke's forest court in *As You Like It*, a liberal, inclusive and relaxed sylvan pastoral community, describing this play as 'Shakespeare's most explicitly personal play', with its celebration of the mythic Forest of Arden, the conversation between Touchstone and William a playful shadowy dialogue 'between the wealthy and quick-witted playwright and the provincial youth he has left behind him in the Forest of Arden'.[72] Yet both William Hazlitt's and Duncan-Jones's reading of Arden neglect to include the element of savagery that is either referenced in the ferocity of the lion's attack on Oliver, in the death of Adam, or in Duke Senior's and Jaques's moralising on the hunt as an analogy for the human leaning towards ferocity and the wilful exercise of power over the weak.

Aaron's malevolent counsel to Tamora's wayward sons centres on both imagery of the hunt and the geographic setting in which such pursuits take place.

> My lords, a solemn hunting is in hand;
> There will the lovely Roman ladies troop:
> The forest walks are wide and spacious;
> And many unfrequented plots there are
> Fitted by kind for rape and villany:
> Single you thither then this dainty doe,
> And strike her home by force, if not by words
> (*Titus Andronicus*, 2.1.113–119)

Barton observes that the forest of *Titus Andronicus* 'keeps shifting not only its character, but even its definition'.[73] Aaron's outline for the gratification and revenge of the barbarian princes underscores the forest as an unstable setting that changes to suit the needs and temperament of those who enter its bounds. The ritualistic 'solemn hunting' is corrupted to the malicious pursuits of rapine and murder, the 'unfrequented plots' a metaphor for the darker, hidden recesses of his nature. 'Wide and spacious' forest paths play on the Christian imagery of 'wide is the gate, and broad is the way that leadeth to destruction, and many there be which go in thereat' (Matthew 7:13), charting man's predisposition to follow an ultimately destructive self-interest. Thus, Aaron illustrates the necessity to find external spaces or activities that will reflect and nurture inner thoughts and feelings – in this case the forest as a setting and the hunt as a sport can be manipulated or corrupted to suit the savage inclinations of man. As Berry notes, the whole process of the hunt is ritualised, enacting 'human domination over wild nature while at the same time acknowledging implicitly the wildness in human nature itself'.[74] This imposition of character on setting highlights the fluidity, malleability and flexibility of liminal spaces, sites of contestation that explore the murkier convolutions of human consciousness.

The carnival forest

It is in the woods of *A Midsummer Night's Dream* that all the elements of gender, darker Freudian motifs and violence combine in mocking inversions of social order that may initially seem to conform to Frye's vision of transformative green worlds but that actually adhere more to Bakhtinian concepts of the carnivalesque. As in the sinister sylvan setting of *Titus Andronicus*, there is more than simply a modicum of carnival contrariness taking place in Shakespeare's midsummer fantasy. Liminal characters such as Bottom and Puck play with power, whether innocently or deliberately, the ripples of which are not entirely contained by the play's conclusion. Subverting the status quo, the four lovers flee from patriarchy and pursue their own agendas outside of Athens. Yet they are then subjected to another act of subversion as they are denied their own right to choose their partners when Puck misapplies his love potion. In each of these cases carnival inversion reaps disturbingly aberrant results, with more than a hint of bestiality, gross disruption of class, and the permanent bewitching of Demetrius, a man no longer in charge of his own will. Does Shakespeare here imply that there are repercussions for straying from the well-established and morally laudable tenets of society, or does he simply reveal that once social norms have been breached there is no containing them? Is he suggesting that the human tendency towards rebellion will inevitably exert itself, even violently, to counter the structures and restraints of contemporary codes? Whatever the reason, the forest provides the arena for change, and it is not Frye's benign vision of transformation. Rather, the forest allows those bound by social conformity, constrained by class, religion and patriarchy, to disrupt the status quo and experiment with alternate structures that are then subsumed or absorbed into the social norm.

Mikhail Bakhtin's pivotal *Rabelais and his World* (1968) opened up new ways of looking at the dynamics and the play of power in literature, notably in his theory of the carnivalesque: an often disrespectful or satirical experiment to subvert authority and the conventional social order. Challenging traditional hierarchies and social structure was not a Renaissance literary innovation but, as Bakhtin proved, a common theme throughout the Middle Ages. Its purpose was twofold, first, the 'negative' application of carnival, which served to draw attention to the disparities between classes, a 'moral condemnation' of the behaviours of the aristocracy and clergy.[75] The positive aspect of carnival was its regenerative aspect, a means by which social frustrations and anxieties could be released; effectively a pressure valve that once opened could temporarily invert the balance of power before social stability was restored.[76] What is significant about the presence of carnival within Shakespeare is that it is rarely contained within the locus of the play, rather spilling out and including the audience in its subversive and festive action. Michael Holquist notes of this phenomenon that 'carnival does not know footlights, in the sense that it does not acknowledge any distinction between actors and spectators'.[77] Thus, when the carnivalesque is manifest with Shakespeare's drama the effect is that it creates a unique social geography, crossing from locus to platea, from play to audience. As previously noted, Weimann described the division of the stage in terms of the locus being both the central stage space and fantasy realm of the play and also symbolic of a place within the social hierarchy, notably that of privilege. Carnival inverts or disrupts this boundary; effectively extending the platea to include the audience within the space of the play. This is in part what occurs when the settings change in *Dream*, shifting from central Athens to the mysterious woods on its margins.

A Midsummer Night's Dream begins in the city, moving into the forest for the bulk of the play before returning briefly to Theseus's court. Alvin Kernan asserts that this clear structure of contrasting locales highlights the 'sharp opposition of place that characterises Shakespeare's geography', a formulaic dichotomy of 'two place structure' that explored the 'possibilities of meaning' in society.[78] For *A Midsummer Night's Dream* the wild woods become a carnival inversion of the city. For Kernan the city represents 'civility, reason, law, tradition, family, manners, order [and] government', a structure of man-made principles that have tamed the wilder side of human nature just as the physical streets and city walls have brought order to the former wilderness.[79] The woods and forests outside of Athens hark back to a time of less restraint often manifest in dramatic changes to human behaviour that becomes governed by the visceral, primal and carnal. This latter place is where the man-made world is inverted and challenged, a place where freedom exists, released from the bounds and strictures of the social status quo surrounding morals, concepts of identity and place. The effect of the sylvan wild is in the formation, however temporary, of an alternate social model and falls in line with the concept of liminal spaces exerting pressure on the centre of social order, an order upheld by law, morals, manners, faith and tradition; and that such pressure shifts the centre, forcing it to relax its stance on certain social issues. However, what Kernan does not acknowledge in his contrasting city with forest is that freedom also goes hand in hand with an element of danger. The restraint exerted within the strictures of the city's civic code serves to curb the coarser extremities of human behaviour and once this is removed such primal urges pose a threat to new-found freedom.

The opening exchanges between Helena and Demetrius may initially seem to be the petty bickering of unrequited lovers. However, the speech of both is punctuated with references to violence and gender-inversion of the Petrarchan model of lovers. Helena's pleas invite Demetrius to treat her in the most unchivalric manner –

> I am your spaniel; and, Demetrius,
> The more you beat me, I will fawn on you.
> Use me but as your spaniel: spurn me, strike me,
> Neglect me, lose me; only give me leave,
> Unworthy as I am, to follow you.
> What worse place can I beg in your love –
> And yet a place of high respect with me –
> Than to be used as you use your dog?
>
> (2.1.203–210)

Here is a vision of love upended; rather than the tender stereotypes of love, Helena is prepared to accept a version of *eros* that involves violence, neglect and abuse, a fetishised deviation of the ideal.

Demetrius's reply hints at the allure of such an offer as he does not reject her outright but says:

> You do impeach your modesty too much,
> To leave the city and commit yourself
> Into the hands of one that loves you not;
> To trust the opportunity of night
> And the ill counsel of a desert place
> With the rich worth of your virginity.
>
> (2.1.220–226)

The setting of the 'desert place' at night brings out Demetrius's alter ego, just as it did with the Demetrius of *Titus*. Here the woods are personified as an ill counsellor, the dark adviser who whispers encouragement to pursue instant, cruel gratification. Yet in a strange carnival twist it is Demetrius who flees the huntress, to 'hide in the brakes' with a parting threat that if Helena follow he shall 'do thee mischief in the wood' (line 237). The word 'mischief' here denotes 'inflicting injury upon; to bring to grief or ruin', and not the more modern meaning of 'prank' and thus carries with it the threat of physical and sexual violence.[80] The whole interchange within this woodland setting is a corruption and inversion of accepted behaviour and gender roles. As in *Venus and Adonis*, the female takes the role of hunter and pursues her lover, putting her own virtue at risk whilst the male retreats before her using the strongest and most vicious language and imagery. Jillian Keenan reimagines the relationship between these two mismatched lovers in terms of sexual identity, their exchange highlighting 'the fundamental question at the core of every sadomasochistic relationship', Demetrius asking Helena 'how she could trust him enough to submit herself to physical risk at his hands'.[81] Though such a reading may be somewhat extreme, Keenan does underscore the unconventional nature of this exchange, its language perverting stereotypical or socially acceptable sexual behaviours in early modern England.

What this brief scene illustrates is that liminal landscapes open the way for carnivalesque reversals of natural order and the established hierarchies of power. The human agency and licence within these woods becomes manifest, as Keenan writes, 'as a condition of freedom and the free play of certain basic human passions and appetites'.[82] As with Peter Brook's emphasis on the sexually grotesque and bizarre, Russell T. Davies's adaptation of *Dream* for the screen in 2016 approached the text and setting in what is perhaps one of the darker yet peculiarly fitting interpretations of the forced marriage of Hippolyta. The Amazonian queen is wheeled in strapped to a trolley and confined in a straightjacket – once again triggering images of sadomasochistic inversions of traditional marital union. Davies's explorations appeared to be centred primarily on the sexual, underscoring homoerotic potential and at times reworking the text dramatically to labour his point. The Indian boy is no longer the source of the feud between the fairy monarchs, but it rather hinges on Titania's love for Hippolyta (who is actually a fairy queen held against her will by the fascist Duke). However, Davies's representation of the woods is particularly noteworthy. As Lysander proposes to elope with Hermia he plots their course on a touchscreen map that displays Athens, his widow aunt's house and the expanse of the forest stretched between. Highlighting their proposed route, a red line through the forest, he reassures the nervous Hermia that, once this threshold is passed, 'the sharp Athenian Law / cannot pursue us' (1.1.162–163). Here the forest serves as the edge of Athenian power, order and control, a place where, upon entry, the visitor leaves both the protection and the censure of political and social hegemony. The significance of this dangerous and deceptive liminal space is when it encroaches on the city itself, the fairies effectively storming Theseus's palace and relishing his controversial death before turning the wedding into a carnival romp. Here, patriarchal power structures and social order are truly undermined, upset beyond repair with the subversive fay-folk extending the forest's power to overthrow that of the city. Thus, the carnival element to the forest serves to satirise and ultimately subvert the status quo, offering visions of alternate or contrary behaviours that exist outside of social approval but are ever present and inherent in those who conform to such systems of authority.

The edge of the wild

In her foray into the political and religious boundaries of the early modern world Lisa Hopkins traced the edges of the physical and spiritual limens, describing them as 'unstable, permeable and open to the possibility of cross-border traffic'.[83] It is just such an 'edge' that Shakespeare crosses in his forests. Between the green wilderness and the ordered, structure of urbane society, the playwright was able to study the possibilities that lay beyond the confines of civilisation. As shown, the forest takes on a dual, paradoxical meaning. It is both sanctuary and slaughterhouse, elite retreat and commoner's refuge, royal preserve and haven for outlaws. This unstable sylvan setting serves to intensify the pressure on the individual to explore their darker side by releasing them from the confines of social, moral, legal and religious limitations. The result is that Shakespeare's wooded realms can present themselves as fierce, hazardous and a risk to social stability, yet at the same time attractive in their promise of societal freedom. This liminal landscape comprises aggressive change, inversion and rebellion. Hopkins observes that the edge is 'always a place of power' that can 'always potentially be crossed'.[84] The significance of this statement must not be downplayed – edges will inevitably be crossed, borders will eventually be broken and thresholds broached. In short, subversive challenges to authoritarian limitation become impossible to contain and control. Under Shakespeare's wooded canopy we witness patriarchal subversion, the transposition of gender binaries, the unmasking of repressed human psyche and the carnival inversions of social geography and the principles of courtship. This liminal forest setting promotes both friction and fluidity, opening the way to explore alternative practices as characters move beyond the strictures of social proprieties.

Notes

1 'Inventory of Elizabeth Nott, late of Stratford-upon-Avon, widow, deceased' (Shakespeare Birthplace Trust Collection, BRU15/1/24), p. 1. http://collections.shakespeare.org.uk/search/archive/bru15124-inventory-of-elizabeth-nott-late-of-stratford-upon-avon-widow-deceased-9-mar-1597-item/exhibition/shakespeare-connected-not-to-be-death-in-the-collection/exhibition_object/shakespeare-connected-not-to-be-death-in-the-collection-inventory-of-elizabeth-nott/page/9654 [accessed 27 Nov. 2018]

2 Vin Nardizzi, *Wooden Os: Shakespeare's Theatres and England's Trees* (Toronto: University of Toronto Press, 2013), p. 10.

3 John Manwood, *A Treatise and Discourse of the Lawes of the Forrest* (London: Adam Islip for Thomas Wight and Bonham Norton, 1598), p. 2
4 Robert Pogue Harrison, *Forests: The Shadow of Civilization* (Chicago: University of Chicago Press, 1992), p. 73.
5 Arthur Standish, *The Commons Complaint* (London, 1611), p. 2.
6 Eco-critical approaches to Shakespeare's natural worlds have been the subject of several recent scholarly monographs and collected essays. Whilst these more modern critical methodologies have been significant in reimagining the dramas in light of contemporary environmental concerns, this is not the primary focus of this study that seeks to link liminal geographies with subversion of the social status quo and the compulsion for change. For more on economic and environmental interpretations of the Shakespearean forest see Nardizzi, *Wooden Os,* and Charlotte Scott, *Shakespeare's Nature: From Cultivation to Culture* (Oxford: Oxford University Press, 2014).
7 Harrison, *Forests*, pp. 79–80.
8 Keith Thomas, *Man and the Natural World: Changing Attitudes in England 1500–1800* (London: Penguin Books, 1983), pp. 192–194.
9 Ibid., pp. 194–195.
10 Harrison, *Forests*, p. 69.
11 Anne Barton, *The Shakespearean Forest* (Cambridge: Cambridge University Press, 2017), pp. 19, 20.
12 Thomas Mallory, *Le Morte d'Arthur* (London: J. M. Dent, 1947), book XI, chapter VIII.
13 Lodovico Ariosto, *Orlando Furioso*, trans. William Stewart Rose [online access] http://www.gutenberg.org/cache/epub/615/pg615.html
14 In 1980 the Metropolitan Museum of Art assembled an exhibition, titled 'The Wild Man: Medieval Myth and Symbolism', that looked in detail primarily at the late medieval depictions of wild men in art. For further reading on the exhibition and the cultural and ideological contexts of the manuscripts, tapestries, woodcuts and other pieces see Timothy Husband's book, *The Wild Man: Medieval Myth and Symbolism* (New York: Metropolitan Museum of Art, 1980).
15 *Timon of Athens* is widely believed to have been a collaborative effort, most likely between Shakespeare and Thomas Middleton, and whilst there is no concrete consensus over which passages were written by whom, the editors of *The Oxford Shakespeare* attribute this particular passage, and all the following excerpts, to Shakespeare. *The Oxford Shakespeare: The Complete Works*, ed. John Jowett,

William Montgomery, Gary Taylor, Stanley Wells (Oxford: Oxford University Press, 2005), p. 943.
16 One might argue that use of the word 'woods' was merely a means of maintaining metre; however, the change from first person to third person in Timon's reference to himself would not have been necessary should he have said 'I will to the forest; where I shall find' thus maintaining both narrative perspective and metre. It would appear that this demarcation of 'woods' and 'forest' is deliberate.
17 Barton, *The Shakespearean Forest*, p. 95.
18 Ibid., p. 46.
19 Abigail Scherer, '*Mucedorus*'s Wild Man: Disorderly Acts on the Early Modern Stage', in *Renaissance Papers*, ed. T. H. Howard-Hill and Philip Rollinson (Rochester: Camden House, 1999), p. 56.
20 '*As You Like It* review – out with merriment, in with humour', *The Guardian,* 8 Nov. 2015, www.theguardian.com/stage/2015/nov/08/as-you-like-it-polly-findlay-review-national-theatre [accessed 30 Dec. 2020].
21 Dominic Cavendish, '*As You Like It*, National Theatre, review: "I felt I'd aged fourscore years by the end"', in *The Telegraph*, 4 November 2015 www.telegraph.co.uk/theatre/what-to-see/as-you-like-it-national-theatre-review [accessed 30 Dec. 2020]. www.telegraph.co.uk/theatre/what-to-see/as-you-like-it-national-theatre-review/ [accessed 30 Dec. 2020].
22 Alice Saville, '*As You Like It*', *Time Out*, 4 Nov. 2015, www.timeout.com/london/theatre/as-you-like-it-19 [accessed 30 Dec. 2020].
23 Northrop Frye, *Anatomy of Criticism* (Princeton: Princeton University Press, 1957), p. 182.
24 Ibid.
25 Ibid., p. 184.
26 Raymond Williams, *The Country and the City* (London: Chatto & Windus, 1973), p. 129.
27 Ibid., p. 220.
28 Edmund Spenser, *The Faerie Queene* (Book III, Canto VI, 22).
29 Jan Kott, *Shakespeare our Contemporary* (London: Routledge, 1991), pp. 176, 178.
30 Ibid., p. 182.
31 This image of sexual liberation in the forest echoes that of Tamora's advances towards Aaron and the rape of Lavinia in *Titus Andronicus* as well as Cloten's pursuit of Innogen through the forest in *Cymbeline*.
32 Philip C. MacGuire, 'Hippolyta's Silence and the Poet's Pen', in *A Midsummer Night's Dream: Contemporary Critical Essays*, ed. Richard Dutton (London: Macmillan Press, 1996), p. 151.

33 Trevor R. Griffiths, *A Midsummer Night's Dream* (Cambridge: Cambridge University Press, 2000), p. 151.
34 Edward Berry, *Shakespeare and the Hunt* (Cambridge: Cambridge University Press, 2001), p. 167.
35 Michael Foucault, *The Archaeology of Knowledge* (London: Tavistock, 1997), p. 194.
36 Lefebvre, *Production of Space*, pp. 3, 42.
37 Ibid., p. 117.
38 Jeffrey S. Theis, *Writing the Forest in Early Modern England: A Sylvan Pastoral Nation* (Pittsburgh: Duquesne University Press, 2009), p. xiv.
39 Ibid., p. 5.
40 Ibid., p. 23.
41 Tim Fitzpatrick, *Playwright, Space and Place in Early Modern Performance* (Farnham: Ashgate Publishing, 2011), p. 32.
42 Ibid., p. 33.
43 Michael Hattaway, *Elizabethan Popular Theatre: Plays in Performance* (London: Routledge, 1982), p. 47.
44 It should be noted that Werner Habicht insists on the inclusion of large stage properties, including trees, in his thesis on 'Tree Properties and Tree Scenes in Elizabethan Theater', *Renaissance Drama*, ns 4 (1971), pp. 69–92. Habicht acknowledges the paucity of evidence for tree properties used on the Elizabethan stage but nevertheless puts forth an argument for their existence based on 'the interaction between the scene qua set and the scene qua literary unit' (p. 70). He asserts that visual emphasisers in the form of stage properties enhanced the command of a scene, not simply indicating its setting. Thus, a throne would not simply indicate a court scene but 'visually emphasize the presence of royal power' (p. 70). Drawing on the evidence of tree properties necessary in staging medieval mystery plays in which the Tree of Life may have come to represent the entire Garden of Eden, Habicht proposes that such properties were 'no less impressively tied up with one's recollection' of later plays such as 'Herne's Oak in *The Merry Wives of Windsor*' (p. 72). Evidencing the Vitruvian *scena satyrica*, reproduced in E. K. Chambers's fourth volume of *The Elizabethan Stage* (1923), and Campion's *Description of a Masque* (1607), Habicht argues that distinct forest sets were indeed in use on the early modern stage. Regarding tree properties he concludes that 'it is fairly obvious that only one or a few single trees or tree elements were possible, and that their function was therefore symbolical and evocative rather than localising and decorative' (p. 76). He goes on to evidence his postulation with textual references within plays that use the pronoun determiner 'this' before 'tree' or 'garden' or 'wood',

'which surely implies gestures that establish a relationship between the spoken words and the visual impressions' (p. 77). To these onstage visual properties Habicht adds the element of sound, offstage 'acoustic symbols' enhancing the dramatic representation of the forest (p. 81). Whilst there may be little physical evidence in the form of extant props or detailed reviews that substantiate Habicht's theories, they nonetheless are a useful imagining of possibilities for the stage that look forward to more modern productions and older theatre to place tree properties on Shakespeare's stage. Tackling naysayers who posit that large properties would have proven problematic for storage and movement on and off stage between scenes, he offers the 'discovery space' and 'stage trap' as solutions to these issues, though there is little time spent on the logistics of this (p. 90). For Habicht, there must be a tree-presence on stage, and vertical pillars or the power of imagination are not enough to conjure a theatrical forest.

45 Nardizzi, *Wooden Os*, p. 20.
46 Ibid., p. 23.
47 Ibid., p. 5.
48 Ibid., p. 24.
49 Berry, *Shakespeare and the Hunt*, p. 82.
50 Sigmund Freud, *The Ego and the Id*, trans. Joan Riviere (London: Hogarth Press, 1927), pp. 29–30.
51 Ibid., p. 30.
52 Harrison, *Forests*, p. 61.
53 Dante Alighieri, *The Divine Comedy*, trans. C. H. Sisson (Oxford: Oxford University Press, 1993), p. 47.
54 Sarah Carter's *Ovidian Myth and Sexual Deviance in Early Modern English Literature* (Houndmills: Palgrave Macmillan, 2011) provides an insight into the Ovidian imagery utilised by Shakespeare and proposes that, in the eventual sacrifice of Lavinia, the playwright borrowed more from Livy's Lucrece and Verginia than Ovid's Philomel.
55 Jeanne Addison Roberts, *The Shakespearean Wild: Geography, Genus, and Gender* (Lincoln, NE: University of Nebraska Press, 1991), p. 36.
56 For further reading on Freud's theories surrounding psychic impotence see Uwe Hartmann, 'Sigmund Freud and his Impact on our Understanding of Male Sexual Dysfunction', *Journal of Sexual Medicine*, 6(8) (2009), 2332–2339.
57 Chiron's reference to his 'mistress' grace' may actually be yet another Chaucerian reference from *The Merchant's Tale* which says of Damian's congress with January's wife: 'And fully in his lady grace he stood' (line 804), grace being a homonym for grass, which in turn is a euphemism for pubic hair. Interestingly, this does not appear in

Eric Partridge's otherwise exhaustive concordance of Shakespearean billingsgate. Whether this is the case or not, there is certainly precedence for this sort of innuendo in *Venus and Adonis* as will be discussed further in this chapter.

58 Richard Tuch, 'Murder on the Mind: Tyrannical Power and Other Points along the Perverse Spectrum', *International Journal of Psychoanalysis*, 91 (2010), 141–162, p. 145.
59 Ibid., p. 152.
60 Roberts, *The Shakespearean Wild*, p. 36.
61 Berry, *Shakespeare and the Hunt*, p. 15.
62 For a more explicit glossary of these terms see Eric Partridge, *Shakespeare's Bawdy* (London: Routledge & Kegan Paul, 1968).
63 Roberts, *The Shakespearean Wild*, p. 28.
64 Peter J. Smith, 'A "Consummation Devoutly to be Wished": The Erotics of Narration in *Venus and Adonis*', in *Shakespeare Survey*, 53 (Cambridge: Cambridge University Press, 2000), 25–38, p. 28.
65 Ibid., p. 36.
66 Harrison, *Forests*, p. 89.
67 Barton, *The Shakespearean Forest*, p. 17.
68 Berry, *Shakespeare and the Hunt*, p. 217.
69 Ibid.
70 William Hazlitt, *Characters of Shakespeare's Plays* (London: Oxford University Press, 1966), p. 240.
71 Katherine Duncan-Jones, *Shakespeare: An Ungentle Life* (London: Methuen Drama, 2010), p. 8.
72 Ibid., p. 30.
73 Barton, *The Shakespearean Forest*, p. 124.
74 Berry, *Shakespeare and the Hunt*, p. 78.
75 Bakhtin, *Rabelais and his World*, p. 63.
76 Ibid., p. 79.
77 Michael Holquist, 'Introduction to Rabelais and his World', in *Rabelais and his World* (Bloomington: Indiana University Press, 1984), p. 7.
78 Alvin Kernan, 'Place and Plot in Shakespeare', *Yale Review*, 47 (1977), 48–61, pp. 48, 49.
79 Ibid., p 51.
80 *OED*.
81 Jillian Keenan, *Sex with Shakespeare* (New York: Harper Collins, 2016), p. 20.
82 Ibid., p. 52.
83 Lisa Hopkins, *Renaissance Drama on the Edge* (Abingdon: Routledge, 2014), p. 2.
84 Ibid., p. 8.

4

Corrupted Eden: The liminal garden and cultures of resistance

In 1884, the Reverend Henry N. Ellacombe wrote what is, to date, the most detailed concordance of botanical references to Shakespeare's works, listing not just their occurrences but also cross-referencing them with the contemporaneous work of John Gerard's *Herball, or Generall Historie of Plantes* (1597).[1] What is immediately evident from *The Plant-lore and Garden-craft of Shakespeare* is the sheer volume and diversity of allusions to flora within Shakespeare's works. The vast botanical miscellany, from the common cabbage to alien towering cedars that, unless he travelled to the Levant, it is unlikely the poet ever saw, as well as the diversity of gardening terms and processes such as blights and grafting, would seem to indicate that horticulture held a certain fascination for the playwright. Indeed, the Reverend Ellacombe goes so far as to assert: 'a lover of flowers and gardening myself, I claim Shakespeare as equally a lover of flowers and gardening'.[2]

Though this may be a somewhat tenuous assumption, it is one that Kenneth Branagh's 2018 imagining of the final years of Shakespeare's life, *All Is True*, develops. Much of Ben Elton's screenplay takes place in the grounds of New Place in which the recently retired poet cultivates a garden. At one point, as the writer uses stakes and rope to plot the boundaries of his allotment, he likens the process of gardening to that of writing a play – 'all begin with an idea, from a compulsion to create something of beauty or of need'.[3] It is a charming and whimsical conception of the enigmatic period before the death of Shakespeare, with the playwright weeding, digging, potting, planting and warning his pet pooch against urinating on the rosemary. However, for Elton and Branagh's ageing playwright, the garden is more than simply a setting; rather it becomes a metaphorical parallel to his desire to find his place in his family, to rekindle connections with his wife and children, and finally to give himself the opportunity emotionally to process the death of his son. The weeds and wilderness created by his absence are thus tamed and brought into harmony as he nurtures his relationships within his family; as his husbandry of the land progresses so too does his husbandry of Anne. Though a purely fictional representation of the end of Shakespeare's life, Branagh and Elton engage with the semiotics of this allegorical space, something that Shakespeare himself did throughout his works to bring both social context and meaning to certain plays and poems. Indeed, as has long been recognised and as Caroline Spurgeon articulates, 'all through his plays he thinks most easily and readily of human life and action in the terms of a gardener'.[4]

This chapter engages with the ways in which Shakespeare used cultivated spaces – parks, gardens, orchards and vineyards, as well as horticultural and botanical sources – as a means to invoke their cultural associations and play with the dynamics of power on the stage. It seeks to identify where the playwright uses either specific stage directions or textually implied cultivated settings, or else employs horticultural language and metaphor to create pockets of resistance. The garden is a liminal space, rendered so by its links both to the domicile, of which it is an extension, and to the wilderness, in that it represents a controlled version of uncultured nature. This opens the way for thought-provoking negotiations of power. What is more, I propose that the figuratively theocentric garden of cosmic order is subverted or sup*plant*ed by Shakespeare's very human vision of such symbolic spaces that focuses not so much on the outward order but on the fundamentally negative, fallible and corrupt aspects within such structures. Employing the models of biblical, medieval and Renaissance garden allegory, he emphasises the flaws in such models – that we are always cast out from Eden; that despite the best efforts to impose systems of governance on the actions of men and women, they will inevitably fail to maintain control; and that the wilderness of humankind's postlapsarian nature is ever present and seeks constantly to overthrow his best intentions.

As with the other spaces discussed in this book, semiotics plays an important part in unravelling the cultural significances of Shakespeare's georgic metaphors. However, I would argue that the garden is one of the most semantically complicated in terms of the sheer scope of what it may represent. Michel Foucault's explorations into the limits of representation underscore the issues one must face when unravelling the multiplicity of meanings wrapped around a seemingly innocuous space. He writes:

> There will be things, with their own organic structures, their hidden veins, the space that articulates them, the time that produces them; and then representation, a purely temporal succession, in which these things address themselves (always partially) to a subjectivity, a consciousness, a singular effort of cognition, to the 'psychological' individual who from the depth of his own history, or the basis of the tradition handed on to him, is trying to know.[5]

In tackling the Foucauldian conundrums over the diversity and ambiguity of significances we also have the issue of what the theorist describes as 'the space that articulates them'. When we apply this to consideration of the Shakespearean garden, this would refer to the stage, or in more recent times, the screen. James H. Kavanagh advances the idea that 'discursive and dramatic practices [...] disturb or displace prevailing forms of social and sexual subjection through an address to the unconscious', pointing to the effects theatrical representation has in appealing to, and indeed altering, individual and collective ideologies.[6] It is this point that is crucial in establishing the subversive potential of the playwright's horticultural spaces and inferences. As Kavanagh asserts, the processes of writing and performance establish 'a productive ideological practice that *transforms* the raw materials it takes up, producing a new ideological ensemble that was not there before'.[7] Thus, in the combination of semiotics and dramatisation, Shakespeare could potentially transform, subvert or manipulate existing ideological precepts associated with garden imagery.

This approach to Shakespeare's garden spaces runs contrary to what, up until recently, has been some of the foremost scholarly opinion on early modern paradigms tied up with such places. In *The Idea of the Garden in the Renaissance* (1979), Terry Comito proclaims that the garden symbolised divine order, love, symmetry, balance, poetry and the sacred. These perspectives echo the earlier work of Stanley Stewart in *The Enclosed Garden: The Tradition and the Image in Seventeenth-Century Poetry* (1966) where early modern concepts of the garden revolve predominantly around King Solomon's love poetry from his *Song of Songs*. Yet Stewart's approach becomes problematical when we consider the representations of the garden not just in Shakespeare's works, but also in the Bible, medieval literature and early modern poetry. Rather, what I propose is that Stewart's and Comito's views constitute but one extreme on a sliding scale of constant changeability that takes in everything between Edenic, ordered spaces under the constraints of divine, legislative, moral and social proprieties, through to the decaying or unkempt garden that is a representation of an Edenic fall from grace, under threat from the machinations of postlapsarian men and women.

In recent years the constrictive ideologies of Edenic perfection have been challenged, not least by theorists such as Foucault and Kavanagh, but also by historians such as Lynn Staley whose approach to the establishment of a Renaissance English identity, in *The Island Garden: England's Language of Nation from Gildas to Marvell* (2012), reads garden imagery as far more fraught, synonymous with national anxieties and disquietude. The collection of essays curated by Andrea Mariani, titled *Riscritture dell'Eden: Il ruolo del giardino nei discorsi dell'immaginario* (2015), complicates recurring historical and modern-day literary and dramatic garden motifs through the lenses of current theories and performances. Charlotte Scott's *Shakespeare's Nature: From Cultivation to Culture* (2014) offers a far more complex and nuanced reading of Shakespeare's cultivated spaces and horticultural language. Identifying the theme of cultivation as 'a form of both power and expression' that 'imposes human patterns of control on an otherwise non-human world', Scott tackles the early modern ideological framework of husbandry and its associated language as a means to interpret relationships between 'nature and culture; the individual and social'.[8]

Yet despite scholastic advances in theoretical methodologies on such spaces, there has been little advance on Comito's classifications that break down Shakespeare's cultivated spaces into the genera of historical, tragic and comic gardens. To this end, I propose that fully to realise the substance of the playwright's numerous garden settings and allusions a recategorisation is needed that reflects the underlying socio-political possibilities for their inclusion. As such, new terms or reinterpretations of existing categories are required, and this chapter introduces classifications of the garden metaphor that encapsulate the three dominant themes Shakespeare explores in his works. I've coined two of these three terms in order to allow me to explore these ideas in wholly new ways.

The *hortus conclusus*, originally a medieval term that deals with several ideas surrounding divine will, female chastity and romantic intrigue, is a recurring theme throughout Shakespeare's plays, and not simply confined to the romantic comedies as Comito and Stewart suggest. Inclusions of these horticultural representations manifest undercurrents of resistance to patriarchal control. As it insinuates, the Garden of State, or the *hortus res publica*, applies to scenes and allegories of national import. Adapted from Cicero's *De Re Publica*, this new term conflates the imagery of the garden with the idea of commonwealth. The metaphorical garden comes to epitomise the vigour and resilience of the state and often contains Edenic themes of resistance and rebellion. The third category pertains to ancestral heritage and the propagation or promotion of the family tree, or *truncus*. Once again, this category of understanding Shakespeare's horticultural metaphor necessitates a new term, and the Latin *truncus* carries within its meaning concepts of both the organic and the human body. Concerns over the continuance of dynasties differ from the *hortus res publica* in that they serve to further individual interests rather than those of a nation state. The inclusion of these 'trunk' motifs unmasks apprehensions over legacy and reveals a more sinister garden in which violent 'pruning' decides the fate of families. Between order and disorder, cycles of renewal and degeneration, these three central classifications serve to focus readings of Shakespeare's gardens, pointing to significant structures of power and the means by which they are challenged and changed.

Eden reimagined: the Renaissance garden

> God Almighty first planted a Garden; and, indeed, it is the purest of human pleasures; it is the greatest refreshment to the spirits of man; without which buildings and palaces are but gross handyworks: and a man shall ever see, that, when ages grow to civility and elegancy, men come to build stately, sooner than to garden finely; as if gardening were the greater perfection.[9]

So begins Francis Bacon's essay, *Of Gardens* (1625), in which the writer seeks to describe the ideal layout and contents of a contemporary garden. The ageing statesman and philosopher's 'princely garden' initially seems to read as a flight of fancy, a fantasy of fine flora and fragrant flowers, of ordered hedges and copses, manicured lawns and elegant fountains. His grandiose grounds contain plants that fruit or flower in each month of the year, and include sensory titillation in the form of caged songbirds, trickling water, perfumed plantation and imposing vegetable architecture. However, the ideas Bacon develops are firmly grounded in religious allegory: 'God Almighty first planted a Garden'. For Bacon, the great architectural edifices such as stately homes were simply the works of man – impressive, yet ultimately removed from Edenic 'perfection', an agricultural endeavour sanctioned by God and tied in with his will for both the earth and its human occupants.[10] Yet his enthusiasm for such horticultural pursuits must not be confused with the more emotive notions of nature later embraced by the Romantic poets.[11] Rather, Bacon's vision of a magnificent, no-expense-spared garden is a far more cerebral undertaking – a reminder of the space between God's original design for earthly order and the future promise of paradisiac perfection restored. Gardening is as much a reminder of what was lost by humankind's first parents as it is a striving to achieve what they could not and a yearning for the future return of God's blessing and the fulfilment of his purposes with regards to the earth. Thus, these gardens are liminal places – situated in the pause between paradise lost and paradise found. Furthermore, such cultivated spaces are positioned between the domestic home and the wilderness, the seemingly permanent structure and representation of human jurisdiction and power, and the more uncontrollable forces of nature, vitality and independence from the imposition of individual authority.

What is noteworthy in Bacon's exposition is his insistence on the garden being enclosed, 'encompassed on all the four sides with a stately arched hedge'.[12] Once more, this specific physical structuring of space recalls biblical motifs of the enclosed Eden – a garden in which the divine principles of order, discipline and love might flourish expressed in both ideological and physical manifestations. Outside of these boundaries is the wilderness, an untamed and godless contrast to celestial order. Terry Comito argues that such spaces engender the Renaissance 'nostalgia for Paradise', a 'search for an equilibrium' or constancy manifest prior to the fall of mankind.[13] Yet this implies that garden settings are principally affirmative, constructive and even sacred. Such a view, as expressed by Bacon and Comito, does not consider the ambiguity of the Edenic garden that also saw the appearance of the Devil in reptilian form, the first lie and the conspiring of the first human pair to contravene the divine mandate. These aspects of challenging the balance of power, of political realignment and low scheming must also be factored into any consideration of the Renaissance garden. Jack Cade's retort to Stafford's denigration of the rebel's lowly origins and occupation, 'And Adam was a gardener' (*2 Henry VI*, 4.2.131–133), becomes a far more complicated line with the application of biblical garden metaphor. Is the occupation of gardening honourable due to it being the first work assigned man? This is certainly the outlook of the gravediggers in *Hamlet* who philosophically observe 'There is no ancient gentlemen but gardeners, ditchers and gravemakers; they hold up Adam's profession' (*Hamlet*, 5.1.29–31). Shakespeare here reworks the original couplet attributed to John Ball, 'when Adam delved and Eve span, who was then the gentleman?'[14] Ball was instrumental in rousing the peasantry to rebel against their landowners in the Peasants' Revolt of 1381 and used the Genesis account in a proto-Marxist sermon highlighting that God had not imposed a feudal class system in prelapsarian Eden. Whilst Shakespeare humorously plays with the original quotation, implying gardeners are gentlemen, the link to rebellion is still present.

So too does the Archbishop of Canterbury's description of Henry V's transformation from degenerate prince to Christian monarch use blatantly adverse Edenic imagery: 'Consideration, like an angel, came / And whipp'd the offending Adam out of him, / Leaving his body as a paradise' (*Henry V*, 1.1.66–68). The biblical setting of Adam's first home is both expressive and appropriate in the clergyman's summation of the dramatic alteration in the King's behaviour following his coronation – renouncing rebellion and embracing the celestial purpose for rulers. Thus, when we reconsider Jack Cade's employment of Edenic garden imagery to link both his origins and purpose to divine will, it conversely carries with it the corollary of rebellion.

Hence, the Renaissance garden encompasses not only the idea of striving to achieve that which was lost in Eden but also the Judaeo-Christian doctrines of the Fall of man, original sin, temptation, rebellion and separation from God. In early modern England, gardens and garden settings carried a host of connotations, implications and inferences generated by the ubiquity of religious imagery and the familiarity with biblical metaphor.

Edmund Spenser's tale of the birth of Belphœbe in *The Faerie Queene* (1590) describes the Garden of Adonis in terms of the Genesis account, the cycle of expulsion due to 'fleshly corruption', its occupants cast into the 'changeful world', and their eventual reinstatement: 'Till thither they returne, where first they grew: / So like a wheele around they runne from old to new' (Book III, Canto VI, 33).[15] The themes of Edenic love and virtuousness run through the popular 'All in a Garden Green', listed in *A Handful of Pleasant Delights* (1584), Clement Robinson's collection of folk songs, where, 'All in a garden green, two lovers sat at ease, / As they could scarce be seen above the leafy trees'.[16] Within the ballad there are references to prelapsarian bodies of clay, innocence and the absence of deceit. Boccaccio's *Decameron* frequently uses medieval garden motifs synonymous with love and religion and it is the Horatian *locus amœnus* (pleasant place), the gardens of the villa, to which the young couples retreat in their self-imposed isolation from the plague.[17] By the time Shakespeare was writing, Edenic allegory and drama already had a significant precedent in medieval and Tudor morality and mystery plays. Raymond Williams argues that 'a shared and conscious point of view towards nature' in this period gave extra weight to georgic settings in terms of social significance.[18] All of this meant that, in terms of Shakespeare's theatre, due to previously significant cultural conditioning, garden settings and horticultural references had the potential to create a far more complicated space than a modern audience might imagine. As Oksana Moskina observes: 'the garden is never just an element of the setting; it always penetrates the rhetoric and semiotic structure of the text, turning into an extended metaphor of Shakespeare's artistic universe'.[19] Thus, the diverse significances of the garden offered Shakespeare not only a rich seam of cultural capital to expose and explore, but also, and most importantly, a problematic and complex space in which its very ambiguity presented the opportunity to question the nature of those who entered it.

There is yet another compelling reason for the significance of garden imagery in Shakespeare's dramatic works – its inherent paradox. A rudimentary third-century Roman fresco fittingly encapsulates this paradox in its depiction of Adam and Eve framing the Tree of Knowledge about which is entwined the unmistakable Devil in his serpentine form. It is an exceptional space in which both the divine and diabolical, the perfect and defective, are realised. Such images recur throughout the Middle Ages in devotional texts or church friezes, often with the addition of walls enclosing the first human pair, but always with the fundamental and centralised corruptive element of the serpent. The J. Paul Getty Museum contains one such fascinating version of the Edenic Fall in the Boucicaut Master's 'Story of Adam and Eve', a complicated piece that portrays the biblical demise of the original pair with the serpent depicted as having a human head, the ejection of the sinners, their toiling outside the walls of Eden and their eventual decrepitude, looking back towards their first home.[20] The representation of the Fall, both in the visual arts and literature, juxtaposes these ethical polarities. Thus, whenever Edenic allusion occurs, the canker that always exists within the garden must accompany beauty, and disorder must always threaten stability.[21]

The appeal of the Edenic juxtaposition is evident in Shakespeare's repeated use of similar imagery. When the apparition of Hamlet's father describes the means by which he met his end it is in his own orchard or garden. Though he disabuses the Prince of a certain popular theory involving a snake, the ghost does play on the Edenic motif of a snake within the garden that upsets the whole balance of a kingdom in its poisonous machinations.

> Now, Hamlet, hear.
> 'Tis given out that, sleeping in my orchard,
> A serpent stung me. So the whole ear of Denmark
> Is by a forged process of my death
> Rankly abus'd.
>
> (*Hamlet*, 1.5.34–38)

It is noteworthy that, when the ghost describes the effect of Claudius' devilish machinations, it is with horticultural metaphor.

The primary meaning is one of abusing the 'ear' of the people of Denmark through the propagation of a lie. There is also the literal act of Claudius's pouring of poison into King Hamlet's ear. Yet the ghost's language potentially contains further meaning than the immediately obvious. The *Oxford English Dictionary* lists numerous definitions for 'ear', two of which have early modern agricultural connotations. 'Ear' may pertain to the head of grain, implying that the state of Denmark corresponds to a diseased crop. It may also refer to the process of ploughing, a violent 'ear' of the soil in which the old is uprooted. What is clear from this wordplay is that the orchard setting and serpent are clearly biblical, representative of the rebellious acts committed within Eden's bounds. So too does Lady Macbeth use prelapsarian imagery of gardens and serpents in advising her husband on how to bring his ambitions to fruition: 'look like the innocent flower / But be the serpent under't' (*Macbeth*, 1.5.64, 65). When Richard's Queen hears the news of her husband's deposition at the hands of Bolingbroke, she rebukes the gardener with the words:

> Thou, old Adam's likeness, set to dress this garden,
> How dares thy harsh rude tongue sound this unpleasing news?
> What Eve, what serpent, hath suggested thee
> To make a second fall of cursed man?
>
> (*Richard II*, 3.4.74–77)

In each case, the use of georgic metaphor is subverted by a transgressive element – a corruption of the ideal, not from without, but from within. Edenic allegory speaks to the flaws within the systems of state, namely, the snake in the grass or the deception and weakness inherent in the *hortus res publica*.

Genesis's portrait of betrayal recurs in *Romeo and Juliet* where Juliet bitterly laments: 'O serpent heart, hid with a flowering face!' (3.2.73–85). Reeling from the realisation that the man she wed that very morning has just slain her cousin in a street brawl, the young Capulet resorts to intense oxymoron to describe her husband: 'beautiful tyrant! fiend angelical! / Dove-feather'd raven! wolvish-ravening lamb!' (lines 75–76). Though the contrasts that lace her expression of incredulity initially seem like youthful petulance, there is significant traction in her incorporation of the intrinsic Judaeo-Christian metaphors of perfection and corruption together in one place. The Edenic imagery of devils in utopia are strongly called to mind when she cries: 'O nature, what hadst thou to do in hell / When thou didst bower the spirit of a fiend / In moral paradise of such sweet flesh?' (lines 80–82). That paradise can contain 'vile matter' (line 83) and that beauty hides bitterness and rot is an appealing motif – one that Shakespeare returned to time and again.[22] Robert Adger Law painstakingly counted all the allusions to Adam, Eve and Cain in his essay on 'Shakespeare in the Garden of Eden' but failed to take the next logical step in asking why such references are so frequent. His tentative and non-committal suggestion was that this either 'express[ed] Shakespeare's own doubts' or 'reflect[ed] popular sentiments of the day' on theological and philosophical teachings.[23] Such hypothesising aside, what is apparent in the frequency of Shakespeare's Edenic opposites is their value in creating dramatic tension and introducing the idea that containing happiness, moral purity and the like is a fundamentally flawed ideology. A space of power that inadvertently contains the very means of its own destruction is a potentially subversive space. Thus, whilst the gardens of King Hamlet, King Richard and the Capulets symbolically proclaim that nature has been cultivated and tamed by higher ideals, they are also sites of contestation where the very nature they claim to control fights back, liminal gateways to cruder, wilder human frailty.

As a locale, the garden yields a rich vein of religious, cultural and philosophical possibilities. Stanley Stewart notes that 'no matter how hard we hang on to the single, synthetic Form, it always (with our present state of knowledge) changes in our grasp'.[24] By this definition, garden imagery, with its myriad connotations is a multivalent symbol both spatially and semantically. Stewart's notion of synthetic forms implies amalgamation of personal, cultural and spiritual concepts that mean the garden is always liminal, unfixed and fluid. What is evident from Shakespeare's use of garden motifs is their being rooted in traditionally established biblical metaphor, particularly surrounding Eden, the first garden. However, rather than the metaphor being one of man's aspirations to achieve the divine, as with Bacon, it is the complex and often-conflicting elements and themes synonymous with paradise that are appealing. Innocence and rebellion, the challenge to systems of power and governance, the fall from grace and the fallibility and duality of humanity are all intrinsically linked to prelapsarian visions of the garden.

The changeable garden: control and neglect

What outwardly appears to be an observation of utmost simplicity, yet is at the root of the garden's artistic and literary value, is that it is a *living* thing. The use of a garden setting, with its associated metaphors and images, in just about any context, is that such a space is first and foremost a location of growth. More accurately, it is a place of *controlled* growth, governed by those who dictate its content, arrangement and maintenance. Hence, the garden relies on order – an order imposed by humans – to function. As Bacon asserted, a garden is an extension of the domicile. When the garden is used as a setting, as an accessory or appendage of a house such as the Capulet residence or the red and white rose gardens in *1 Henry VI*, such scenes reflect the imposition of human will over nature, of controlling, taming and refining a setting that, without such cultivation, would revert to its wild origins. In *Titus Andronicus* the cultured hunt in the wooded parks outside of Rome's walls is initially augmented by Tamora's glowing speech of harmony and natural accord that is echoed in Bacon's description of the princely garden – 'when everything doth make a gleeful boast' and 'birds chant melody on every bush' (2.3.11, 12). Yet there is also the promise of Edenic corruption, 'the snake lies rolled in the cheerful sun' (line 13) and as tranquil park imagery is eventually overtaken by the darker forest motif, Shakespeare maps not only the decaying Roman system of governance and the increasingly predatory behaviour of the protagonists, but the deterioration of familial relations, specifically, that of the Andronici. We are thus reminded of the ties between wilderness and forest settings, that allow the baser elements of human nature to reveal themselves, and more cultivated settings that, when neglected, or with mismanagement, will eventually revert to their wild state.

There have been attempts at qualifying Shakespeare's horticultural metaphors and settings in such a manner as to draw parallels with his contemporary social environs. As has been demonstrated already, one cannot engage with the topic of

Renaissance conceptions of the garden without considering Terry Comito's substantial critical contributions. *The Idea of the Garden in the Renaissance* (1978) establishes much of the significance and cultural connotation of the garden with the religious, political and social structures of early modern Europe. However, it is in Comito's essay 'Caliban's Dream: The Topography of Some of Shakespeare Gardens' that he attempts to impose his model of the three 'norms and forms' onto the garden imagery and metaphor within Shakespeare's plays. Though he may be somewhat limiting and general in his 'political garden' being synonymous with histories, the 'fallen garden' with the tragedies and the 'garden of love' with romances, his reading of garden symbols does shed light on the means by which the writer employed, adapted and manipulated established garden images to challenge the very social models and values they were based on. He writes: 'such forms as the garden of love, the garden of state, and the garden of tragedy are not isolated or arbitrary images. They are *complex norms*, the very shapes of which by particular understandings of the worlds are manifested in the imagination of the dramatist' (my italics).[25] There is a seeming contradiction in Comito's generalised imposition of strict rules for reading garden allegory in each of Shakespeare's dramatic genres, and his acknowledgement of the complexity of garden allegory and symbolic significance.[26] There are indeed complications when looking at the types of horticultural references and settings within the plays but they are not simply explained away by dramatic compartmentalisation. Rather, their complexity lies primarily in the nature of the garden as a locus for transformation.

Before focusing on categorisations or claiming that Shakespeare followed generic models for representing the garden, I propose that for Shakespeare, the garden represented a place of *continual* contestation, a space in which moral, political and social order is constantly put under pressure by forces of nature that seek to upset balance and structure. Through cyclical and often violent processes the garden is a place of liminal transition between states. Even Comito admits to the processual nature of garden scenes, where there is 'no absolute distinction' between 'the order of the garden and the mutability of the wilderness outside'.[27] Hence, whether garden allegories are political or personal, pertaining to great matters of state or to familial bonds, their significance is in their being widely comprehensible yet equally nuanced metaphors, with the scope to correspond to healthy, flourishing environs or to overlooked, mistreated and deteriorating states.

However, if we are to attempt to classify the tropes Shakespeare most commonly associated with cultivated green spaces then a new model is necessary. Rather than imposing broad rules to georgic metaphor, I propose an alternate means of quantifying the symbolic space of the garden. Comito's theory relies on arbitrarily applying dramatic genres, designations that were introduced by Henry Condell and John Heminges following Shakespeare's death. The First Folio's three kinds of play, histories, tragedies and comedies, does not even acknowledge the original titles of certain plays such as the 1597 quarto of the *Tragedie of King Richard the Second*, listed as a history in the First Folio, or the 1608 quarto of *Lear* as *M. William Shak-speare: His True Chronicle Historie of the life and death of King LEAR and his three Daughters*, titled *The Tragedie of King Lear* in later folios. This is not to open up debates over genre, but merely to illustrate that attempts to use First Folio taxonomy to clarify types of garden symbolism is problematic. Instead, I recommend that an understanding of Renaissance garden allegory opens the way to challenge the means by which we perceive the dynamics of power inside the social, political and religious structures of Shakespeare's poetry and plays. As such, it is these structures that must form the basis for categorisation.

Starting with individual and more intimate relationships, Shakespeare's garden metaphors are used to tease out the complexities and extremes of love and desire. Comito's comic gardens of love are loosely based on the concept of the *hortus conclusus* that, as I will demonstrate, is itself a label heavy with ambiguity and double meaning. The gardens of tragedy and political history do not aptly fit either genre, nor do they describe a type of garden symbolism. Instead, I believe the terms *hortus res publica* and *truncus* designate the ideas of gardens as a representative of the state and of the family tree. These three motifs recur throughout Shakespeare's works and display not only the poet's appreciation of all things horticultural but his engagement with the relational politics of power.

Hortus conclusus

One of the most common usages of garden setting and its attendant metaphors within Shakespeare's works is that of the medieval *hortus conclusus*. The term literally translates as 'enclosed garden' and, according to Stanley Stewart, in medieval and early modern times, was synonymous with the Virgin Mary and the protection of the Mother Church.[28] This figuratively protective or safe space for the virtuous is described by Liz Herbert McAvoy as 'simultaneously physical, spiritual, symbolic, curative, and restorative – and iconographically, frequently housing Christ, the Virgin, or the "Lady" of medieval romance'.[29] Yet, despite the *hortus conclusus*'s association with high ideals, McAvoy's reading of such emblematic spaces acknowledges that 'literary treatments of the medieval enclosed garden' offer a 'subtle critique and disruption of established hegemonies whether gendered, theological, spiritual, spatial, or temporal'.[30] Indeed, the garden of love is layered, ambiguous and open to intricate readings of female authority, the nature of love and the systems that attempt to regulate its expression. I would argue that Shakespeare's use of both the figurative or allegorical textual referents and literal or staged enclosed garden draws on a tradition of nuanced understandings and representations of this space. Furthermore, such depictions often serve to destabilise established socio-religious mores.

To fully understand the abstruseness of the *hortus conclusus* and the manner in which Shakespeare used and interpreted garden imagery and settings synonymous with the female body and the complexities of love, it is necessary to look at how this theme was used in other literature, both before and contemporary to Shakespeare's day. The tradition of the enclosed garden and its corresponding cultural significances can be traced from its biblical origins, through medieval literature and into the Renaissance. At times the *hortus conclusus* has a physical manifestation and at others it appears in figurative language and allegory. However, within each iteration its associations betray a complexity of meaning and counter-cultural significance that make it one of the more complex literary motifs.

One of the earliest literary allusions to the enclosed garden is that of King Solomon's evocative biblical serenade in his Song of Songs or Canticles which also contains an abundance of horticultural allusions:

> A garden inclosed is my sister, my spouse; a spring shut up, a fountain sealed.
>
> Thy plants are an orchard of pomegranates, with pleasant fruits; camphire, with spikenard,
>
> Spikenard and saffron; calamus and cinnamon, with all trees of frankincense; myrrh and aloes, with all the chief spices:
>
> A fountain of gardens, a well of living waters, and streams from Lebanon.
>
> Awake, O north wind; and come, thou south; blow upon my garden, that the spices thereof may flow out. Let my beloved come into his garden, and eat his pleasant fruits.
>
> (Song of Songs 4:12–16)

What is noteworthy in Solomon's suggestive Hebrew epithalamion is the dialogue that flows between the two lovers, each using the metaphor of a walled garden. It is a private space in which love is considered and defined between the two lovers, and not by outside influences. Further to this, as Stanley Stewart observes, 'the passage shrouds the speaker's identity', as the 'singers' are unnamed.[31] This element of anonymity is heightened by the image of the enclosed garden of love, full of sensory pleasures and redolent with sensuous inference in which the paramours find a safe haven to express their affections. It is a gendered space, the bucolic metaphors applied to the female body. What is more, there is also the element of possession, the woman inviting her lover to come into 'his garden', denoting his ownership over her body and calling to mind the Edenic garden of the first human couple. However, though the poetic biblical image serves as an ideal for the *hortus conclusus*, as previously contended, the scriptural archetype also contains the means to institute its own collapse – a complication that recurs throughout classical, medieval and early modern literature.

To some extent, this process plays out in Shakespeare's gardens – love becomes transactive, the enclosed bower where lovers ponder and negotiate their own judgement on matters of the heart, often in ways that contravene the patriarchal rubric. The directives given by fathers and princes in Shakespeare's houses and palaces are undermined in the gardens of these same edifices. There is the idea of the female being dictated to by contemporary power structures yet within the bounds of the garden the female comes into a power of her own – it is a space in which she exerts her own will. One example of this complication of patriarchal authority occurs in the opening scenes of *Cymbeline*. Knowing full well that 'the King hath charged you should not speak together' (1.1.83, 84), Innogen's stepmother engineers a space of resistance to patriarchal control within her garden when she contrives a tryst for the two lovers. In this scene, the garden becomes a space of female empowerment and resistance to centralised, masculine supremacy. Whilst Cymbeline is at least nominally in charge of the interior spaces of state, his queen utilises the liminal space of the garden to effect her own plots. It is a place in which the Queen feels comfortable to conspire and scheme on how she will 'move' or sway her husband (line 104), and a place where the two innocent lovers find a reprieve and shelter from the strictures of court.[32] As such, the garden is a complicated and gendered space – elements of resistance stretching from the sinister machinations of the Queen to the morally justifiable actions of Posthumus and Innogen.[33] What does emerge from *Cymbeline*'s garden scene is that it is a liminal space of contestation where male control is challenged. As the scenes eventually shift towards the forest, an aberration of patriarchal influence attempts to reassert itself in the savagery of Cloten.

This contradictory and polysemic allegorical space is alluded to by the melancholic Jaques who utilises the contrasts inherent in horticultural metaphor in his somewhat sceptical appraisal of life and love: 'And so from hour to hour we ripe and ripe / And then from hour to hour we rot and rot' (*As You Like It*, 2.7.26, 27). Mikhail Bakhtin describes this inversion of meaning as 'negation', 'the opposition to the official world and all its prohibitions and limitations'.[34] This negation of ideologically elevated social protocols and religious allegories through their subversive and oppositional representations is evident in yet another text Shakespeare would have been familiar with. Chaucer's *Merchant's Tale* depicts the enclosed garden as the masculine possession of the feminine body but then negates or subverts this ideal through subterfuge and cuckoldry – the undermining of matrimonial sanctity. The Merchant tells us that, amongst all the Knight's possessions, his garden is that which he guards most closely:

> Amonges othere of his honeste thynges,
> He made a gardyn, walled al with stoon;
> So fair a gardyn woot I nowher noon.
>
> (lines 2028–2030)[35]

Old January's walled garden doubles as a second bedroom, effectively becoming a symbol of his young bride's body – owned and locked away to be enjoyed by none other than him. McAvoy urges such spaces to be understood as allegorically gendered as much as spiritual or theological, and January's jealously protected walled garden certainly fits with the former metaphor.[36]

> And whan he wolde paye his wyf hir dette
> In somer seson, thider wolde he go,
> And May his wyf, and no wight but they two;
> And thynges whiche that were nat doon abedde,
> He in the gardyn parfourned hem and spedde.
>
> (lines 2048–2052)

However, this image of patriarchal privilege and power is inverted when the jealous nobleman goes blind and his enterprising May counterfeits the key and invites her lover into the garden. Using January as a ladder to climb the pear tree, where Damian waits, May seizes the opportunity to cuckold the elderly knight, in doing so mocking both the institution of marriage and the so-called sacrosanct honour of women. What is more, even when January's sight is miraculously restored, only for him to witness the lovers' congress in the branches, May manages to turn her infidelity into a selfless medicinal act with the aim of healing her husband. Cuckoldry complete, the tale ends with the hallowed patriarchal institutions of marriage and women's honour lambasted and in tatters. The walled Eden is no longer a place of male control over the female body, or a symbol of chastity and virtue. Rather, as Jenny Stevens observes, 'the allegorical force of the Tale's finale brings into sharp focus the biblical Tree of Good and Evil and the inevitable failure of January's hubristic project to create a new Eden'.[37]

Chaucer's poetic transposal of the *hortus conclusus* is later recalled in Shakespeare's *Venus and Adonis*, where the Edenic setting plays host to yet another inversion of patriarchal control. Jeanne Addison Roberts notes the 'analogy between [...] body and landscape' within this poem.[38] More than this, there is a distinct merging of symbolic landscapes. As stated in the chapter on the Shakespearean forest, there is a conflation of wild and pastoral settings and imagery in this poem. Remonstrating with the sexually inflamed goddess, Adonis pleads that his 'unripe years' (line 524) stand in the way of knowing his heart: 'The mellow plum doth fall, the green sticks fast / Or, being early plucked, is sour to taste' (lines 527, 528). How quickly is the georgic imagery replaced with that of the animalistic and wild as Venus overwhelms the young man with the strength and ferocity of her passions: 'With blindfold fury she begins to forage / Her face doth reek and smoke, her blood doth boil / And careless lust stirs up a desperate courage' (lines 554–556). The violence and language Shakespeare uses for Venus's impassioned assault on Adonis is later echoed in *Julius Caesar*, where the assassins' 'purpled hands doth reek and smoke' (3.1.159). It is a shocking turn from the idyllic setting; a juxtaposition that calls to mind the Edenic serpent in paradise. This time, however, the snake is in feminine form, taking the place of the innocent Eve. Shakespeare not only parodies contemporary gender stereotypes with the predatory Venus, he upsets peaceful garden imagery using references to blood and savagery, with the female as the dominating force. The inversion of gender roles continues with the lines: 'He now obeys, and now no more resisteth / While she takes all she can, not all she listeth' (lines 563, 564). This possible transposition of the anonymously attributed idiom, 'men must do as they can, not as they would', further emphasises the role Venus has taken that has dramatically shifted the balance of power. As with Chaucer's *Merchant's Tale*, the *hortus conclusus* becomes the arena of female domination and empowerment, where the woman exerts authority over her own body. In contrast, the male is emasculated, and overtly gendered language and analogy are used to destabilise the social norm. Venus's description of Adonis's death itself is marked by sexual imagery synonymous with penetration and submission: 'nuzzling in his flank, the loving swine / Sheathed unaware the tusk in his soft groin' (lines 1115, 1116). Whilst Roberts maintains that the withdrawal of Venus to Paphos suggests 'the victory of male principles over female', I would argue that

Venus's gardens and parks open the way for a sustained Bakhtinian negation in their disruption and subversion of patriarchy, rendering Roberts's conclusions on the ultimate containment of social transgression as questionable.[39]

The literary tradition of the *hortus conclusus* progresses throughout the early modern period, continuing to complicate fundamental social mores. The classical scenes, horticultural motifs and their dissident interpretations that occur in *Venus and Adonis* echo in the later works of Andrew Marvell.

> When we have run our passion's heat,
> Love hither makes his best retreat.
> The gods, that mortal beauty chase,
> Still in a tree did end their race:
> Apollo hunted Daphne so,
> Only that she might laurel grow;
> And Pan did after Syrinx speed,
> Not as a nymph, but for a reed.
>
> ('The Garden', lines 25–32)[40]

Filled with the paradisaical imagery of the original 'Garden-state' (line 57), Marvell's poem associates such cultivated spaces with love, courtship and chastity. The garden is a place of communion with nature, both that which grows from the ground and that of one's own internal, human struggles pertaining to the cultivation of morally elevated qualities. Yet despite its peaceful and contemplative bent, the poem also challenges such corollaries with more sinister implications. For Marvell, the retreat of love, or divine garden of tenderness, is tainted by its association with lust, rapine and jealousy. Apollo's lustful pursuit of Daphne results in the metamorphosis of the latter into a laurel. That the only recourse to concord is achieved through the confinement of the aggrieved party upsets the image of the garden as a feminised, safe space. The second Ovidian reference, this time to Pan's unrelenting stalking of Syrinx, once again results in the transformation of the nymph into hollow reeds that echo Pan's frustrations when he blows across them. Clearly, for Marvell, the garden of love was a far more complex space than a haven of chastity. Thus, from Solomon's Hebraic verses through to Marvell's pessimistic poems there exists a literary convention of dealing with affairs of the heart through garden metaphor and imagery. Shakespeare's garden settings and motifs are part of this tradition, painting such spaces as ambivalent and ambiguous, and in doing so challenging some of the more high-minded ideals associated with love.

Shakespeare's horticultural worlds had the potential to reach beyond the page and onto the stage in their physical representations. In order to appreciate Shakespeare's approaches to the garden of love it is important to consider specific garden settings within his works. Whilst we owe a great debt to Heminges and Condell's posthumous assemblage of Shakespeare's plays into the First Folio, we must acknowledge that there is much they did not manage to collate, including the settings of individual scenes. This should not, however, been seen as an editorial failure. Rather, such seeming oversights actually speak of the scenic fluidity of the early modern stage – a dramatic blank canvas that could shift, even mid-scene, between settings. Thus, the responsibility often lies with the text to reveal setting rather than specific props or stage directions. It is not until the eighteenth century that Shakespearean editors such as Nicholas Rowe, Alexander Pope and Edward Capell began to suggest settings and stage directions that would make dramatic 'sense' of the text. If anything, these anachronistic measures limited the subversive potential of liminal settings that came into existence through the language of the text, dragging with them a host of cultural connotations that served to nuance the scenes in which they occurred. There are, however, occasions when the text reveals specific use of certain settings.[41] The garden is one such setting that is either textually implied or suggested from a scholarly standpoint. In each instance the setting evokes certain cultural significances that the writer plays with, either using them to augment his argument or to challenge their inherent cultural connotations through inversion. In some cases, parks and gardens provide the environs for much of the play or poem. The backdrop for *Venus and Adonis* is that of the hunt which in Shakespeare's day, as Edward Berry notes, took place primarily in managed parks and royal forests.[42] So too is *Love's Labour's Lost* set in the King of Navarre's capital and its surrounding parks, and begins with hunting and pastoral motifs, the action shifting between the King's quarters and the Princess's pavilion outside of the city and within the park where she goes to hunt.[43] *The Merry Wives of Windsor* also has several scenes referencing Windsor Park that draw on hunting imagery yet are notably used in the exposure and humiliation of Falstaff.[44] The Capulets' walled orchard in *Romeo and Juliet* forms the backdrop for at least three scenes.[45] Constituting a space reserved for the private and honest conversation of females, in scaling the walls of this sanctuary Romeo becomes the invader of protected chastity. In a similar vein, the opening scene to *Cymbeline* concerns the subject of forbidden love and likely takes place in the garden of Cymbeline's palace where the two lovers, Innogen and Posthumus, reaffirm their wedding vows against the wishes of the King. Love's complications and entanglements continue to be the thematic focus in *Twelfth Night*,[46] where three scenes take place in Lady Olivia's garden, and in Leonato's gardens in *Much Ado About Nothing*.[47] So too is the love scene in *Troilus and Cressida*[48] set in a garden or orchard.[49]

In each of these instances, what becomes apparent is that the setting itself has a certain fluidity. When necessary, there are verbal signposts to a specific setting – significantly, when it is called on to introduce cultural implications that either augment or challenge the argument. Thus, it is the meaning of the metaphor that is of import, rather than simple stage dressing.

The idea of a garden motif or setting complicating scenes in which they are employed is furthered when we consider Terry Comito's conceptualisation of Shakespeare's gardens of love as 'equivocal places, even sinister ones' that contain both the attractive charms and promise of love but equally a 'potential wildness' and 'mutability'.[50] Passions such as those of Romeo and Juliet, Benedick and Beatrice, and Posthumus and Innogen may be fostered in such a place, but they are also illusory spaces that constantly work against the will of those who move through them. In *Much Ado About Nothing*, Hero aptly encapsulates this when she describes the arbour in which her cousin Beatrice is to secrete herself:

> Bid her steal to the pleached bower
> Where honeysuckles, ripened by the sun,
> Forbid the sun to enter, like favourites
> Made proud by princes, that advance their pride
> Against the power that bred it
>
> (3.1.10–14)

This description of a complicated garden setting with its respective imagery bears some consideration. First, Hero uses the entwined foliage of the bower as a symbol of resistance and defiance. The sun caused the growth that now defies its benefactor by blocking it out and creating a place of shade and secrecy. That Shakespeare reinforces this image with yet another metaphor is telling. Princes, like the sun, exert power and influence, raising 'favourites' who in time may actually usurp their privileged position and seek to challenge the very power that elevated them. This is not an image of harmony and love such as we might expect from the virginal Hero. It is a nuanced, deeply cynical reading of the enclosed garden that portrays a space that works against the very ideals it purports to embody. This is played out by the mockery made of love within this setting as both Benedick and Beatrice are hoodwinked by contrived love. The paradoxical nature of such spaces is confirmed by Benedick who, after being tricked into believing Beatrice is in love with him, then attempts to make sense of her brusque invitation to dinner, saying, 'there's a double meaning in that' (3.1.249). The control Beatrice establishes over Benedick in these garden scenes is eventually put to the test following the slight against Hero, as Beatrice leverages Benedick's love to 'kill Claudio' (4.1.288).

These inversions and intricacies of horticultural connotation also play out in *Twelfth Night*, Malvolio reading Maria's forged love note in the garden whilst the plotters and pranksters observe from within the concealment of the box-tree hedge. In these scenes the garden becomes a space of subterfuge, where Malvolio's misguided love is preyed upon and becomes a source of mocking amusement and hurtful entertainment. Thus, there is an element of carnival contempt about the garden – where romance and love are made to look foolish and, furthermore, within such manufactured spaces grow false fruits that in turn may conceal ugliness and decay. The grotesque satire of chaste love and chivalric romance takes place in their burlesque perversion. These ideals are trivialised and shown to be open to manipulation. Hence, the allegorical interpretations of the *hortus conclusus* open the possibility that 'scriptural meanings might legitimately be construed on several levels'.[51] The enclosed garden is not, as McAvoy states, always 'curative and restorative', but can be an equally treacherous, even unsafe space – just as in Eden. It is a locus in which the guileless come to feel safe, yet by their very innocence open themselves to be misdirected and abused.

Corrupted Eden 143

What becomes increasingly apparent in Shakespeare's inclusion of garden imagery synonymous with biblical and medieval concepts of the *hortus conclusus* is that such references, inferences and representations manifest traces of resistance to patriarchal control. Far from being havens of chastity and the sacred in which the male-imposed epitomes of love and virtue are enclosed, the gardens of love are often liminally unfixed, complicated through substantial ambiguity, subversion and deception. Rather than being safe spaces devoted to the ideals of love, they form figurative arenas in which the idea of the feminine, the place of the woman in patriarchal Renaissance England and the archetype of matrimonial hierarchy might be contested.

Hortus res publica

There is another way in which the language of horticulture and the image of the walled garden occurs in Renaissance England – that of national identity and geographic politics. Lynn Staley notes that 'early modern political rhetoric reflects a similar (and sometimes conflicting) set of interests in insularity and law as they help to provide a focus for a conception of the identity of the realm'.[52] This distinctive national character is closely linked with the garden. As David Rollison observes, 'before England became a nation of shopkeepers, it was, metaphorically at least, a commonwealth of gardeners'.[53] Probably the most notable of Shakespearean references to this conceptual garden is the speech of an elderly and infirm John of Gaunt:

> This royal throne of kings, this sceptred isle,
> This earth of majesty, this seat of Mars,
> This other Eden, demi-paradise,
> This fortress built by Nature for herself
> Against infection and the hand of war,
> This happy breed of men, this little world,
> This precious stone set in the silver sea,
> Which serves it in the office of a wall
> Or as a moat defensive to a house,
> Against the envy of less happier lands,
> This blessed plot, this earth, this realm, this England.
> (*Richard II*, 2.1.40–49)

The entire passage is included above as it is replete with horticultural inference and metaphor. Here, England as a nation is depicted as a walled garden, a blessed plot reminiscent of Eden as a divinely cultivated state separate from the wilderness surrounding it. Within this enclosed utopian dominion, immune to the 'infection' or blight afflicting foreign nations, is contained a particular 'breed' of men, whose husbandry constitutes a happy realm. Yet this oft-quoted, seemingly patriotic effusion is part of a much longer diatribe that explains why the aged Duke of Lancaster likens England to Eden, though in this case as an inferior, demi-paradisaic copy. The neglect with which Richard has treated his divine allotment has reduced him to the level of an inattentive 'landlord' (line 114) who has carelessly leased his lands out, thereby sullying the garden that was England. Once again, the Edenic imagery serves as a complicated metaphor that encompasses both a divinely blessed realm but also the idea that the carers of this walled paradise have been neglectful of their duties and are subsequently cast out. In this case, the garden allegory foreshadows the deposition of Richard. For Gaunt, Eden represents a state that contains divine harmony as well as the seed of rebellion.

Shakespeare's likening of Richard to a gardener who is entrusted with a precious and fertile plot does not just borrow from biblical precedence. Cicero's *De Re Publica* (54–51 BC), a dialogue on Roman politics, describes the duties of a leader in horticultural terms:

> Therefore, as a farmer is acquainted with the nature of his soil, a steward with the nature of letters, and each can turn from the amusement of theory to the greater utility of practice; so this our ruler may be thoroughly conversant with the knowledge of rights and of laws; he may have looked even into the very fountains of them: but let not his consultations, his constant readings, and his writings occupy him too much; but let him be as it were both steward and farmer to the commonwealth.
>
> (*De Re Publica* 5.3)[54]

Here, the Roman statesman likens the role of a potentate to that of a farmer or field-overseer (*agri novit*). The implications are that for a commonwealth (*res publica*) to flourish, its rulers must cultivate it with the same attention and skill as a gardener. Yet Cicero also lived through the most turbulent of political epochs, witnessing the bloody transformation of the Republic of Rome into the Roman

Empire. He knew that when those in authority neglected the garden of state, this could only lead to trouble amongst the masses: 'As if to a virtuous, brave, and magnanimous man there could be a juster reason for seeking the government than this – to avoid being subjected to worthless men, and to prevent the commonwealth from being torn to pieces by them' (1.9).[55] Though it is not essential that we know whether Shakespeare had read Cicero, the ideas implicit in the pre-Christian treatise amalgamate with the biblical picture of the first 'State', a garden whose 'landlords' were entrusted with its cultivation and upkeep yet whose neglect led to the loss of that state. Cicero's philosophy is one of resistance to any in positions of authority whose poor husbandry has resulted in ruination; and these themes recur throughout Shakespeare's political gardens.

The idea of a monarchy or commonwealth being represented in the form of garden allegory is most pronounced in Shakespeare's histories and tragedies – where power has decayed or been corrupted. When employed within these settings, the garden motif encourages the audience to look beneath the pleasing exterior of order to the hidden flaws and inevitable corruption that, despite all attempts to conceal, is a truer indication of the state of the nation. *Hamlet*'s 'unweeded garden that grows to seed' (1.2.135, 136) is one of the most powerful images employed within the play – the idea of a garden-state that has been overrun with choking weeds indicts all within its bounds. The garden is a place of treachery – an Eden complete with poisonous serpents juxtaposed against banks of flowers. These ambiguous Edens encapsulate the process of interchanging and constantly shifting power. Rather than places of peace, Shakespeare's garden topographies become spaces of contestation in which we come to expect social commentary, conflict and change. Higher ideological principles are at war with base nature. As Comito observes:

> The garden is an image of fruition, order, and completeness; and at the same time, and by the same token, it is an image of growth, process, and mutability. It is at once a privileged place and witness to the effects of time. What is ambiguous and endlessly suggestive in the image is the way it evokes these antinomies, spatial form and temporal process, simultaneously, in a single intuition, as dimensions of a single possibility. A garden, we might say, is an image of time turning itself precariously into space'.[56]

Thus, the significance of gardens as dramatic capital is in their use as metaphorical spaces and allegorical backdrops that enable the concepts of temporality and space to be conflated. Orlando may observe that 'there's no clock in the forest' (*As You Like It*, 3.2.295), but *there is* in the garden where a strict set of rules govern the husbandry and taming of growth and decay and where seasons dictate progress and degeneration.

With the temporal implications attached to such settings what we are presented with is an ideal liminal space in which to upset notions of permanence. As with seasonal successions of growth, fruition and death, the garden setting fosters a cyclical view of time. The garden of Denmark that has been allowed to rot since the assassination of its King is eventually violently pruned, yet even this cycle is perpetuated with doubtful outcomes in the appearance of Fortinbras at the play's conclusion. So too with *Titus Andronicus*, a play that opens with a new regime (a new garden of sorts), and goes through the same tragic cycle as *Hamlet* in its final scenes which witness the birth of yet another administration that promises to unite the fractured realm, or at the very least, take up where the previous regime ended.[57]

As with the *hortus conclusus*, when such a space is represented on the stage it imitates Bacon's association of the garden as an extension of, yet distinct from, the domestic abode and becomes a space of contestation to centralised authority. In this setting, the dwelling is exchanged for the state-sanctioned structures of power. If the *hortus conclusus* carries with it connotations of the feminine, the cultivation of love and, crucially, the resistance to patriarchal control, then it is necessary to differentiate such figurative spaces from the *hortus res publica*, or garden of state. The latter, by its association with, yet suitable removal from, the Court, great hall or commons, also carries with it elements of opposition and change. Hence, Shakespeare's use of garden scenes depicts socio-political proceedings inside the theatre of state. Act 2, scene 4 of *1 Henry VI* is set in the Temple Garden, one of the Inns of Court, and precedes the official declaration of civil war. The roses within this setting become emblematic of allegiances to the Houses of York and Lancaster. So too does the scene in Brutus's orchard herald the enormous shift in Roman hierarchies of power in *Julius Caesar*. These examples of plotting and political pruning project apt representations of a garden-state in which figures of authority exert their influence in shaping the political landscape.

What is telling about such spaces is that they are removed from the central seats of authority such as throne rooms, courtrooms and senates, hence fostering or representing the insubordinate nature of the actions taken there. Though much of the Machiavellian manoeuvring and statecraft has already taken place by the end of *King John*, the final scene is set in the orchard of Swinstead Abbey. Revealingly, though it is the scene in which the King dies, Philip, the Bastard, intimates that the political and religious meddling from foreign powers will henceforth cease in England, and a clear definition of national identity will emerge from the death of England's monarch. Once again, it is the idea of enclosure and separation from outside influences that is called to mind – this time from international politics and not patriarchal privilege. So too is the notion of political pruning and the uprooting of anything that would threaten the health of the *hortus res publica* conveyed in slaying of the rebel, Jack Cade, in the garden of Anthony Iden.[58]

However, it is not only these georgic settings that draw on Renaissance cultural understandings of the allegorical garden. Just as the idyllic setting of certain scenes affected an audience's understanding, so too does comprehending these semiotic signposts bring to bear associated complicated symbolisms within their respective texts – fertilising and, in some cases, altering contemporary conception.

Rollison's description of England as a metaphorical 'commonwealth of gardeners' points to an interesting way of reading relationships of power in such settings. Gaunt's likening of Richard to a gardener is more than simple allegory – it essentially levels the hierarchical standings of kings and commoners who share occupancy in the garden commonwealth. This is reinforced in the garden scene where Richard's queen notes that the gardeners 'talk of state, for everyone doth so / Against a change' (3.4.27, 28). First, she notes that politics is the interest of all, not just those who make policy. As with the cycles and husbandry peculiar to the garden, such forms exist also within the garden of state in which all, the great and the humble, play a part. Hence, the garden in which the Queen walks may belong to her, yet it is reliant on the efforts of common men to maintain. The result of this is a space in which both commoners and nobility inevitably rub shoulders, a phenomenon shared with the battlefield, as the next chapter will explore. What happens to the order of authority is also of interest in Richard's garden, attested to by the gardener's reply to the Queen berating him for what she sees as his insensitive and ignorant political prattling. Rather than an ingratiating apology, the workman bats back the Queen's reproaches with:

> Pardon me, madam: little joy have I
> To breathe this news; yet what I say is true.
> King Richard, he is in the mighty hold
> Of Bolingbroke: their fortunes both are weigh'd:
> In your lord's scale is nothing but himself,
> And some few vanities that make him light;
> But in the balance of great Bolingbroke,
> Besides himself, are all the English peers,
> And with that odds he weighs King Richard down.
> Post you to London, and you will find it so;
> I speak no more than every one doth know.
>
> (3.4.81–91)

It is an irregular exchange between social opposites, the inequality of their stations strangely inconsequential in this setting. Far from retracting his statement and claiming ignorance, the gardener reinforces his statements with an illustration of weighing, a doubling of the very situation he and the Queen are in as to the knowledge they each possess. The gardener's ability to weigh the state of the kingdom is akin to his ability to comprehend the condition of the garden in which he labours, and on both counts, his matter-of-fact appraisal puts the Queen on uneven footing. His assessment goes as far as to pass judgement on those 'vanities' or weak nobles who stick to Richard, something for which he goes unpunished and actually results in the alarmed Queen leaving with the passing insult, 'pray God the plants thou graft'st may never grow' (line 100), effectively a curse on the very garden in which she walks.

The second argument that arises from Isabella's scorn for the gardeners' political gossip is that she sees such conversations as precursors to 'a change' (line 28). As the gardener elucidates, echoing Gaunt's earlier appraisal of the commonwealth, a neglected allotment results in the flourishing and strengthening of only one thing – weeds: 'our sea-walled garden, the whole land, / Is full of choking weeds, her fairest flowers choked up' (lines 43, 44). Such neglect necessitates change. The humble gardener reads Richard's situation all too well as he explains that 'the weeds which his broad-spreading leaves did shelter, / That seemed in eating him to hold him up, / Are plucked up, root and all, by Bolingbroke – / I mean the Earl of Wiltshire, Bushy, Green' (lines 50–53). Seeing England as a garden overrun by useless administrators, with ironically horticultural names, and a 'wasteful King' (line 55), the gardener understands that there is only one way to restore order – through violent change. Here, his imagery borrows from both horticultural metaphor and that of battle:

> O, what pity is it
> That he had not so trimm'd and dress'd his land
> As we this garden! We at time of year
> Do wound the bark, the skin of our fruit-trees,
> Lest, being over-proud in sap and blood,
> With too much riches it confound itself:
> Had he done so to great and growing men,
> They might have lived to bear and he to taste
> Their fruits of duty: superfluous branches
> We lop away, that bearing boughs may live:
> Had he done so, himself had borne the crown,
> Which waste of idle hours hath quite thrown down.
>
> (lines 55–66)

Wounding, blood, lopping and the eventual cutting down of a tree whose 'crown' has been weighed down by superfluous branches are all the duties of a responsible gardener. When a garden or orchard lies unloved and unkempt it requires significant, even brutal, change to restore any semblance of order. What is remarkable about this 'relentlessly poetic study' of Richard's decaying commonwealth is that, as Rollison notes, 'Shakespeare has working men speak their own proverbial wisdom'.[59]

Thus, the political gardens of *Richard II* are ripe with allegory – from Gaunt's nostalgic remembrance of England being another Eden to the labourers in the King's garden. The *hortus res publica* carries with it the idea of pruning and cutting back, of the imposition of human will over nature, that beauty and order often comes only after the axe, and that the enclosed garden is an illusion – the reality being that such borders, and all they encompass, are constantly subject to change and corruption. For Comito, these are the gardens of history and he notes that 'gardens of the histories are [...] rhetorical, cut off from and commenting upon the substance of the plays. They are not so much places into which the imagination is invited as ideas.'[60] Whilst this may outwardly appear to be the case, I would argue that this is generally the circumstance in all of Shakespeare's gardens – that ideological norms are always contested within the liminal space that lies between the court and the wild. Staley notes that, rather than the early modern horticultural depictions of England's political geography expressing the sacred and enclosed, 'it is the permeability of those boundaries that frequently preoccupies efforts to describe or celebrate England, the garden whose inviolability is constantly at risk and with it the very identity of England itself'.[61]

It is important to note that Shakespeare's use of the complicated allegorical imagery of gardens, which includes both the serene and the vicious, is not simply historical allegory but is rooted in contemporaneous social anxieties over the future of the English commonwealth. The turbulent seesawing of religious and political power that defined the latter half of the sixteenth century continues into the seventeenth with what would become one of the bloodiest chapters in England's history – the civil war and Interregnum. Shakespeare's inclusion of such politically charged imagery suggests a significant public awareness and concern that stretched from central positions of governance to the edges of a society that would ultimately feel the aftereffects of mismanagement. The concept of the *hortus res publica* recurs in Marvell's various depictions of mowers. In 'The Mower's Song' the mower's frustration moves him to express his pent-up anguish against the pastoral setting:

> But what you in compassion ought,
> Shall now by my revenge be wrought;
> And flow'rs, and grass, and I and all,
> Will in one common ruin fall.
> For Juliana comes, and she
> What I do to the grass, does to my thoughts and me.[62]

This motif recurs in 'Upon Appleton House' where Marvell's mowers' maintenance of the pastoral setting is likened to a violent massacre, stressed in the unwitting death of a fledgling corncrake or water rail.

With whistling Sithe, and Elbow strong,
These Massacre the Grass along:
While one, unknowing, carves the Rail,
Whose yet unfeather'd Quils her fail.
The Edge all bloody from its Breast
He draws, and does his stroke detest;
Fearing the Flesh untimely mow'd
To him a Fate as black forebode.[63]

What both these stanzas accomplish is to take the pastoral, synonymous with peace and order, and associate it with the destructive. The outwardly tranquil vista of mowers and harvesters tending the land is brought into sharp contrast by the individual thoughts and actions of two mowers, each harbouring feelings of either revenge or ruin, battles and bloodshed. The very acts of husbandry and cultivation are unfortunately and necessarily severe, even punitive – something attested to first-hand by Marvell who witnessed England's garden subjected to civil war and the 'detest'able' execution of Charles I. Peter Stallybrass and Allon White highlight these 'points of antagonism' as providing 'some of the richest and most powerful symbolic dissonances' within a culture – a 'carnivalesque and transgressive anti-structure [...] marking out new sites of symbolic and metaphorical intensity in the ideological field'.[64] What emerges from these inversions and perversions of allegorical and symbolic spaces is a tradition of resistance. In the case of the garden, it provides a rich polysemy in which idealistic structures may be challenged using the very same imagery by which they seek to establish themselves.

Truncus: familial metaphor

There are few scenes in Shakespeare's body of works that come close to the sheer horror of Lavinia's rape, both its prelude and its aftermath. Augmenting the spectacle of Tamora's sons' torturous lusts is the language used, heavy with imagery of the hunt and, in particular, horticultural allegory. Yet this particular use of garden metaphor does not easily sit within either of the categories previously discussed. What we are presented with is something of a conflation of the *hortus conclusus*, Lavinia's 'chastity ... nuptial vow, her loyalty' (2.3.124, 125), and her 'nice preserved honesty' (line 135), and the idea of the *hortus res publica* as Titus attempts to secure Rome under the rule of the Andronici. Yet what ensues focuses more on the anxieties surrounding dynasties, the preservation of the genealogical or family tree. The Latin, *truncus*, is a horticultural term pertaining to the trunk or genus, and carries ideas of familial stock resulting from the body or trunk of the family head. In *Coriolanus*, the titular hero uses this metaphor as his family enters: 'My wife comes foremost; then the honour'd mould / Wherein this trunk was framed, and in her hand / The grandchild to her blood' (5.3.22–24). The Duchess of Gloucester refers to the bloodline of Edward III in terms of 'seven fair branches springing from one root' (*Richard II*, 1.2.13). So too does Henry refer to himself as the progenitor of a new Lancastrian dynasty, albeit a dying one, when he says to his son, 'Thou bring'st me happiness and peace, son John; / But health, alack, with youthful wings is flown / From this bare wither'd trunk' (*2 Henry IV*, 4.3.355–357). Prospero's vitriol against the brother who sullied his name and cast him out is also expressed in horticultural allegory as he declares of 'now he was / The ivy which had hid my princely trunk, / And suck'd my verdure out on't' (*The Tempest*, 1.2.85–87). In *Titus Andronicus* the metaphor is played out in the systematic tit-for-tat eradication of the scions of both Titus's and Tamora's houses. For Tamora, letting her 'spleenful sons this trull deflower' (line 191) is more than an act of spite against the Andronici, it is but one exploit in a grand scheme to effectively 'raze their faction and their family' (1.1.448). Furthermore, deflowering connotes not only the act of separating Lavinia from her chastity, but also the act of familial pruning, albeit so thorough a lopping as to kill off the entire family tree.

Demetrius's petition for his mother to stay her hand in slaying Lavinia incorporates a somewhat sadistic play on harvests: 'first thresh the corn, then after burn the straw' (line 123). Husbandry of the land involved the cultivation of crops, one part of which involved the threshing or beating of certain grains to remove the chaff that, along with the stalks, was later burnt or disposed of. For the violation of Lavinia's womanhood to be likened to the forceful acts of harvesting and threshing, followed by the careless disposal of her unwanted body once appetites had been sated, is a bleak and brutal treatment of classical garden motifs. The familiar cycles of planting, growth and reaping are now associated with sinister intent, and the dark harvest of Lavinia's chastity, not to mention her tongue and hands, corrupts the metaphor.[65] Yet there are greater implications for the murder of Bassianus and the mutilation and rape of his betrothed. Chiron endorses the use of Lavinia's dead husband as the bed on which she is to be ravaged: 'drag hence her husband to some secret hole / and make his trunk pillow to our lust' (lines 129–130). Apart from the offensiveness of such an act, effectively provoking even greater repulsion from an audience, the play on 'trunk' is telling. Both referring to the torso and the body of a tree, 'trunk' conjures up images of *truncus*, the family tree, implying that the potential for expanding the genealogical line of Andronicus has been irreparably damaged in the killing of his son-in-law and the defilement of his daughter. What is of particular significance is the reiteration of both harvest and family tree motifs at the play's close. With Rome in political disarray in the aftermath of Titus's obscene cookery, Marcus entreats those left to let him 'teach you how to knit again / This scattered corn into one mutual sheaf / These broken limbs into one body' (5.3.69–71). Lavinia's rape and disfigurement, previously likened to a macabre harvest, prefigures the state of Rome (*hortus res publica*), a figurative, and in some cases literally, disastrous crop of dismembered nobility. So too are the genealogical inferences in 'trunk' repeated as Lucius beckons his uncle to 'shed obsequious tears upon this trunk' (line 151) in mourning the passing of Titus. Though Tamora's ultimate plan to eradicate the family tree of the Andronici failed, the recurring pastoral images of broken branches, toppled trunks and horrific harvests suggest the damage to both Titus and to Rome are devastating.

This idea of linking the *hortus conclusus*, *hortus res publica* and *truncus* is strikingly portrayed in Julie Taymor's *Titus* (1999). Following the assault and disfigurement of Lavinia, Marcus discovers his mute and mutilated niece in a marshland, enclosed by mire and the skeletons of dead trees. It is very much a dead garden, a wasteland, with its centrepiece the broken Lavinia standing on a lopped tree trunk, virginal white dress torn and spattered with mud. Instead of hands she has had twigs thrust into the ruined wrists, a darkly parodic representation of Daphne's metamorphosis into the laurel tree to escape the lusts of Apollo. In this case, semiotics and 'non-verbal systems' or staging work together to reinforce the overall theme.[66] Later flashbacks recall the scene with bestial imagery; a detail which, Peter J. Smith notes, 'picks up the language of Shakespeare's play but also figures the helplessness of Lavinia confronted by the male tigers of Chiron and Demetrius'.[67] However, Taymor's horrific depiction of Lavinia's rape not only draws on Shakespeare's language, it essentially conflates the thematic milieu of female chastity with the downfall of a great family and the failure of state.

Albert Tricomi attests to the 'thematic matrix' within *Titus Andronicus* being a combination of grandiose Senecan horror and pastoral images, exposed in the imagery of Lavinia's 'mutilated garden'.[68] As Marcus looks upon the appalling picture of his niece's ruined and bleeding body, his speech is heavily punctuated with pastoral metaphors:

> Speak, gentle niece, what stern ungentle hands
> Hath lopped and hewed and made thy body bare
> Of her two branches, those sweet ornaments
> Whose circling shadows kings have sought to sleep in.
>
> (2.4.16–19)

Whilst the analogy of the brutally trimmed branches is unmistakable in its implications of female defilement, it is the last line that is of particular import in associating Lavinia's mutilated form with affairs of state. Bassianus was indeed from the line of Roman kings and emperors, and his death, followed by the rape of his wife, ensured that the Andronici's legitimate ties to the throne are all but destroyed. Thus, Marcus's focus is not only on spoiled womanhood, but the now shattered hope of creating dynasties from this royal stock – that Titus's legacy is intrinsically linked with Lavinia's ruin. Marcus continues with the horticultural theme, likening Lavinia to a bubbling fountain, her severed wrists and tongue 'three issuing spouts' (line 30). Bacon's definitive princely garden's centrepiece is the fountain, a 'great beauty and refreshment'.[69] There is a marked contrast between these two images, the culturally elevated generative motif of life bubbling forth and its appalling, disfigured and bloody mockery. In Taymor's *Titus*, Lavinia's ghastly fountain within the dead marsh is an image of the neglected garden, overgrown and lifeless. In the background is the sinister bulk of the forest, a reminder that the two motifs of park and forest, as

I showed in the last chapter, are constantly in a state of unrest – the human imposed orders of patriarchy and governance persistently endangered by man's baser nature. Taymor's vision is not simply poetic licence, but a visual representation of Shakespeare's setting. As Marcus describes it, it is 'a park' (3.1.88), a civilised preserve of hunting that becomes a much darker place, a 'ruthless' and 'dreadful' forest (2.1.128) in which humans are preyed upon. For Tricomi, this is not merely poetic ornamentation and romantic embellishment. Rather, he sees the two settings of park and forest conflating or changing from the former to the latter as in the Fall of man, stating: 'the idyllic pastoral world always contained the possibility of becoming its opposite'.[70] There is a significant link to be made between the pastoral and the wildness of the forest in *Titus Andronicus* – two liminal settings each with their own set of images and social subtexts, here expressing the idea of moral and social regression. Indeed, one might actually express the overthrow or inversion of the Edenic park imagery with the wild and dangerous forest as expressing a widening gap between divine will and the more visceral nature of mankind.

Thus, when Shakespeare used images associated with cultivated space in his plays there is significant evidence for categorising dynastic anxieties within their manifold allegorical applications. In an age that bridged the gap between feudal and capitalist England, the aristocratic houses still formed an integral part of the political structure. Early modern concerns over Elizabeth's successor, the creation of an heir and the potential end of the house of Tudor all had momentous national consequence. Shakespeare's plays harness these national apprehensions through the application of nuanced horticultural referents and raise questions as to the sustainability and viability of these antiquated modes of authority.

Weeds in Eden

> But if that flower with base infection meet,
> The basest weed outbraves his dignity:
> For sweetest things turn sourest by their deeds;
> Lilies that fester smell far worse than weeds.
>
> (Sonnet 94)

Shakespeare loved gardens. We cannot say for certain, as the Reverend Ellacombe proclaimed, and Ben Elton envisioned, that the playwright was a gardener himself. However, we do know that Shakespeare returned again and again to a unique space that contained a layered cultural meaning and significance – open to multiple interpretations and connotations. The biblical Eden offers a semantically complex framework that, as Northrop Frye expressed, 'enables the pastoral poet to use a highly concentrated metaphorical imagery without any breach of decorum'.[71] 'Decorum', or propriety is key here, as to assist in social commentary a metaphor must be well established and accepted, but also malleable enough to present multiple, even conflicting perspectives. I would argue that, in this, the garden is exemplary.

Shakespeare's georgic settings draw on complicated biblical analogies that tend towards either political dissidence or patriarchal subversion. The garden of state calls to mind prelapsarian rebellion whilst the garden of love draws on the imagery of Hebrew love poetry and the nature of relationships decided exclusively by paramours and not peripheral authorities. In each case, the garden is a liminally private space outside of the centralised structures of authority that provides its temporary occupants with the reprieve or shelter, albeit illusory, they require to set in motion events that will challenge those self-same power structures.

What stands out in Shakespeare's garden motifs, whether they be the patriarchal visions of the *hortus conclusus*, the *hortus res publica* of the functions of state, or themes of dynasty and family stock lineage in *truncus*, is that, in each case, there is a level of subversion, social anxiety and corruption that is inherent in their very structure. As Shakespeare's ninety-fourth sonnet articulates, weeds and decay inevitably exert themselves, a constant reminder of fallibility and change. Hiram Haydn attributes these pessimistic views to Shakespeare undergoing a radical change in his philosophical beliefs, 'moving from a traditional humanistic (and explicitly Stoic) position to a semi-cynical, wholly disillusioned one'.[72] Yet, as I have shown, the seemingly idealistic Edenic garden contains the very means of its demise, the serpent around the tree, the first lie and the original sin. So too is the literal garden subject to seasons, blight and the depredation of weeds. Rather than attempt, as Haydn does, to read this as the personal inclinations of the playwright, I would argue that Shakespeare's prolific use of garden metaphors and settings throughout his writings attests to their adaptability within multiple socio-political settings and their power to point out the weaknesses inherent in such systems. Furthermore, when we look at the Shakespearean garden in relation to new historicist concepts of the containment and control of the movement of power, what we are presented with is an inherently complex and slippery space that resists attempts to regulate subversion. As such, where horticultural comparisons and locations are employed, they represent resistance to authority, the inevitability of change and the impossibility of containment.

Notes

1 In more recent times Gerit Quealy, co-editor of *Fifty Things to Do When You Turn Fifty* (2005), put together an illustrated compendium of Shakespeare's botanical references in his works under the lengthy title, *Botanical Shakespeare: An Illustrated Compendium of All the Flowers, Fruits, Herbs, Trees, Seeds, and Grasses Cited by the World's Greatest Playwright* (New York: Harper, 2017). Whilst it claims to be the 'most comprehensive' work to date, its lack of academic approach situates it more in in the region of the coffee table than the scholar's library.
2 Revd Henry N. Ellacombe, *The Plant-lore and Garden-craft of Shakespeare* (London: W. Satchell & Co., 1884), p. 2. www.gutenberg.org/files/28407/28407-h/28407-h.htm#Page_333 [accessed 30 Dec. 2020].
3 *All Is True*, dir. Kenneth Branagh (Sony Pictures Classics, 2018).
4 Caroline Spurgeon, *Shakespeare's Imagery and What it Tells us* (Cambridge: Cambridge University Press, 1952), p. 86.
5 Michel Foucault, *The Order of Things* (London: Tavistock Publications, 1970), pp. 239, 240.
6 James H. Kavanagh, 'Shakespeare in Ideology', in *Alternate Shakespeares*, ed. John Drakakis (London: Methuen & Co., 1985), p. 146.
7 Ibid., p. 148; emphasis mine.
8 Charlotte Scott, *Shakespeare's Nature: From Cultivation to Culture* (Oxford: Oxford University Press, 2014), pp. 2, 4, 28. Whilst this particular research does not apply ecocritical literary theories to Shakespeare's literal or figurative settings, Scott approaches

land-husbandry from an economic standpoint that ties in more recent developments in ecocritical thinking. For further reading on these approaches to Shakespeare's cultivated world see the collection of essays edited by Lynne Bruckner and Dan Brayton in *Ecocritical Shakespeare* (London: Routledge, 2011).

9 Francis Bacon, *Of Gardens* (London: Hacon & Ricketts, 1902), p. 6. www.gutenberg.org/files/46964/46964-h/46964-h.htm [accessed 30 Dec. 2020].

10 As is later discussed in Andrew Marvell's garden poetry, the early modern country house genre becomes a literary arena for competing discussions of outdoor spaces and their symbolism.

11 On specifically Romantic conceptions of nature and their influence on Shakespeare, see the two publications by Jonathan Bate: *Shakespeare and the English Romantic Imagination* (Oxford: Clarendon Press, 1986), and *The Romantics on Shakespeare* (London: Penguin, 1992).

12 Bacon, *Of Gardens*, p. 13.

13 Terry Comito, *The Idea of the Garden in the Renaissance* (Hassocks: Harvester Press, 1979), p. xi.

14 For a more extensive study into the subversive origins and uses of this quotation in medieval Europe, see Paul Freedman's *Images of the Medieval Peasant* (Stanford, CA: Stanford University Press, 1999).

15 Edmund Spenser, *The Faerie Queene* (London: Penguin Books, 1987), p. 470.

16 John Playford, *The Dancing Master: Or, plain and easie Rules for the Dancing of Country Dances, with the Tune to each Dance, to be play'd on the Treble Violin* (London: John Playford, 1653).

17 Edith G. Kern, 'The Gardens in the *Decameron* Cornice', *PMLA*, 66(4) (June 1951), 505–523, pp. 507, 508.

18 Raymond Williams, *The Country and the City* (St Albans: Granada, 1975), p. 42.

19 Oksana Moskina, 'The Garden Scene in *Romeo and Juliet*: Its Representation on Stage, Canvas, and Screen', *Riscritture dell'Eden: Il ruolo del giardino nei discorsi dell'immaginario*, 8 (2015), 75–108, p. 75.

20 Boucicaut Master, 'The Story of Adam and Eve' (fifteenth-century), J. Paul Getty Museum, Ms. 63 (96.MR.17), fol. 3.

21 What is to this day probably the most quoted Virgilian line, *latet anguis in herba* or 'the snake in the grass' from his *Eclogues* (3.93), is yet another example of the danger hidden within seeming beauty. The expression is framed in the context of boys picking flowers and strawberries and forms a warning that what is outwardly good may also conceal harmful elements. This theme occurs again in William

Blake's 'The Sick Rose' (1794) where the 'invisible worm' destroys the beauty of the cultivated flower, a juxtaposition of life and decay, perfection and humanity.
22 Shakespeare's Sonnet 94 declares, 'for sweetest things turn sourest by their deeds; / Lilies that fester smell far worse than weeds' (lines 13, 14) and Jaques observes that all that ripens eventually rots (*As You Like It*, 2.7.26, 27).
23 Robert Adger Law, 'Shakespeare in the Garden of Eden', *Studies in English*, 21 (1941), 24–38, p. 38.
24 Stanley Stewart, *The Enclosed Garden: The Tradition and the Image in Seventeenth-Century Poetry* (Madison, WI: University of Wisconsin Press, 1966), p. xi.
25 Terry Comito, 'Caliban's Dream: The Topography of Some Shakespeare Gardens', *Shakespeare Studies*, 14 (1 Jan. 1981), 24–40, p. 24.
26 It is worth noting that scholarship has largely moved away from strict delineation of genres. For further reading on this see the collection of fourteen essays edited by Antony R. Guneratne that explores current thoughts on the subject in *Shakespeare and Genre: From Early Modern Inheritances to Postmodern Legacies* (New York: Palgrave Macmillan, 2011).
27 Comito, 'Caliban's Dream', p. 24.
28 Stewart, *Enclosed Garden*, p. 49.
29 Liz Herbert McAvoy, 'The Medieval *Hortus Conclusus*: Revisiting the Pleasure Garden', *Medieval Feminist Forum*, 50 (2014), 5–10, p. 5.
30 Ibid., p. 8.
31 Stewart, *Enclosed Garden*, p. 10.
32 Whilst there is no hard and fast referent either in the stage directions or the body of the text as to where this scene occurs, I would argue that the action takes place either within or adjacent to the royal gardens, as when the Queen exits to take her turn around the garden she re-enters eighteen lines later to urge the lovers to make haste. Her proximity to and control over both the lovers and Cymbeline within this scene indicates it is a place she feels comfortable in challenging the royal edict and can hover on the edge of the action to step in as she sees fit. Dramatically, it would make sense to have this scene within a garden as it parallels similar 'romantic' scenes in *Much Ado About Nothing, Twelfth Night* and *Romeo and Juliet*.
33 Though the later scene of Pisanio and Innogen's plot to counter the accusations of Posthumus would appear to take place in the fields and wilderness of rural Wales it contains ripples of Ovidian transformation as Innogen becomes 'Fidele' in order to protect her

chastity, a repetition of the action of Viola in *Twelfth Night*. It is noteworthy that the only scene set in the garden in *Titus Andronicus* borrows from Ovid's *Metamorphoses*, likening Lavinia's rape to that of Philomel as the former victim attempts to communicate the heinous act in a series of signs in the earth. This fusion of female sexuality and influence is manifest in Lavinia's drawing the names of her assailants in the earth, facilitating their demise.

34 Bakhtin, *Rabelais and his World*, p. 412.
35 All references to Geoffrey Chaucer's tales are taken from *The Canterbury Tales* (London: J. M. Dent, 1939).
36 McAvoy, 'The Medieval *Hortus Conclusus*', p. 8.
37 Jenny Stevens, 'A Close Reading of Chaucer's "The Merchant's Prologue and Tale"', *British Library* (2018). www.bl.uk/medieval-literature/articles/a-close-reading-of-chaucers-the-merchants-prologue-and-tale [accessed 18 Feb. 2020].
38 Roberts, *The Shakespearean Wild*, p. 28.
39 Ibid., p. 35.
40 Andrew Marvell, *The Complete Poems*, ed. George Lord (London: Random House, 1993), p. 49.
41 Note that, although there is always a measure of debate over specific settings of scenes, those that have been listed follow current academic opinion and evidence. In this regard, the Arden Shakespeare and opensourceshakespeare.org have been valuable sources of individual scene settings.
42 Edward Berry, *Shakespeare and the Hunt: A Cultural and Social Study* (Cambridge: Cambridge University Press, 2001), p. 15. Whilst the physical setting of *Venus and Adonis* is nominally a park, garden imagery is most prolifically used in metaphor, Venus's 'cheeks were gardens full of flowers' (line 65), her body likened to a 'park' (line 231), her 'lower' regions to 'fountains' (line 243). There is also the sense of time and seasons that regulate growth become allegories for sexual increase and propagation: 'by law of nature thou art bound to breed' (line 171). The poem also contains horticultural referents with interesting contrasts such as the likening of Adonis to a flower where the masculine becomes subject to feminine representations of chastity, and the reversal of the social norms when Venus, representative of the feminine, single-mindedly pursues the male.
43 Act 4, Scene 3, takes place when 'the king is hunting deer' and Biron is 'coursing' (lines 1, 2) and the King later appears from behind a bush (line 135). The following act seems to take place in the fields wherein the Princess has encamped, the disguised King stating he has travelled

some distance 'to tread a measure with her on this grass' (5.2.186). The Princess later refuses entry to court, empowered as she is in 'this field' (line 345) in which she and her ladies in waiting have established a rival court.

44 The final ruse set by Mistress Page revolves around Hearne's Oak in Windsor Forest: 'Falstaff at that oak shall meet with us' (4.4.41), and the final scene appears to take place in this part of the park with John declaring, 'for me, I am here a Windsor stag, and the fattest I think i'th' forest' (5.5.12, 13).
45 2.1.30 indicates Romeo has 'hid himself in trees' and in the following scene Juliet expresses her wonder at Romeo having scaled the garden walls: 'the orchard walls are hard to climb' (2.2.63). Capell proposes 2.5 is set within the Capulet's garden. Once more, Juliet's room overlooking the orchard is given attention in 3.5. Romeo's brief interlude with his wife ends with his departure via the window to the garden below – 'one kiss and I'll descend' (line 42).
46 According to Pope, 2.5 is set in Olivia's Garden. This fits in with Maria's urging her fellow schemers to, 'get ye all three into the box tree' (line 15) from whence they may observe Malvolio's actions. In 3.1, Olivia would seem to receive the disguised Viola in her garden as she instructs her staff and relatives to 'let the garden door be shut and leave me to my hearing' (lines 91, 92). Capell recommends 4.3 as set in Olivia's Garden.
47 Benedick requests a book be fetched by a boy and brought to him 'in the orchard' (2.3.4), and later on Hero and Ursula 'walk in the orchard' (3.1.5) in order to spring the trap for Beatrice.
48 Pandarus's instruction to the expectant Troilus is to 'walk here i'th' orchard. I'll bring her straight' (3.2.15).
49 Aside from references to garden settings, both direct and inferred, we have only the imaginations of directors and the suppositions of scholars from the eighteenth century onward to fall back on. Kurt Schlueter imagines a garden setting for the conversation between Julia and Lucetta in his edition of *Two Gentlemen of Verona* (Cambridge: Cambridge University Press, 2012), p. 72; and Capell envisages a similar setting involving the plotting for Jessica to be freed of her father in *The Merchant of Venice*.
50 Comito, 'Caliban's Dream', p. 24.
51 Stewart, *Enclosed Garden*, p. 15.
52 Lynn Staley, *The Island Garden: England's Language of Nation from Gildas to Marvell* (Notre Dame, IN: University of Notre Dame, 2012), p. 108.

53 David Rollison, 'Shakespeare's Commonwealth', in *Shakespeare and the Politics of Commoners: Digesting the New Social History*, ed. Chris Fitter (Oxford: Oxford University Press, 2017), p. 78.
54 Cicero, *De Re Republica*, trans. G. W. Featherstonhaugh (New York: G. & C. Carvill, 1829). www.gutenberg.org/files/54161/54161-h/54161-h.htm [accessed 25 Aug. 2020].
55 Ibid.
56 Comito, 'Caliban's Dream', p. 40.
57 Though gardens are not mentioned in *Titus Andronicus*, its conclusion sees Marcus apply horticultural metaphor and the language of cultivation and husbandry to the ruined commonwealth when he declares, 'O, let me teach you how to knit again / This scattered corn into one mutual sheaf / These broken limbs into one body' (5.3.69–71).
58 Though Anthony Iden is a historical figure there is traction in the notion that Shakespeare's audience would have made the connection between his surname and the garden setting of Cade's demise and the Garden of Eden in which the rebellious occupants were delivered their death sentence.
59 Rollison, 'Shakespeare's Commonwealth', p. 79.
60 Ibid., p. 31.
61 Staley, *The Island Garden*, p. 115.
62 Marvell, *The Complete Poems*, p. 45.
63 Ibid., p. 75.
64 Stallybrass and White, *Politics and Poetics of Transgression*, p. 25.
65 The *OED* indicates that there are commonalities in the etymological origins of 'rape' and 'reap', both implying seizure.
66 Alessandro Serpieri, 'Reading the Signs: Towards a Semiotics of Shakespearean Drama', in *Alternate Shakespeares*, ed. John Drakakis (London: Methuen & Co., 1985), p. 121.
67 Peter J. Smith, 'The Roman Plays on Film', in *The Cambridge Companion to Shakespeare on Screen*, ed. Russell Jackson (Cambridge: Cambridge University Press, 2020), 119–133, p. 128.
68 Albert H. Tricomi, 'The Mutilated Garden in *Titus Andronicus*', *Shakespeare Studies*, 9 (Jan. 1976), 89–105, pp. 89, 90.
69 Bacon, *Of Gardens*, p. 17.
70 Tricomi, 'Mutilated Garden', p. 93.
71 Northrop Frye, *A Natural Perspective: The Development of Shakespearean Comedy and Romance* (New York: Columbia University Press, 1965), p. 62.
72 Hiram Haydn, *The Counter-Renaissance* (Gloucester: Charles Scribner's Sons, 1966), p. 638.

5

Theatres of war: Shakespeare's ideological battlefields

Some twenty-odd years ago, a few friends and I went on a brief holiday north, across Hadrian's Wall and into the wilds of Scotland. Amongst the many places visited was the site of the most celebrated Scottish victory over the English – the Battle of Bannockburn, fought over two days in late June 1314. The modern-day field of Bannockburn contained a monument to Robert the Bruce, a vast blue flag emblazoned with the white saltire of Scotland and a visitor's centre complete with audio-visual aids, wooden swords and fridge magnets. As I looked over the fields and streams I attempted to imagine the movements of Edward II's cavalry, the hail of arrows, the dispositions of the Scottish schiltrons and the various manoeuvres the two armies would have taken over the terrain. It was only at this point that a friend who was more assiduous than I looked up from his *Lonely Planet* guide and said, 'Of course, you know this wasn't the real battlefield – nobody really knows where it was!' This was a truly baffling revelation, yet not the first of its kind.

In more recent times, the discovery of what are believed by many to be the remains of Richard III in a car park in Leicester sparked national interest in the Battle of Bosworth, yet another engagement – and one Shakespeare brought back to life – that is hotly contested not only as to where it was fought but the size of the forces and their various factions. Such disclosures raise poignant questions. What can be said of the construction of identity and the memorialisation of certain historical events through their association with certain physical spaces? What happens when a place of national significance, the most celebrated of triumphs, is contested and debated by historians who, in the case of Bannockburn, place the actual battlefield up to, and for a few over, a mile away in almost every direction – everywhere but where the monuments and national emblems marked the engagement?

Battlefields have always been associated with the establishment of identities, whether they be national, religious or otherwise. What is curious about Bannockburn, Bosworth and countless other historic battlefields is that, for such decisive events, the spaces in which they occurred are often indefinite, ambiguous and disputed. In turn, such incongruities open the way for contestation of the events themselves, or at the very least, the means by which these events have been recorded and passed down through the ages. With such uncertainties there is the potential to view such spaces and the historical/legendary/notorious events associated with them from a number of different and even conflicting positions. Thus, acts of heroism might also be seen as wanton cruelty, chivalry may serve as a veneer for egocentrism and righteous ideals theoretically become a façade for shameless self-promotion and greed.

This conundrum over the contestation of spaces of significance lies at the heart of Shakespeare's battlefields. Within his plays he recognises that such spaces and the events that unfold in them are first and foremost the violent manifestation of human failure to resolve differences outside of primitive and vicious means, raising questions over the motivations of those who engineer these events, as well as the men who ultimately carry out the action – those who choose war and those for whom war is chosen.[1] What's more, such events create unique and temporal spaces: yesterday non-existent, today a battlefield and tomorrow a place forever located and memorialised within the collective social consciousness, such as the fields of Flanders after the First World War and the beaches of Normandy after the Second World War. These aspects of memorialisation and the manner in which time and place are affected by violent events are challenged and manipulated within Shakespeare's plays, both out of necessity related to the limitations of staging and the obvious constraints of play-length, but also in the writer's choice of what to depict and when and, tellingly, what to withhold and the potential political motivations behind such suppression.

Surprisingly, within the not inconsiderable body of scholarly works devoted to Shakespeare, there is very little written on the imagined and theatrically reproduced space of the battle. In recent years there have been forays into Shakespeare and the world of war, most recently the excellent collection of essays compiled and edited by Patrick Gray on *Shakespeare and the Ethics of War* (2019), in which the question is examined from present perspectives, contemporary conflicts and recent productions. Janette Dillon's *Shakespeare and the Staging of English History* (2012) is particularly valuable in its look at spatial symbolism on the stage – particularly in situating this concept within the playwright's various representations of battles and duels. Charles Edelman's focus on the staging of martial encounters on the early modern stage in *Brawl Ridiculous: Swordfighting in Shakespeare's Plays* (1992) contextualises contemporaneous attitudes towards chivalry and considers the use of metaphor and parody to introduce more subversive elements into the plays. In some ways, these modern works develop the more rudimentary depictions of the Renaissance conceptualisation of war and peace that were the subjects of Paul Jorgensen's *Shakespeare's Military World* (1956). Each of these works has contributed to our understanding of certain concurrent attitudes to battlefields and the ideologies of war in Shakespeare's world. Yet there has been no real foray into the reasons behind why such events were represented theatrically or why such liminally important spaces were pivotal in establishing alternate perspectives and divergent belief systems that ultimately challenged centrally endorsed social dogma.

What this chapter seeks to uncover is, first, the idea of a battlefield, both in terms of its early modern cultural significance and spatially – its theatrical representation and the means by which the immense clash of armies may be translated onto a stage with limited actors. In examining the physical, geographical and temporal properties of the battlefield what becomes apparent is that it is the quintessential liminal space – quite literally a place of contestation and subversion, ideally suited to dissident narratives. So too are the cultural, political and religious resonances important in understanding the way staging battles could present the means by which social institutions and their incumbent ideological derivatives were challenged. In this regard, consideration of how ideals surrounding war were disseminated complicates the idea of a homogeneous or socially static conceptualisation of chivalry, heroics and the justification for conflict. Furthermore, and related to this idea of presenting alternate histories on the stage, is the idea that the battlefield ironically offers the playwright a unique space in which to introduce carnivalesque subversion – that the classical arena of masculine power and chivalric prowess is in fact often inverted, as indeed are social hierarchies and ideological principles. Finally, we are inevitably drawn back to the question of remembrance – how the re-enactment or retelling of history shapes, and indeed challenges, social identity. Despite the considerable array of Shakespeare's fields of war, it is the siege of Harfleur and Battle of Agincourt that have become the theoretical battlefields for numerous critics who have sought to understand the poet's inclusion of such scenes of violence; and creating a dialogue with these often-disparate conclusions necessitates revisiting these recreated spaces. As such, whilst diverse Shakespearean battlefields will be considered in exploring the themes above, *Henry V* forms the central case study for this chapter. I will establish that Shakespeare's battlefields were inherently subversive spaces that provided an ideal arena in which to present, compare and challenge disparate social ideologies.

What is a battlefield? This seemingly innocuous compound word actually carries with it a more complex meaning. The *Oxford English Dictionary* defines the first part of the word as referring to 'a hostile engagement or encounter between opposing forces on land or sea'. Yet the word, and its straightforward explanation, does not allude to the contexts of such events – the religious acrimony or political rancour that preceded wholesale bloodshed. A battle is not a randomly occurring event or natural phenomenon; it is an engagement that carries with it culturally layered connotations and justification. In essence, the battlefield is a space in which a final and decisive act serves radically to shift the balance of power through violence.

Yet one might plausibly conclude that such a definition could also apply to the assassinations of Duncan and Julius Caesar, or the street-wars between the houses of Montague and Capulet. Indeed, all violence is an attempt to upset the status quo and stimulate new structures of authority. What separates the battlefield from these other bellicose acts is its legitimisation. It is no wonder that battlefields recur throughout Shakespeare's plays, their fundamental principles and accompanying intricate rationalisations providing a glimpse of humanity on the cusp of anarchy. As Paul Jorgensen observes, 'war was one of the most precariously ordered and civilised of human enterprises; far more serious than peace-inspired institutions like government and marriage, it threatened to revert to chaos'.[2] It is noteworthy that battle scenes primarily occur within Shakespeare's dramatic representations of history. Agincourt, both Battles of St Albans, Angers, Barnet, Bordeaux, Bosworth, Crecy and Poitiers (should we admit *Edward III* to the canon), Harfleur, Orleans, Shrewsbury, Tewkesbury, Towton and Wakefield all take place either on stage (excursions) or behind it (alarums). Of course, battlefields are present in other plays: *Antony and Cleopatra, Coriolanus, Julius Caesar* and *Cymbeline* each contains scenes devoted to the clashes between Rome and her adversaries both on land and sea, and *King Lear, Macbeth* and *Troilus and Cressida* also include battles. Furthermore, although confrontations are not staged in some of Shakespeare's plays, there is mention of pervasive conflict. Theseus's war against the Amazons precedes the opening of *A Midsummer Night's Dream*, the events that immediately follow the defeat and capture of Don John become the subject of *Much Ado About Nothing, Titus Andronicus* takes place after the defeat of Tamora's Gothic armies, Antonio's fear of capture in Illyria following a sea-battle in which he fought against Duke Orsino adds an added level of tension to *Twelfth Night*, and *Othello* follows the exploits of a successful Venetian general. However, the sheer volume of battles in the histories pertaining to the English crown suggests their inclusion was not simply a means to break the tempo and provide a change to dynamics of stage play.

Stephen Greenblatt's alarm at the rise of Donald Trump prompted the literary critic's response in the form of *Tyrant: Shakespeare on Politics* (2018). In it he proposes that the popularity of staging histories was their remove in time from the events they depicted, providing 'a certain immunity' from censure, whereas setting plays in more contemporary settings would arouse the ire of public officials.[3] Further, he notes that 'censorship inevitably generates techniques of evasion', hence, subtlety and discretion would be needed if an audience were to draw parallels to existing events, systems of power and institutions.[4] Dissident themes were more comfortably incorporated within comedies or tragedies that could be suitably 'removed' or distanced from the English bodies of monarchy and Church whether by time, location or purely fictional or fantastic content. Yet history had to be handled with kid gloves. In fact, it still does – if we learn anything from Oskar Eustis's 2017 production of *Julius Caesar* in Central Park, the 'political firestorm' that ensued from his depiction of 'the assassination of its Caesar-as-Trump figure' shows that some parallels may sail a little too close to the wind.[5] However, what is important to note is that histories and their respective battlefields enabled a critique of systems of authority at the very point at which they were openly contested and the void of power threw wide the way to change.

Theorists on the battlefield

There exists an argument that Shakespeare's incorporation of historic battles into his plays was *not* a means to subvert the status quo. Hence, it is important that we revisit new historicist critical theories over the ultimate containment of any dissident threads within theatre. Stephen Greenblatt's 'Invisible Bullets', his pioneering essay in which he outlined the close relationship between orthodoxy and subversion, used Shakespeare's history plays to model his concept. For Greenblatt, containment implies that change is minimal and that when there is subversion it serves ultimately to maintain the status quo. Thus, we still have monarchies, we still have religious principles and we still have social dogma – these societal structures never truly disappear, nor are they radically reorganised. As Greenblatt puts it, in the end, these plays force us to 'pay homage to a system of beliefs whose fraudulence only confirms their power, authenticity, and truth'.[6] Hence, any attempt at subverting, satirising or subjecting these institutions to theatrical vilification only reinforces their power and presence within society. That there is a voice of resistance is acknowledged; however, he asserts that 'subversive voices are produced by and within the affirmations of order; they are powerfully registered, but they do not undermine that order'.[7] Greenblatt's insistence is that even theatrical subversion and its exposure of hypocrisy and malfeasance in the institutions of power ultimately reinforces such structures, that theatre both reflects social order and is a tool of it, but never truly stands apart from it. It is a pessimistically monochrome and unpromising view of what subversion actually is, not to mention the power of the stage. For Greenblatt, there must be a clear outcome, a manifest social change, in order to prove that a subversive theatrical gibe at a political system had definitive social ramifications.

However, as Peter Stallybrass and Allon White observe, there are multiple 'symbolic domains' that are fundamental to 'ordering and sense-making in European cultures'.[8] What is more, any change to or transgression of established hierarchies within any one these domains (social order, the body politic, geographical space) has the potential to 'have major consequences in the others'.[9] As will later be demonstrated, without the inclusion of Falstaff, *1 Henry IV* would conceivably be, for some, a rather dry chronicle of the preamble to the War of the Roses. Yet the comic element Shakespeare introduces does more than merely function to lift the tone and add flavour and colour to the past. Falstaff is uncontainable, the most slippery of characters. D. S. Kastan observes that 'Falstaff's exuberance refuses to be dominated by any authority, resisting incorporation into or containment within the stabilising hierarchies of the body politic or indeed of the well-made play'.[10] The battlefield was traditionally a place of martial prowess and feats of arms, the anvil on which manhood, kingship and power were shaped and determined. Yet Falstaff upsets these ideological parameters, bringing a whole new approach to the battlefield – that of the irrepressible human traits of selfishness and self-preservation. As a comic character he succeeds in projecting his worldview with minimal censure due to the faux charm with which he attempts to win over his audience. What's more, history itself has been changed – it is no longer contained in respected historical texts and documents, it is no longer the possession of the learned. Rather, in its retelling or re-enactment, it is subject to the whims of the playwright's pen, the actor's voice and the stage's geography. Rebecca Schneider describes this phenomenon as 'cross-temporal slippage', that 'despite or perhaps because of the error-ridden mayhem of trying to touch the past, something other than the discrete "now" of everyday life can be said to occasionally occur – or recur'.[11] History is manipulated through remembering, presented from political slants and with social agendas. It bestows on kings and princes words, feelings and motivations that are purely imagined yet stir the audience to pass judgement; and fictional characters and clowns that tint perspectives and sway verdicts populate it. Greenblatt's hierarchical structures look far less invulnerable from this point of view – subject to the scrutiny of playwrights, the theatrical flourishes and whims of players and the variety of audience responses.

Though it may be argued that plebeian perspectives often overlapped politically popular points of view, Paola Pugliatti proposes that there are voices that are not represented by these prevalent ideologies:

> Dramatists, in particular, as subjects that mastered the most widespread popular, even plebeian source of information and opinion-shaping, may have been, in those years, the only mouthpieces of the many strata of society which did not have a public voice of their own; those who did not belong to either the intellectual caste (which made itself heard through books) or to the political, military, and religious castes (which made themselves heard through statutes, ordinances, proclamations, sermons, and so on).[12]

Thus, through the playwright, the commoner is given a voice and is no longer contained within the same social parameters as before – the very shape of society has shifted, even if the substance may not have appeared to have changed significantly. One of the ways Shakespeare demonstrates this alternate perspective and manipulation of hierarchies is in *3 Henry VI*. In what is perhaps the battle scene most infused with pathos, Shakespeare's treatment of the Battle of Barnet aptly illustrates the means by which the battlefield is employed to bestow power upon the commoner. As the King sits on a hillock in the midst of the battlefield, imagining himself as a shepherd, two mirrored events interrupt his solipsistic reverie. The stage directions indicate that from one door enters a soldier carrying a dead man in his arms. The initial motive for this action is revealed when the soldier soliloquises that he slew the man in combat whom he has now dragged to the edge of the field with the intention of robbing the corpse. However, on removing the dead soldier's helmet, he is confronted with the face of his father:

> Who's this? O God! it is my father's face,
> Whom in this conflict I unwares have kill'd.
> O heavy times, begetting such events!

From London by the King was I press'd forth;
My father, being the Earl of Warwick's man,
Came on the part of York, press'd by his master;
And I, who at his hands received my life, him
Have by my hands of life bereaved him.

(2.5.61–68)

The bleakness of the young soldier's lament is underscored by the reason such a tragedy occurred in the first place – both he and his father were 'press'd' into service based, not on any ideological choice on their part, but on the quirks of their geographical positions at the time conflict broke out. David Underdown notes that in the civil war preceding the Interregnum 'the armies of both sides were heavily recruited from the poor and the marginal' and were composed of 'men who served under compulsion', that being either through impressment, poverty or obligation to a landowner.[13] Falstaff's levying of troops in *2 Henry IV* sheds light on such undertakings as being open to abuse when both Bullcalf and Mouldy bribe their way out of being drafted. Yet not all could afford such avoidance, a fact attested to by the Calendar of State Papers that lists a sharp increase in conscription in the late fifteenth century.[14]

As if to emphasise through repetition, and certainly, from a theatrical perspective, to balance the stage with a parallel episode, from the opposite door we witness yet another soldier enter, bearing a body. Once again, it is material gain that precedes calamity:

Thou that so stoutly hast resisted me,
Give me thy gold, if thou hast any gold:
For I have bought it with an hundred blows.
But let me see: is this our foeman's face?
Ah, no, no, no, it is mine only son!
Ah, boy, if any life be left in thee,
Throw up thine eye! See, see what showers arise,
Blown with the windy tempest of my heart,
Upon thy wounds, that kill mine eye and heart!
O, pity, God, this miserable age!
What stratagems, how fell, how butcherly,
Erroneous, mutinous and unnatural,
This deadly quarrel daily doth beget!

(2.5.79–91)

As with the first account, this brief scene follows a pattern. The base motivations of common soldiery (fiscal gain) lead to the revelation of the personal cost of war (individual loss), which in turn lead to the allocation of blame (the system). In each instance the King, unseen by the lowly soldiers, is forced to confront the reality of his actions at a level not just of human loss but also of their effect on families. As with the surreptitious 'Harry le Roy' at Agincourt, the battlefield once again enables Shakespeare to throw together the opposite ends of society in a way that calls to account those in positions of power. Jorgensen, whilst acknowledging the poignancy of these scenes of social juxtaposition, asserts that:

> On the whole, however, whatever insights Shakespeare achieves into the mentalities of his common soldiers are focused upon their less admirable traits: their reluctance to be drafted, their ridiculous poverty, their fear of battle, their pursuit of booty rather than honour, and their grumbling and insubordination.[15]

This claim seems to ignore Shakespeare's intimation that the common soldier is a product of the system in which he has no say, a system that does not consider him anything more than a pawn on a chessboard, effortlessly pushed forward and easily sacrificed. The King himself attests to this when he declares: 'O piteous spectacle! O bloody times! / Whiles lions war and battle for their dens, / Poor harmless lambs abide their enmity' (lines 74, 75). The King's Bo-Peep daydreams take on a reality he had not previously considered – that if he is indeed God's representative, if he adheres to the Christian codes of kingship, then he is *already* a shepherd. What's more, his 'lambs' have taken the brunt of disputes wrought from greed or grievance – as Falstaff so bluntly expresses it 'food for powder' (*1 Henry IV*, 4.2.65), a term Greenblatt aptly turned into 'food for power, [...] consumed by the great'.[16] Are these common voices truly consumed, repressed or quashed by the more powerful central systems of social governance? We cannot dismiss the amassed 'subversive voices' of the Falstaffs, Pistols, Williamses and the hosts of rustics and common soldiery that amount to a veritable shout of no confidence in the system.

The mutability of power evidenced in Shakespeare's dramatic representations of battlefields links with more recent anthropological and social studies. That these temporary historic spaces and brief theatrical performances did not seem to significantly 'change' anything, or lead to the immediate overthrow of institutions, does not detract from their *potential* to do so, nor of the long-term effects of dramatic exposés in realigning such institutions with the will of the masses. Both Arnold Van Gennep and Victor Turner proposed that such liminal stages and settings are part of a cyclical process, one that is constantly renewing, rebuilding and refashioning social structures. Society, with its hierarchies and orthodoxies, maintains certain familiar structures; however, it constantly experiences incremental shifts. Van Gennep wrote that cultural action takes place over three stages: pre-liminal, liminal and post-liminal.[17] Turner expanded on this theory as 'structural aspects of passage [...] in which behaviour and symbolism are momentarily enfranchised from the norms and values that govern the public lives of incumbents of structural positions'.[18] For Turner, structure, specifically social structure, becomes peripheral, systems and hierarchies are at once both simplified and rendered ambiguous due to their structures being reduced or eliminated within a liminal space. His conclusions are that 'if liminality is regarded as a time and place of withdrawal from normal modes of social action, it can be seen as potentially a period of scrutinization of the central values and axioms of the culture in which it occurs'.[19] This is what takes place through dramatic cultural input, and is never clearer than when Shakespeare remembers or reimagines history – the status quo seems to be maintained but it has actually shifted through the liminal medium of theatre and its unique space. This cultural phenomenon is evidenced in theatre as carnivalesque inversions and hierarchical reversals; it is also the province of the battlefield where the simple rule of kill-or-be-killed eclipses societal structures. However, whilst these liminal spaces and events may seem to simply segue between pre- and post-liminal states in which social order is restored, Turner warns that society is never static; rather it is 'a dialectical process with successive phases of structure and communitas', driven by the social 'need to participate in both modalities'. Hence, to view the dramatically satirical and playfully transgressive content of the theatrical battlefield as simply contained within various social structures that 'permit' temporary licence to invert social orthodoxies is narrow. It fails to recognise the fluidity and flux by which social and cultural activities move from the peripheries to the centre, each testing the other's limitations and strengths.

Shaping ideologies

In order to understand how Shakespeare manipulated the battlefield as a liminally fraught space it is important to understand the contemporary ideologies attached to great conflict. From an early age, Shakespeare would have been exposed to literature that concerned the wars of the Greeks and Romans. Plutarch's *Parallel Lives*, translated in 1579 by Thomas North, provided a rich seam of historical material that later appeared in Shakespeare's Roman tragedies.[20] It is possible that, in learning the art of rhetoric, students would have studied the essays and treatises of Cicero, in which he expounds on the ethics associated with war and the moral obligations of combatants.[21] However, it is to the works of Raphael Holinshed that Shakespeare makes considerable reference in his history plays. Holinshed's *Chronicles* were first published in 1577 when Shakespeare was only 13 and thus it is most unlikely to have appeared in any of the curricula to which he would have been exposed, not least because his schooling at King Edward VI Grammar School in Stratford-upon-Avon would probably have been drawing to a close by this point. However, by the time Shakespeare was writing plays, in the latter half of the 1580s, Holinshed's historical volumes were in their second edition and, if the poet did not possess a copy himself, then he certainly had access to one. As will be demonstrated later, Shakespeare readily drew on Holinshed not just for content but also for the dramatic structure and staging of battle scenes. In addition to historical reference works, Ros King argues that Shakespeare was likely to have also perused Thomas Syward's *The Pathway to Martiall Discipline* (1581) and William Garrard's *The Art Of Warre* (1591), manuals in which directives for soldiery and ethical justifications for war are expounded.[22] However, whilst such texts form a backbone to the history plays and their attendant battlefields, I would argue that the playwright's approach to such spaces is influenced by more than his schoolbooks, conduct books and history texts.

War was everywhere. The protracted Anglo-Spanish War (1585–1604), the Dutch War of Independence (1566–1648) and the French Religious Wars (1562–1598) meant that territorial conflict and naval warfare were never very far away. Moreover, all of these engagements saw the involvement of English troops. And what becomes of veterans once their service is terminated? Shakespeare's plays are populated by a variety of soldiers and his dexterity in expressing their language and attitudes would seem to indicate that he had met more than a few veterans of battles both on land and sea. Duncan Salkeld's exploration of *Shakespeare and London* (2018) mentions the brothels, pubs, gambling dens, bear-baiting pits and theatres of Southwark and the various citizens to be encountered in the vicinity of The Globe. He remarks that Shakespeare would have come across not only those who plied their trade in the theatres but also 'parishioners, tradesmen, shopkeepers, lawyers, merchants' and a host of other persons involved in 'the seamier aspects of life in the suburbs'.[23] Yet he omits any mention of veterans and soldiers of fortune who must inevitably have inhabited and moved through London, either on their way to or returning from campaigns abroad. Jorgensen notes that wounded soldiers who returned from war may well have received a small annuity but that the Crown's issue to such veterans of an official licence to beg attested to the insufficiency of such pensions – such beggars would no doubt have availed themselves of the crowds who gathered outside London's many theatres. Those fortunate to return without significant bodily harm still met with the prospect of having to find employment, or to try their hand at more nefarious trades. Ros King observes that 'the evidence of war in Shakespeare's London was never far away [...] Mercenaries and private soldiers, returning destitute and probably traumatised, constituted a social problem at home, becoming the subject of successive royal proclamations'.[24]

Shakespeare's contemporary, Robert Greene, wrote a series of pamphlets published in 1592 that were largely taken from the extant *A Caveat or Warning for Common Cursitors, vulgarly called vagabonds* (1566) by Thomas Harman. Although a certain amount of authorial licence may have been taken, Greene's collection of stories of vagrants and rogues who lived by their wits and their ability to sell themselves or take advantage of the innocent gives us a glimpse of a dirtier, more dangerous London, a tradition of urban satire later embellished by Defoe, Fielding, Johnson and Dickens.

One such account is that of Ned Browne, an opportunist, thief, swindler and one-time soldier of fortune:

> I thought indeed that Tyburn would at last have shaked me by the neck: but having done villainy in England, this was always my course, to slip over into the Low Countries, and there for a while play the soldier, and partly that was the cause of my coming hither: for growing odious in and about London, for my filching, lifting, nipping, foisting and cross-biting, that every one held me in contempt, and almost disdained my company, I resolved to come over into France: by bearing arms to win some credit, determining with myself to become a true man. But as men, though they change countries, alter not their minds: so given over by God into a reprobate sense, I had no feeling of goodness, but with the dog fell to my old vomit, and here most wickedly I have committed sacrilege, robbed a Church, and done other mischievous pranks, for which justly I am condemned and must suffer death.[25]

Browne's villainy mirrors that of the condemned Bardolph and his band of unruly drinking companions-cum-soldiers who steal a pax from a church. Though this account follows Holinshed's *Chronicle* where 'a souldiour tooke a pix out of a church, for which he was apprehended, & the king not once remooued till the box was restored, and the offendor strangled', it would appear that such deeds were more widespread and the common soldiery more kleptomaniac than Holinshed's account admits.[26] Indeed, as Ros King and Paul J. C. M. Franssen note, a series of royal proclamations were issued in the 1580s following the public misconduct of 'disillusioned and quarrelsome soldiers returning from the wars in France and the Netherlands'.[27] After the theft of items from a church, Pistol's supplication for Fluellen to intercede in the sentence to execute the lieutenant falls on deaf ears. Following the battle, the disenchanted and cynical Pistol vows: 'To England will I steal, and there I'll steal; / And patches will I get unto these cudgelled scars, / And swear I got them in the Gallia wars'. (*Henry V*, 5.1.88–90). It is just such veterans that Greene speaks of – referring to them by the popular term: the soldado, or soldier of fortune.[28]

> These soldados, for under that profession most of them wander, have a policy to scourge ale-houses [...] now sir they have sundry shifts to maintain them in this versing, for either they creep in with the

goodwife and so undo the goodman, or else they bear it out with
great brags if the host be simple, or else they trip him in some words
when he is tipsy that he hath spoken against some justice of peace or
other, or some other great man, and then they hold him at a bay with
that, till his back almost break. Thus shift they from house to house,
having this proverb amongst them: Such must eat as are hungry, and
they must pay that have money.[29]

Veterans of the wars in the Low Countries and of the protracted Anglo-Spanish conflict would no doubt have sought entertainment in London's theatres and drinking establishments, brawling, begging and exchanging stories. As such they would have constituted a valuable source not only of the experiences of battle but of the attitudes of the common soldier towards conflict.[30] Thus Shakespeare's approach to staging the battlefield would have been shaped as much by the real-life experiences of the soldiery he rubbed shoulders with on the city streets as by the education and higher social ideals taught within the classroom and portrayed in tales of chivalry. These disparate philosophies form the focus not only of the struggle for power, as enacted in battle, but the war of contemporary ideologies.

One ideological meaning of battle is that used by the King in *1 Henry IV* as he chastises his wayward son for not measuring up to the patriarchal, dynastic, chivalric ideals of Hotspur, who he goes on to describe:

> He hath more worthy interest to the state
> Than thou the shadow of succession;
> For of no right, nor colour like to right,
> He doth fill fields with harness in the realm,
> Turns head against the lion's armed jaws,
> And, being no more in debt to years than thou,
> Leads ancient lords and reverend bishops on
> To bloody battles and to bruising arms.
> What never-dying honour hath he got
> Against renowned Douglas! whose high deeds,
> Whose hot incursions and great name in arms
> Holds from all soldiers chief majority
> And military title capital
> Through all the kingdoms that acknowledge Christ
>
> (3.2.98–111)

Here, Percy is depicted as an energetic prodigy, displaying all the desirable qualities and actions of a prince amongst men, or as the King articulates, 'Mars in swaddling-clothes' (line 112). The young Percy is a god of battle, blood and honour intrinsically linked, feats of arms not only associated with greatness, but with Christ himself. Here Henry fuses a Roman pagan god of war with the symbol and founder of the Christian faith. Christ's gospel of peace and the love of one's enemy are jarringly juxtaposed in the King's speech with the mention of this rapacious belligerent leading 'reverend bishops' to war. Somewhat ironically, battles are portrayed as the commendable Christian pursuit, the proving ground for masculinity and the means to establish a worthy name.[31] In this Shakespeare reflects contemporary attitudes and popular values promoted by the English Court. Ralph Berry notes that 'court spectacle and pageantry proclaimed chivalric values. No mere cult, this revival had its roots in reasons of state'.[32]

Henry's attitude to battle was forged in an earlier play where he further nuances the understanding of combat. Bolingbroke's dispute with Mowbray results in the former's recourse to battle to decide who is right. 'I say, and will in battle prove' (*Richard II*, 1.1.92), declares Bolingbroke. In this case, battle represents the hand of Providence in deciding a legal case – effectively, a trial by combat. Keegan notes that in the Middle Ages, 'theologians reluctantly conceded the morality of combat when conducted to impose or restore a sovereign's lawful rights'.[33] In turn, the Crusades developed the ideology behind honourable combat, chivalric actions being modelled on Christian principles where knights effectively became the gauntleted hand of God in the reinstatement of Christianity to its origin in Palestine. The idea of battle and its outcome as divine judgement somewhat complicates the simpler might-is-right power play of combat. It effectively justifies bloodshed and theoretically masks more egotistical or self-serving motives for acts of aggression.

These Judaeo-Christian ideals, mobilised and weaponised under the moniker of chivalry, once again appear in the pious supplications of Henry V on the eve of the Battle of Agincourt. Falling to his knees the King prays, 'oh God of Battles, steel my soldiers' hearts' (*Henry V*, 4.1.286). Once again there is a religious element to the forthcoming conflict, its very foundations and legal justifications plotted by none other than the Archbishop of Canterbury and the Bishop of Ely in the first act. However, Henry's petition is addressed to the Old Testament Lord of Hosts, the God of Heavenly Armies. For Henry, it would appear from his earnest entreaty that the battlefield represents an arena where God himself manifests his power and will, choosing champions to fight his causes and directing the events to reflect his own designs, reminiscent of the words of the psalmist, 'turn to us again O LORD God of hosts, cause thy face to shine, and we shall be saved' (Psalm 80:7). This is indeed the very picture painted of him by his uncle, the Bishop of Winchester, at Henry's funeral: 'The battles of the Lord of hosts he fought' (*1 Henry VI*, 1.1.31). In the tradition of biblical heroes, such as Joshua praying for the sun to stand still that he might bring God's vengeance upon the pagan nations, or David's entreaty to guide his sling-stone into the forehead of the giant who was taunting the God of Israel, Henry humbles himself before God, his contrite supplications those of a penitent who throws himself on the mercy of the Almighty. The disguised Henry's earlier conversation with Bates also focuses on 'his cause being just and his quarrel honourable' (4.1.127, 128) – qualifications that excuse the forthcoming brutality in God's eyes.

Yet this linking of God's will to Henry's campaign for the throne of France is challenged by the lower ranks whose idea of a battlefield is far more pragmatic. For Williams, Christian ideals cannot easily be reconciled with battle – 'I am afeared there are few die well that die in a battle, for how can they charitably dispose of anything when blood is their argument?' (4.1.141–143). The macabre apocalyptic visions of an assembly of lopped heads and limbs uniting to condemn a king whose cause, whether right or wrong, brought a bloody and painful end to so many lives, throws the battlefield's reality into stark relief against high-minded religious epitomes and chivalric stereotypes. There is an echo here of an ode Shakespeare may well have come across in his schooling:

> With you I shared Philippi's rout,
> Unseemly parted from my shield,
> When Valour fell, and warriors stout
> Were tumbled on the inglorious field
>
> (Horace, *Odes* 2.7.9–12)

Horace's encounter with battle does not recall splendid deeds and glorious acts but rather ignominy and despair – sentiments amplified in Williams's condemnatory reflection. What's more, Henry's ruthless commands to slay French prisoners somewhat sully the image of piety and providence he displayed prior to the battle. In terms of performance, Donald Hedrick notes that Shakespeare's Henry V displays a 'paradox of his personality' that complicates the Shakespearean theatre of war yet has been carefully steered away from in some modern productions.[34] Berry too avers that in most of Shakespeare's histories, chivalry is treated with an irony that interprets it as a 'vestigial residue of past thinking'.[35] Thus, the battlefield presents the playwright with a space in which ambiguity is at home – an environment that by its grim nature calls into question the morality of the belligerents, primarily that of its kings and generals, those who set the events in motion that will ultimately result in mutilation and mortality.

Temporal fields: staging battles

A battlefield differs significantly from a field, a street, a city or a wood. in that it comes into existence for a period, is used as the arena for monumental power struggle, before it is again overtaken by nature and returns to an otherwise indistinguishable space. There is something to say for its temporality, its relationship as a physical space to time. This can be seen reflected in the rapid scene changes with minimal scenery indicating specific places and times that make the stage an abstraction of reality – history twice removed, slowed down or sped up depending on the manipulation of the playwright. This phenomenon of both temporal and spatial abstraction is noted by Stephen Greenblatt as a 'secularization of space', and the 'abolition of qualitative up and down' resulting in 'the essential meaninglessness of theatrical space, the vacancy that is the dark side of its power to imitate any place'.[36] In the fourth act of *Henry V*, we are subjected to this speeding and slowing of the temporal plane. The close of the third act sees the Duke of Orleans state: 'It is now two o'clock; but let me see, by ten / We shall have each a hundred Englishmen' (3.7.155, 156). From this time and space we are then transported to the other side of the field, the Chorus opening with 'Now entertain conjecture of a time' (4.0.1). The subject of time recurs here, showing both its swift passing for the audience (within sixteen lines it is now 'the third hour'), and yet the slow and dreadful progress of time for the English soldiery who anticipate the morning's battle. This act is divided into eight scenes, which in turn are split into sub-scenes within each camp. This constant movement takes us back and forth between common soldiers and heralds, nobles and kings, French and English, and the battle's margins and its nucleus, and serves to mimic the stages of action in battle from its prelude through to its denouement. Within this loose structure and ambiguous playfulness with space, and the manner in which time appears to either compress or expand, all manner of social behaviours and standards are tested and even broken. It is a space of extreme licence where hierarchies are thrown into confusion, where a peer may yield to a commoner, where a low-born foot soldier might kill a nobleman and yet be celebrated for his actions, and where a common goal dictates that aristocrats and peasant militia work shoulder-to-shoulder in the filth and blood. This latter levelling is certainly evident in Montjoy's description of princes' and peasants' mingled blood at the conclusion of the Battle of Agincourt:

> I come to thee for charitable licence,
> That we may wander o'er this bloody field
> To look our dead, and then to bury them;
> To sort our nobles from our common men.
> For many of our princes – woe the while! –
> Lie drown'd and soak'd in mercenary blood;
> So do our vulgar drench their peasant limbs
> In blood of princes; and their wounded steeds
> Fret fetlock deep in gore and with wild rage
> Yerk out their armed heels at their dead masters,
> Killing them twice.
>
> (*Henry V*, 4.7.75)

The French Herald's plea to scour the battlefield is tellingly framed by his revulsion at the comingling of noble and vulgar blood. The inference is that, as terrible as the battle's outcome is for the French, the greater offence is in the hierarchical subversion of common and aristocratic bloodlines among the dead!

The creation and temporary nature of a battlefield is also highlighted in the way Shakespeare refashions familiar pastoral and urban settings into liminal locations of affray. The significance of such a location was in the memorialisation of an event, whether a grandiose affair or a light skirmish, where power was drastically disrupted and redistributed. The Battle of Shrewsbury may have been fought in a field of peas yet the agricultural history of that location changed forever with the clash of armies.[37] So too was the obscure field on which Henry's army laid waste to the flower of French nobility, previously a nondescript plot roughly adjacent to a small castle named Agincourt. Yet at the close of the battle the victorious king sees fit to memorialise the event by naming the space it was fought in – 'Then call we this the field of Agincourt' (4.7.89). The significance of naming or renaming the location of such clashes is first that it becomes forever a marker or symbol of either pride or shame, of victory and celebration or of defeat and subjugation – effectively a social tool that unifies one nation through its overthrow of another (one only need reference the taunts of present-day English football hooligans who chant, 'two world wars and one world cup' whenever their team plays Germany). The French King's warning to his eager generals to consider Henry's lineage before underestimating his prowess as a warrior does just this:

> Think we King Harry strong,
> And, princes, look you strongly arm to meet him.
> The kindred of him hath been fleshed upon us,
> And he is bred out of that bloody strain
> That haunted us in our familiar paths.
> Witness our too-much-memorable shame
> When Cressy battle fatally was struck
>
> (*Henry V*, 2.4.48–54)

The sour taste of their being trounced at the Battle of Cressy, a battle that occurred nearly seventy years earlier and more than likely before the birth of most of those on the French war-council, is employed to curb boasting that is born of miscalculation. So too the realisation of the French defeat immediately triggers a sequence of 'shame' (the word occurs no fewer than six times in twenty-three lines) from the French nobility who dread the memorialisation of such an ignominious and incontestable defeat. Naming solidifies the event and the space within the social consciousness and historical re-enactment on the public stage potentially tapped into such communal memories, generating shared associations of pride or shame, an immediate realignment or manipulation of an audience.

The challenge for any dramatist, both in early modern London and indeed our modern day, is the translation of historical conflict onto a wooden platform within its limited space and without having access to a cast of thousands. The dramatic representation of both large- and small-scale physical clashes is important when considering the historical understanding of and exposure to armed conflict and the reasons why Shakespeare would choose to depict such scenes. Whilst grand battlefields, with their formations, cavalry, cannon and kings, were often removed from the day-to-day realities of the average early modern London playgoer, street fights were not. Charles Edelman notes that Henry VIII outlawed the carrying of certain weapons in the streets of Westminster on pain of death in the attempt to curb public violence.[38] This stipulation is echoed in *Romeo and Juliet* with the Prince's warning to cease public brawling or face summary execution. David Underdown also observes that this kind of civil strife, in the form of 'brawls and quarrels', was to be 'watched, restrained ... and denounced by the authorities' who were all too aware of the larger social impact such fights could have.[39] Thus, when small-scale reproductions of loftier confrontations graced the wooden platforms of London's many playhouses, an audience would doubtless already have been exposed to scenes of public violence. Londoners also had something of a penchant for organised blood sports. Fencing and duelling, bear-baiting and cockfighting were all popular entertainments. Louis B. Wright's study of stage fencing notes that 'the playhouses when not being used for stage plays were frequently given over to exhibitions of fencing and other feats of skill or agility'.[40] The diarist John Manningham's entry on 7 February 1602, regarding a duel at the Swan theatre, reads: 'Turner and Dun, two famous fencers, playd their prizes this day at the Banke side, but Turner at last run Dun soe far in the brayne at the eye, that he fell downe presently stone deade; a goodly sport in a Christian state, to see one man kill an other!'[41] Though Manningham's latter comment may be an attempt to elevate his personal principles, he does paint a somewhat more critical picture of Elizabethan Londoners' fondness for fighting, a predilection any playwright would seek to capitalise on through translating such spectacles, where possible, into dramaturgical experience.

In regard to the subject of staging battles, Jean MacIntyre's essay of 1982 begins by dispelling the idea that staged battles would have been comical affairs with actors arrayed in makeshift armour and wielding blunted weapons, attempting to avoid hurting each other in a mock skirmish. She notes that precisely one third of Shakespeare's plays contain scenes of melee, including single fights, sieges and pitched battles.[42] That does not mean that there may not have been the odd comic element involved in the dramatic representations of combat, such as the duel between Sir Andrew Aguecheek and Cesario/Viola in *Twelfth Night* or the cowardly Falstaff's feigning death after his clash with Douglas in *1 Henry IV*. However, what is clear from MacIntyre's exposition is that, when battle took place on the stage, such scenes did not suffer from any inadequacy in conveying all the energy and weight of mortal combat. Shakespeare's battles are broken down into four methods: 'to separate speech and fighting, which the actors managed at will; to limit battle to a duel between leaders, accompanied by offstage sound; to represent the battle by offstage sounds alone, with or without onstage observers; to order simultaneous or successive duels, fights, and pursuits, introduced and followed by speeches and accompanied by sound effects'.[43] What is of note in these various ways of depicting battle, both visually and aurally, is the presence of offstage sound – the alarum denoting action on a larger scale than that witnessed on stage.

Whilst MacIntyre does not expand on what such alarums would sound like we can piece together from stage directions, lines within plays and historical events that such sounds were not simply a few tin plates being bashed together. Christopher R. Wilson and Michela Calore observe that the term alarum comes from the Italian *all'armi* ('to arms'), and that on the stage 'the sounding of alarums by various instruments, especially trumpets, drums or bells is connected with military atmospheres'.[44] Along with drums, bugles, fifes and jangling bells, one might also have heard various shouts of command, battle cries and, most notably, cannons. The cannon that set fire to The Globe's thatch roof midway through the staging of *Henry VIII* on 29 June 1613 was probably one of several 'chambers', or small cannon used by the theatre for battle scenes.[45] The most notable reference to such staged cannonades is in *Henry V* where the Chorus describes the siege of Harfleur:

> And the nimble gunner
> With linstock now the devilish cannon touches
>   *Alarum, and chambers go off.*
> And down goes all before them.
>
>   (3.0.32–34)

The impact of even a small cannon going off on cue within the theatre's confined space would have had a profound effect on the audience, at the very least on their eardrums, but more importantly in creating the percussive effects, sounds and smells of battle (the smoke of the powder would have created a lingering stench of rotten eggs).[46] Michael Hattaway suggests that the physical space and time it would have taken in choreographing and rehearsing a dramatic fracas on a small platform necessitated the representation of battles offstage, with the sounds and 'choric narration' substituting for onstage action.[47] Jorgensen argues that there is evidence to support the translation of a battle into music, asserting, 'Shakespeare more frequently and effectively enlarged his military theatre through an appeal to the ear'.[48] Though we do not have substantiation of a precursor to Tchaikovsky's 1812 Overture, replete with cannons, there is certainly reference to acoustic spectacle in Canterbury's claim that the newly minted Henry V's martial prowess would cause one to hear 'a fearful battle rendered you in music' (*Henry V*, 1.1.44). Whether this was metaphoric bluster or, as Jorgensen claims, literal, what is apparent is that battlefields offered the dramatist an opportunity to use sounds other than words to move his audience.

Thus, the theatrical battlefield promised an audio-visual spectacle with the potential to bring far more than a diverting clash between protagonists. Rather, on a jutting wooden promontory, roughly half the size of a tennis court, with a limited number of actors, Shakespeare staged skirmishes between opposing philosophical, political, religious, moral and social perspectives, calling into question social structures and their motivations and justifications. Within this unique space plays out the dissociation between those who instigate battles and those who fight them – creating an inherently chaotic zone, a liminal fulcrum between ideological positions and social situations.

The politics of battle

One of the most controversial lines from *Henry V* is spoken on the battlefield and reveals the politically subversive nature of such spaces and the means by which Shakespeare could undermine chivalric stereotypes as well as destabilise the very foundations of monarchy. At one point mid-battle the King enters, accompanied by prisoners of war. When Henry hears the French call to regroup he proclaims: 'every soldier kill his prisoners / give the word through' (4.6.37–38). Later, on learning of the French attack on the baggage boys, the King eschews clemency and declares 'we'll cut the throats of those we have / and not a man of them that we shall take / shall taste our mercy' (4.7.62–64). This battlefield brutality moves beyond the remit of generals and kings, a fact attested to by the officious Fluellen and his loquacious polemology.

The idea that Henry's quest for the French crown is personal and not providential, displaying Machiavellian win-at-all-cost motivations, is reinforced with a striking comical interlude in the form of Pistol and his French captive. Amusing though the fumbling misinterpretation of language may be, yet the disturbing realities of Pistol's ruthless actions revile the common English soldiery, effectively labelling them as mercenaries. Pistol's incentive in battle is pecuniary, and his interaction with the French gentleman he has vanquished displays his concern with only one thing – crowns.[49] 'Peasant, unless thou give me crowns, brave crowns; / or mangled shalt thou be by this my sword' (4.4.38, 39) plays with the parallelism between the uncouth English soldier and Henry – both driven by their desire for 'crowns', and both willing to shrug off gallantry when it may compromise their venality. Shakespeare has previously thrown these two together on the eve of battle where the subject of social status is first discussed. The King, suitably disguised as Harry le Roy, is challenged by the pugnacious Pistol as to his rank – 'art thou officer / or art thou base, common and popular' (4.1.37, 38). The Stygian gloom preceding the morning's battle may conceal Harry's true physical identity, allowing him to pose as someone other than himself and express his alter ego, yet this does not necessarily happen in the heat of battle where, despite rank or uniform, true character is revealed. Indeed, the battlefield constitutes a unique space that becomes the crucible in which man, be he commoner or king, has his motives and beliefs tried, tested and exposed. And in this crucible it is revealed that both Pistol and Henry have similar ideas of what constitute rules of engagement – that the end always justifies the means.

It is noteworthy that in both Olivier's and Branagh's film versions of the play these exchanges are either heavily edited or else removed entirely, presenting a 'sanitised' portrayal of the King.[50] In each of these screen adaptations the massacre of the French prisoners is removed, thus morally exculpating the King. Peter S. Donaldson notes that in Branagh's rendition the sheer quantity of mud serves as a 'ritual immersion', a baptism from which Henry and his men emerge sanctified.[51] So too does the deliberate removal of Pistol's money-or-your-life demand for his prisoner's ransom paint the English soldier in a more favourable light than that which Shakespeare may have envisioned. The significance of these two editorial choices to censor, sanitise or remove any allusions to iniquitous action on the part of the King or the quality of an Englishman is manifold. First, the setting of the battlefield opened an opportunity for Shakespeare to bring the institution of the monarchy down into the mud with the common man. Agincourt becomes an arena in which the true qualities of chivalry, Christian charity and common decency are put to the test for each man – commoners and kings alike. Secondly, on this particular field Shakespeare chooses not to render Henry in the favourable light one might expect of a heroic conqueror – and this opens the way for discussion on the possible effects of this kind of portrayal. Louis Montrose suggests that 'theatricalism may also be the very media through which royal power is demystified', effectively presenting a 'multiplicity of perspectives' that raise important questions.[52] Some of the more radical issues raised surround notions of proto-socialist class levelling, where social hierarchies are portrayed as useless fabrications. So too does the question of divine providence in the appointment of monarchs rear its head, an issue soon to divide England into warring factions, not to mention the killing of its king. What is clear is that uncomfortable home truths were not always shied away from by the playwright, and that the battlefield was a setting that lent itself to presenting subversive matter to his audience. John Sutherland notes that the slaying of the French prisoners *precedes* the scene in which the English 'poys' were killed, but maintains that 'it was motives of military prudence, not condign reprisal' that determined Henry's order to execute the prisoners.[53] In what appears to be an attempt to extricate the King from any associations with war-crimes, Sutherland references Henry's request for the bill of slaughter followed by a list of 'prisoners of good sort' (4.8.73), intimating that the initial commands to kill the prisoners were merely spoken in the 'heat of battle' as 'words only' and carried no weight of command. However, this reasoning is undermined by the fact Shakespeare gives Henry the line to slay the prisoners *twice*. What is more likely, considering the double nature of Henry as both warrior king and cunning statesman, is that 'prisoners of good sort' would have meant nobility, those whose ransoms would have paid for his bloody campaign. As such, the common French POW would be of no worth, merely an unnecessary distraction to the business at hand.

What is of particular interest when it comes to Shakespeare's staging of Agincourt is the way he utilises historical patterns of depicting conflict but manages to remove any sort of aristeia or centrally staged duel as in *1 Henry IV*.[54] Jean MacIntyre argues that Shakespeare appropriated Holinshed's formula when it came to concentrating on (1) the convergence of the armies, (2) negotiations and verbal transactions that ultimately fail, (3) engagement, where 'attention narrows to the exploits of some secondary person', (4) wider actions such as reinforcements arriving and daring rescues, (5) a key dramatic event that ultimately decides the battle's outcome and finally (6) the aftermath including the tolls of dead and wounded.[55] She notes, however, that in *Henry V* Shakespeare does not glorify Agincourt; rather he subverts any sort of national pride when he 'adds to Holinshed's list [of the dead] grim details of blood, wounded horses, and dying men'.[56] There is no onstage action as in the first and second parts of *Henry IV* but rather the bluster of the French nobility and the cowardly murder of the baggage boys, the humorous exchange of the ignorant Pistol with a French prisoner, the King ordering the slaying of all prisoners of war, the comical exchange between Gower and Fluellen, the second order to kill prisoners of war, this time in the presence of Bourbon who is the King's prisoner, and finally the surrender and lists of the dead. Whilst Holinshed's pattern is followed, and we are constantly aware of the sound of battle taking place offstage, Shakespeare denies any sort of heroic single combat, thus diminishing any sort of magnificence or chivalric splendour. Shakespeare deliberately withholds visual displays of honour, choosing to focus on individuals and speech that upsets the ideals of chivalry. Thus, it is not what is included but rather what is excluded from the stage that subverts any traditional approaches to the battlefield as an arena of gallantry, courtliness and masculine prowess, focusing on the more visceral, horrific and imperfect aspects of warfare.

What the battlefield enables Shakespeare to expose is the way power is manifest when faced with the two options of Christian courtliness or cold-blooded calculation. Henry's callous commands reveal his arbitrary revaluation of life based on realpolitik rather than morality, on might and not right. There can be little glorification in either feats of arms or acts of sacrifice, as the whole event is tarnished by the horror of a war without rules. Indeed, the Chorus's opening apology for the limitations of the stage to portray the battle in all its glory is ironically disingenuous as Shakespeare more than adequately represents the duality of man and his propensity to throw the rulebook out when it comes to achieving his ends. As MacIntyre observes, the treatment of the battle 'proves not that Shakespeare's stage was inadequate, but that Shakespeare did not want to clothe this battle in the usual heroics'.[57] One might add to this that Shakespeare paints Henry V in a similar light to Richard III, the only difference being that the latter monarch takes us into his confidence from the opening scene, his Janus-faced approach to court politics made delightfully transparent for his audience through his frequent asides. Yet Henry maintains a detachment from his audience – even his soliloquy is addressed to God and not to the onlookers. We are shut out, left to witness his pretence at piety and politic camaraderie with the common English soldier, masking his Machiavellian choreography preceding, during and following the battle.

Much has been said about the stimulus of Niccolò Machiavelli's controversial treatise, *Il Principe* (1532), on Shakespeare's works.[58] Where *Richard III* presented us with the advanced guide for unscrupulous monarchs, the anatomy of political intrigue, *Henry V* gives us all the subtlety without the explanatory asides – and never more so than on the battlefield. Machiavelli notes that 'there are two ways of doing battle: using the law and using force', and that 'typically humans use law and animals force'.[59] It is evident from Henry's morally confronting battlefield commands that the more bestial side of human nature is here revealed. There is also evidence that Shakespeare recreates a character that fits Machiavelli's criterion where 'a leader doesn't have to possess all the virtuous qualities, [...] but it's absolutely imperative that he *seems* to possess them'.⁶⁰ Thematically, *Henry V* becomes something of a challenge to Shakespeare's audience who are presented with the conundrum of whether to condone or censure such character traits. For Norman Rabkin, the ambiguity of Henry's morality represented 'a crisis in Shakespeare's spiritual life' that was translated onto the stage.⁶¹ Katherine Attié argues that 'for the spectator, moral judgment, and the work of thinking required by it, becomes part of the aesthetic experience of the theatre'.⁶² However, whilst there may be traction in each of these arguments, I would contend that such depictions go beyond mere aesthetics into the realm of subversion. As Paola Pugliatti maintains, we witness the contestation of 'the time-honoured Christian doctrine of responsibility that, since Augustine and later Aquinas formulated it, had served to placate both the leader's and the soldiers' consciences'.⁶³ Further to this, Michael Hattaway proposes that certain Shakespearean battles are 'metatheatrical', and 'demonstrate that war, for dissimulating politicians, is a kind of theatrical game'.⁶⁴ Indeed, Shakespeare's battlefields are testing grounds that often serve openly to critique or darkly to satirise structures of power such as the Church and the monarchy – both of which are embodied in Henry.

Carnival carnage

One way in which Shakespeare undermines the often-vaunted Henry is in the resolution of the argument between 'Harry le Roy' and Michael Williams. There is a pleasing symmetry to the parenthetical posturing of the King and his philosophical, if belligerent, soldier in that their argument precedes the battle and its resolution immediately follows the battle's close. Yet, if anything, its resolution serves to diminish the King's moral standing. Only just having received news that the battle is won and following hard on the heels of news that the baggage boys have been mercilessly slain, the King's memory of his conversation prior to the battle is jogged by the appearance of Williams with Harry's glove still affixed to his helm. What ensues is a jolly jape wherein the King bestows Williams's glove on Fluellen, knowing that the resultant recognition of the token of challenge will potentially result in further bloodshed. That Henry sends Warwick and Gloucester to follow and break up any such fracas does not take away from the fact that, in all the tragedy and carnage that has just ensued, all the King seems interested in is an elaborate practical joke. Over 110 lines are devoted to this incongruous digression that only ends with the appearance of Montjoy and the list of the dead.

What this instance reveals is that, for Shakespeare, the battlefield becomes a space of exposure and inversion – in the above case, that of a carnivalesque prank. As a definitive example of Shakespeare's generic amalgamation, heroic action is destabilised by black humour. Northrop Frye struggled with bonding such seemingly disparate genres in his essays, noting that 'there seems to be a far less direct connection between history and comedy: the comic scenes in the histories are, so to speak, subversive'.[65] What Frye fails to do here is to see histories as more than a category of recording and recreating the past without commentary on its highly political nature. For Frye, history as a genre is subverted through the introduction of comic elements. Yet Shakespeare's inclusions of comic and carnival components within his histories actually serve to anchor history in the present, to comment on the same institutions and ideological principles carried through into the English Renaissance. Thus, Henry's inappropriately timed practical joke does not upset the genre so much as upset the image of monarchy. That a historic battlefield strewn with dead and dying is now a stage for an elaborate jape diminishes and denigrates the victorious young monarch, altering audience perceptions of him from national hero and the exemplar of English kings to a somewhat less heroic standing.

This is not the only instance of the conflation of battlefields and comedy to subvert social structures and their attendant ideologies. As has been previously demonstrated, the battlefield is shown by Shakespeare to be a stage of sorts, with heroic lines written by social custom and ancient codes of honour, spoken by antagonists whose oddly courteous and archaic speeches frame bloody mortal combat. This unnatural and paradoxical combination of chivalric fundamentals outwardly served as a model to which lusty young men could aspire. Comedy would seem peculiarly out of place in such a space and yet Shakespeare insists on inserting the comically chaotic figure of Falstaff with a single purpose: to counter these banal battlefield values with his devastatingly acerbic wit. 'Can honour set to a leg?' (*1 Henry IV*, 5.1.131), begins the fat knight, to which he catechises any who would listen that honour is a painted shield for the dead and is thus valueless. Dragging the body of Blount from the field, Falstaff intones his personal motto: 'Give me life, which if I can save, so; if not honour comes unlooked for, and there's an end' (5.3.59–61). Life is what drives Falstaff, to the point that he is prepared to drop chivalric notions of honour and play dead, carry a bottle of sack on the field rather than a pistol, and throw his followers forward as cannon fodder to save his own neck (4.2.64–66). As Kastan observes, 'Falstaff is never merely the servant of the historical plot. He exists at its margins, observing, willing to take what it offers, but always as its critic, an unruly presence challenging the fundamental assumptions that motivate the political world'.[66] As with Henry's and Pistol's base motivations, Falstaff is but another, albeit more obvious, challenger to the chivalric ideal. Falstaff's anarchic presence on and around the battlefield parodies the very act of power violently negotiated through force and seemingly directed or governed by an old-fashioned sense of honour. Rather, he presents us with a dissident narrative that what really governs the actions of men is a desire to live at all costs. This promotion of the self, life and the celebration of momentary pleasure overrules the principled and elevated mores a society may endorse as a means of social 'resistance to the totalizations of power'.[67] One of the more memorable scenes during the battle is when Falstaff stumbles upon the recently deceased Sir Walter Blount. Here Shakespeare juxtaposes the two knights, one chivalrous and courageous, who was prepared to wear the King's own colours, a disguise that would draw attention to any who would seek glory in slaying a monarch and winning the day, and the other cowardly and egocentric, who attempts to project a façade of chivalry yet is actively avoiding the hostilities and who is more than likely inebriated. In respect of staging, there is a poignant contrast between Blount's heroic sacrificial death and Falstaff's comic self-preservation – the pudgy, pusillanimous knight looking down upon the corpse of one whose rank he shares yet whose principles are worlds apart. Gifting Falstaff with one of the more powerful lines in the play, in one sentence Shakespeare undermines the ideological principles upon which the newly dead Blount has built his life: 'There's honour for you' (*1 Henry IV*, 5.3.32, 33). For Sir John, honour is as dead and useless as the corpse of Sir Walter; it is a weighty social encumbrance that becomes a disadvantage. Turning honour on its head, the corpulent cavalier directs our attention downwards; stating the only weight he intends to carry is 'mine own bowels' (line 35). This is exactly the sort of privileging of the lower bodily strata Mikhail Bakhtin spoke of as reflective of 'a deep awareness of historic time, of the change of epochs' and of 'the fusion of the past and the future' where the 'dual body becomes a dual world'.[68] It would be easy to become distracted by the larger-than-life figure of Falstaff at the expense of all else; however, in this instance the comic knight's behaviour within the space of the battlefield provides an insight into the dualities of Shakespeare's world (past and present, spiritual idealism and physical reality, chivalry and egocentrism) and the ways in which battle scenes enabled the writer to explore such frictions, contradictions and dissonances.

Bakhtin observes that 'fights, beatings, and blows' follow a naturally downward movement towards the lower body in which 'they throw the adversary to the ground [...] but at the same time they are creative; they sow and harvest'.[69] In this sense the battlefield becomes a location of regeneration, of new power structures, restructuring everything from families to governments by the most violent, chaotic and indiscriminate means. Change and inversion, the destruction of the old and the birth of the new, is at the core of carnival. Bakhtin favoured the folk etymology of this word as deriving from the Germanic *karne*, a holy shrine for pagan gods, and *val* or *wal*, meaning death. The resultant 'procession of dead gods' appealed to his ideas of how power evolves over time – never more so than on the battlefield.[70] Though such romantic notions of spiritual rites and cycles of life are ultimately spurious, the idea of carnival revolves around rituals of change, the suggestion of new ideologies, of new structures and of the death of old gods or old systems of power. Presiding over the carnival festivities is the fool or clown, a liminal character whose motley perspectives easily cross between new and old, between disparate points of view. Such characters might outwardly appear incongruous with battlefields, which classically are the province of heroes. Yet Sir John is fantastically malleable in such an environment; his opportunistic and resourceful nature, coupled with his insolent and unruly streak, turns such a setting to his advantage and ultimately undermines not only chivalric, but also monarchical power models. Earlier in *1*

Henry IV, the Prince's portly subordinate likens Hal's future reign to that of Diana, a familiar trope in Elizabethan England as the Virgin Queen too was likened to Diana, chaste goddess of the hunt:

> Marry then, sweet wag, when thou art king, let not us that are squires of the night's body be called thieves of the day's beauty. Let us be Diana's foresters, gentlemen of the shade, minions of the moon, and let me say we be men of good government, being governed, as the sea is, by our noble chaste mistress the moon, under whose countenance we steal.
>
> (1.2.24–28)

Here Falstaff describes servitude to Diana as one in the shade, a follower of the changeable 'mistress moon' and as mercurial as the sea. The obvious pun on night/knight plays with ideas of hierarchy and rectitude – the Prince's entourage depicted as devotees of crepuscular pleasures rather than engaging in morally uplifting pursuits. It is noteworthy that Falstaff also makes reference to other liminal settings discussed within this book – that of the forest and the sea – both of which stand outside of the control of human beings. The resultant picture is not one of solid, unified rule, but rather one of heterogeneous and divided factions wherein carnivalesque licence undermines social order. Though the setting of this conversation is not stated in either the quarto or folio copies of the play, the scene has been imagined in several settings, including the tavern (Howard Staunton), an equally liminal space in that it is a place where the freedom to mingle princes and prostitutes, commoners and nobility, is available to tease out the dynamics and potentiality of power and to dislocate social hierarchies.[71] Once again, it is the clown that is naturally at home in a place that allows wit and a subversive streak to shine.

There is one last scene in which the battlefield is used to appraise socially established norms – that of the duel between Hotspur and the Prince. Edelman notes that at this juncture of the play the Arthurian ideals celebrated in Elizabethan England become embodied in their combat – 'not simply as a matter of kill-or-be-killed between enemies in war, but as a chivalrous test of valour'.[72] What Edelman fails to comment on is that when Douglas and Falstaff enter, the 'battle' takes on a mirror effect – two duels fought in concert on the stage. Falstaff's inclusion introduces an element of carnival that is seemingly out of place considering the subject matter. Of particular interest in this regard is Janette Dillon's look at the staging of Shakespeare's history plays, particularly her ideas surrounding the division of the stage on its horizontal axis. She asserts that the Elizabethan 'audiences expected the stage routinely to communicate through fairly emphatic visual signs', often looking for 'proportion' around a central axis.[73] Where Edelman notes the more obvious simultaneous enactment of two duels in *1 Henry IV*, Dillon sees this as deliberately parodic, with the Falstaff/Douglas duel 'necessarily seeming to comment' on the Hal/Hotspur conflict.[74] She goes on: 'the fight between Douglas and Falstaff quickly turns into parody, as Falstaff plays dead. Not only does one fight set the other in an ironic light, then, but so too does the fake death frame the true death in a way that renders its value questionable.'[75] Falstaff's revivification next to the play's chief protagonist necessarily weakens his heroic demise and questions the values of chivalry, honour and personal sacrifice for a cause (note a parallel to Strumbo, the comical cobbler of the apocryphal *Locrine*, who also plays dead on the battlefield). Any lingering pathos following Hal's brief eulogy evaporates as the comic knight arises and promptly steals both the credit for Percy's death and the scene. This already liminal space, representative of Shrewsbury's fields and recently the scene of the culmination of England's civil unrest, now takes on an equally liminal yet far more personal setting as a moment is shared exclusively with the audience who witness the fleshy bulk of Falstaff stir and rise, probably checking to see he is unobserved, before he opens with a soliloquy that reveals his darkly humorous machinations. What is more, as he mutilates Hotspur's corpse, Shakespeare plays with his audience's moral tolerances as they are pulled between horror and humour, merriment and the macabre. The stage symmetry is upset, destabilised and undermined by Sir John's actions, the duel's original proportion and mirroring now a comic subversion that favours cunning over chivalry, guileful opportunism over honour and duplicity over decorum. Though he does not reference Falstaff in his appraisal of Shakespeare's approaches to the knightly codes of valour, Ralph Berry nonetheless describes the dramatist's depictions of chivalry as ironic 'sketches' and 'vestigial residues' of an 'ideology of unreality'.[76] Shakespeare's chubby caricature of chivalry not only steals Harry's aristeia, but also manages to reduce the entire battle to a farce, shifting the balance of power from the state-sanctioned and ideologically praiseworthy principles of honour and dignity. As Michael Bristol observes, 'by treating honourable death as a joke, Falstaff speaks to a plebeian consciousness that maintains itself despite sacrifices demanded in the name of the nation-state'.[77]

In Shakespeare's inclusion of such comic pauses within his historical play he not only challenges the way history is remembered, but also the sentiments and values of the society remembering such events and persons. Kastan describes these carnival elements of inversion and subversion as far-reaching in that:

> The very existence of the comic plot serves to raise questions about the nature of history. Comedy here isn't subordinated to history, nor does it compete with history. Rather, comedy is revealed to be part of the very same fabric, exposing the exclusions and biases in our usual definition of history.[78]

Sir John's presence on the battlefield, his devotion not to a national cause or a sentimental code but to his own life and its preservation, his comic resurrection and serendipitous claiming of Hotspur's overthrow all serve as a counter-narrative to history. The clownish knight brings a decidedly human element to the events he has been inserted into and allows Shakespeare to strip any sort of propriety or misplaced national pride from the history surrounding Hal's journey to the throne.

Back to Bannockburn

The hackneyed finale to Mel Gibson's *Braveheart* (1995) shows the sentimental Scottish warrior poets' commemoration of William Wallace's rebellion before their slow-motion charge towards the lines of the abhorrent English oppressors. This almost certainly didn't happen. And yet the skirling bagpipes, the defiant expressions and rousing battle cries of the Scots and the dreadful Australian/American/faux-Caledonian brogue of Gibson's narration is aimed at one thing – to affect the audience in such a way as to identify with the heroic rebels (and to create a box office smash). I am ashamed to say that, as I gazed over the 'ground' of Bannockburn, with its enormous Scottish flag flying proudly, it was difficult to dispel such romantic images.

Did Shakespeare do the same thing? Did he manipulate the collective 'memory' of events, and in doing, shape the future perceptions and ideologies of playgoers towards history? This is not a new question, nor is it a novel approach to the staging of history. If we give any credence to Plato's principle of ideal forms, then all art, including re-enactment through theatrical performance, should be regarded as imperfect counterfeit. Yet far from the diminishing or cheapening of the 'original' events, memory (or rememory) adds certain complications and textures that result in far more culturally relevant nuances. Pierre Nora's 'Between Memory and History: *Les Lieux de Mémoire*' (1989) outlined the processes whereby 'memory crystalizes' around certain historical events, but that collective memory, such as with the English patriotism around Agincourt, is not in itself history – it has been embellished and reinvented to the point where 'memory and history, far from being synonymous, appear to be in fundamental opposition'.[79]

It would be easy for us to position these two seemingly disparate concepts as the antipodal extremes on a sliding scale of fact and fiction; dry history, with its dispassionate truths and apparently objective 'facts', and vivid memory, with its selective and romantic 'fictions'. However, this is more the province of the historian than the literary critic. What is perhaps more to the point in considering Shakespeare's representations of history is not whether they faithfully re-enact events but that the human element, with its accompanying moral conundrums and justifications, reconstitutes these events in ways that anchor them in the present, either challenging or reinforcing cultural significances and social memory. The spaces of historic conflicts resonate with feeling through the power of imagination and their connection with incumbent cultural implications. Nora qualifies this act when he explains, 'to interrogate a tradition, venerable though it may be, is no longer to pass it on intact'.[80] Thus, the field of Bannockburn, whether it is situated within its currently marked geographic locale or any other of its contested sites, and augmented with re-enactments, both in media and by living history groups, is imbued with a certain amount of power over the emotions of the pilgrims who cross it. The same phenomenon occurs in Shakespeare's staging of historical battles. These spaces exist between fact and fiction, history and memory. As such they are liminal, powerful and open to interpretation.

Rebecca Schneider points out the value of Hamlet's directive to the players as an insight to how re-enactment can be manipulated to carry subversive themes. His instruction to curb the extemporaneous clown is followed by, 'though in the meantime some necessary question of the play be then to be considered' (3.2.41–42). Giving the audience pause to consider an underlying message is key to understanding Shakespeare's use of battlefields. Such liminally powerful spaces, between history and memory, depicting struggles between elevated chivalric ideals and disreputable power play, necessarily challenge the audience's own, *current*, culturally received memories and archetypes. As Schneider states, the play takes place in

> two times, at the same time, between. The 'question of the play' occurs '*meantime*' in encounter, and it is posed quite explicitly in *Hamlet* as *between* words set down and words taken up, between doing and re-doing as it were. The question of the play is a question of (villainous) 'acts' re-encountered meantime, in double time, or across and in time – a matter of and for the *duration* of one time in (between) another time.[81]

The inevitable correspondences and connections a playgoer makes drag history into the present. Such acts bring medieval Bannockburn into a conveniently modern location, fixed in the minds of modern-day tourists through the necessity of establishing national identity and augmented by the irrepressible potency of artistic recreation. So too does the dramatisation of Agincourt transport the centuries-old field into bloody reality on the early modern and modern stages in such a manner that national pride and collective memory is confronted by less noble realities, unfailingly merging contemporaneous affairs and attitudes. What we can conclude from Shakespeare's treatment of historical battlefields is that they became palimpsests for theatrical forays into extant socially controversial and often-polarised positions on divine will versus monarchical privilege, might or right, personal gain and self-preservation against the ideologies of chivalry. For the playwright as well as for the audience, Holinshed's annals of bygone battles were no longer concrete or reliable once they had been dramaturgically reimagined. Instead, such battlefields were presented not only as spaces of contestation between historically opposing belligerents but also as unstable, incongruous and subversive spaces in which contemporary opposing ideologies could be fought out.

Notes

1. John Keegan, *A History of Warfare* (London: Hutchinson, 1993), p. 94.
2. Paul A. Jorgensen, *Shakespeare's Military World* (Berkeley, CA: University of California Press, 1956), p. 35.
3. Stephen Greenblatt, *Tyrant: Shakespeare on Politics* (New York: W. W. Norton & Co., 2018), p. 23.
4. Ibid., p. 13.
5. Peter Marks, 'Oskar Eustis: "I Felt my Job was to Try to Make the Issues of 'Julius Caesar' as Pertinent as they Could be."', *Washington Post*, 15 June 2017, www.washingtonpost.com/news/arts-and-entertainment/wp/2017/06/15/oskar-eustis-i-felt-my-job-was-to-try-to-make-the-issues-of-julius-caesar-as-pertinent-as-they-could-be/ [accessed 11 Aug. 2020].
6. Greenblatt, *Shakespearean Negotiations*, p. 56.
7. Ibid., p. 52.
8. Stallybrass and White, *Politics and Poetics of Transgression*, p. 3.
9. Ibid.
10. William Shakespeare, *King Henry IV Part 1*, ed. D. S. Kastan (London: Bloomsbury, 2018), p. 39.
11. Rebecca Schneider, *Performing Remains: Art and War in Times of Theatrical Reenactment* (Abingdon: Routledge, 2011), p. 14.
12. Paola Pugliatti, 'Shakespeare and the "Military Revolution": The Cultural and Social Weapons of Reformed War', in *Shakespeare and the Politics of Commoners*, ed. Chris Fitter (Oxford: Oxford University Press, 2017), p. 151.
13. Underdown, *Revel Riot and Rebellion*, p. 183.
14. Jorgensen, *Shakespeare's Military World*, p. 130.
15. Ibid., pp. 122, 123.
16. Greenblatt, *Shakespearean Negotiations*, p. 43.
17. Arnold Van Gennep, *Rites of Passage* (Oxford: Routledge, 2004), p. 11.
18. Victor W. Turner, *The Ritual Process* (Harmondsworth: Penguin, 1969), p. 155.
19. Ibid., p. 156.

20 Dennis McCarthy and June Schlueter, *A Brief Discourse of Rebellion and Rebels by George North: A Newly Uncovered Manuscript Source for Shakespeare's Plays* (Cambridge: D. S. Brewer, 2018), p. 17.
21 Interestingly, in his exposition *On Moral Duties*, Cicero attempts to differentiate between battles waged for self-promotion and honour, and those fought to preserve a way of life and the attitudes the soldiery should have toward their enemies dependent on the reasons for battle.
22 Ros King, ' "The Disciplines of War": Elizabethan War Manuals and Shakespeare's Tragicomic Vision', in *Shakespeare and War*, ed. Ros King and Paul J. C. M. Franssen (London: Palgrave Macmillan, 2008), pp. 15, 16.
23 Duncan Salkeld, *Shakespeare and London* (Oxford: Oxford University Press, 2018), p. 63.
24 Ros King, 'Shakespearean Narratives of War: Trauma, Repetition and Metaphor', *Shakespeare Survey*, 72 (2019), p. 64.
25 Gamini Salgado, ed., *Cony Catchers and Bawdy Baskets* (Harmondsworth: Penguin, 1972), pp. 335, 336.
26 Raphael Holinshed, *Chronicles of England, Scotland, and Ireland*, vol. 6 (1587), p. 552 http://english.nsms.ox.ac.uk/holinshed/ [accessed 19 June 2020].
27 King and Franssen, *Shakespeare and War*, p. 3.
28 This term would appear to be pejorative, being the Spanish word for soldier. As anti-Catholic sentiment ran high during the time of the Anglo-Spanish War, it may be that the depreciative Latinate title of 'soldado' typified the negative views of mercenaries who returned from the continent.
29 Salgado, *Cony Catchers*, p. 361.
30 Not to mention, such individuals would no doubt have formed the basis for characters such as Pistol and Iago, both veterans of war.
31 It might be argued that the imagery employed by the Apostle Paul in his letter to the Ephesians to 'take unto you the whole armour of God' that includes the 'breastplate of Righteousness', 'the shield of Faith', 'the helmet of Salvation' and 'the sword of the Spirit' (Ephesians 6:13–17), is an incitement to war. However the previous verse contextualises this as a spiritual battle and the accoutrements of war as symbolic: 'For we wrestle not against flesh and blood, but against [...] the princes of the darkness of this world, against spiritual wickedness, which are in the high places' (verse 12).
32 Ralph Berry, *Shakespeare and the Awareness of the Audience* (London: Macmillan, 1985), p. 109.
33 Keegan, *History of Warfare*, p. 290.

34 Donald K. Hedrick 'Branagh's *Dirty Harry V* and the Types of Political Ambiguity', in *Shakespeare, The Movie: Popularizing the Plays on Film, TV, and Video*, ed. Lynda E. Boose and Richard Burt (London: Routledge, 1997), p. 217.
35 Berry, *Shakespeare and the Awareness of the Audience*, p. 115.
36 Greenblatt, *Renaissance Self-Fashioning*, p. 195.
37 Hugh Owen, *Some Account of the Ancient and Present State of Shrewsbury* (Shrewsbury: P. Sandford, 1808), p. 26.
38 Charles Edelman, *Brawl Ridiculous: Swordfighting in Shakespeare's Plays* (Manchester: Manchester University Press, 1992), p. 174.
39 Underdown, *Revel, Riot and Rebellion*, p. 15.
40 Louis B. Wright, 'Stage Duelling in the Elizabethan Theatre', *Modern Language Review*, 22(3) (1927), 265–275, p. 266.
41 John Manningham, *The Diary of John Manningham* (Westminster: J. B. Nichols & Sons, 1868), p. 130, www.gutenberg.org/files/41609/41609-h/41609-h.htm [accessed 30 Dec. 2020].
42 Jean MacIntyre, 'Shakespeare and the Battlefield: Tradition and Innovation in Battle Scenes', *Theatre Survey*, 23(1) (1982), 31–44, p. 32.
43 Ibid., p. 37.
44 Christopher R. Wilson and Michela Calore, *Music in Shakespeare: A Dictionary* (Bloomsbury: London, 2014), pp. 2–3.
45 William Shakespeare, *Henry V*, ed. T. W. Craik (London: Routledge, 1995) p. 201, footnote.
46 There is a point to be made here for the inclusion of as many battle scenes as possible to promote a certain theatre's productions. Battles justified the use of cannons, trumpets and other horns, the sounds of which would have carried across the Thames and over the city.
47 Michael Hattaway, '"Thou Laidst No Sieges to the Music-Room": Anatomizing Wars, Staging Battles', *Shakespeare Survey*, 72 (2019), 48–63, p. 52.
48 Jorgensen, *Shakespeare's Military World*, p. 4.
49 It is worthwhile noting that when Shakespeare uses the word 'crown' and its derivatives such as crowns, crowning and crowned, they have a triple significance. A crown may refer to the symbol of rule, to currency as well as to the human head. In *Henry V* there are multiple instances of this playful interchangeability such as the King's observation that 'the French may lay twenty French crowns to one, they will beat us; for they bear them on their shoulders: but it is no English treason to cut French crowns' (4.1.222–225), a comment that would seem to suggest all three meanings are included, French heads,

currency in the form of a wager and the 'one' crown possibly referring to the French king.
50 John Sutherland and Cedric Watts, *Henry V, War Criminal? And Other Shakespeare Puzzles* (Oxford: Oxford University Press, 2000), p. 109.
51 Peter S. Donaldson, 'Taking on Shakespeare: Kenneth Branagh's *Henry V*', *Shakespeare Quarterly*, 42 (1991), 60–71, p. 64.
52 Louis Montrose, *The Purpose of Playing: Shakespeare and the Cultural Politics of the Elizabethan Theatre* (Chicago: University of Chicago Press, 1992), p. 85.
53 Sutherland and Watts, *Henry V, War Criminal*, p. 113.
54 There is precedent for this exclusion in the anti-aristeia of *Richard II*. In the unfinished duel between Bolingbroke and Mowbray, the King's intervention upsets the traditions of chivalry and ultimately weakens his position and reputation.
55 MacIntyre, 'Shakespeare and the Battlefield', p. 37.
56 Ibid., p. 42.
57 Ibid., p. 41.
58 Whilst this chapter does not engage with debates over whether Shakespeare had read *Il Principe* and how far his works were influenced by the Florentine's philosophy, there are several recent texts that reignite these arguments. Notably: John Roe, *Shakespeare and Machiavelli* (Cambridge: D. S. Brewer, 2002), and Hugh Grady, *Shakespeare, Machiavelli, and Montaigne: Power and Subjectivity from* Richard II *to* Hamlet (Oxford: Oxford University Press, 2002).
59 Niccolò Machiavelli, *The Prince*, trans. Tim Parks (London: Penguin, 2009), p. 93.
60 Ibid., p. 95, emphasis mine.
61 Norman Rabkin, *Shakespeare and the Problem of Meaning* (Chicago: University of Chicago Press, 1981), p. 62.
62 Katherine B. Attié, '"Gently to Hear, Kindly to Judge": Minds at Work in *Henry V*', in *Shakespeare and Judgment*, ed. Kevin Curran (Edinburgh: Edinburgh University Press, 2017), p. 95.
63 Pugliatti, 'Shakespeare and the "Military Revolution"', p. 160.
64 Hattaway, '"Thou Laidst No Sieges"', p. 56.
65 Northrop Frye, *Anatomy of Criticism* (Princeton: Princeton University Press, 1973), p. 284.
66 Shakespeare, *King Henry IV Part 1*, ed. Kastan, p. 49.
67 Ibid., p. 43.
68 Bakhtin, *Rabelais and his World*, p. 435.
69 Ibid., p. 370.
70 Ibid., p. 393.

71 Shakespeare, *King Henry IV Part 1*, ed. Kastan, p. 149 footnote.
72 Edelman, *Brawl Ridiculous*, p. 103.
73 Janette Dillon, *Shakespeare and the Staging of English History* (Oxford: Oxford University Press, 2012), p. 30.
74 Ibid., p. 37.
75 Ibid.
76 Berry, *Shakespeare and the Awareness of the Audience*, pp. 110, 115.
77 Michael D. Bristol, *Carnival and Theatre: Plebeian Culture and the Structure of Authority in Renaissance England* (London: Methuen, 1985), p. 183.
78 Shakespeare, *King Henry IV Part 1*, ed. Kastan, p. 16.
79 Pierre Nora, 'Between Memory and History: *Les Lieux de Mémoire*', *Representations* (Spring 1989), 7–27, p. 8.
80 Ibid., p. 10.
81 Rebecca Schneider, *Performing Remains: Art and War in Times of Theatrical Re-enactment* (Abingdon: Routledge, 2011), p. 88.

Conclusion

Time and again, defenders of the Temple of the Bard, those critics who maintain a unique status for the playwright, have quoted Ben Jonson's encomium of Shakespeare being 'for all time'. This quotation is somewhat subjective considering Jonson was a contemporary of Shakespeare and had little in the way of quantitative or qualitative data on which to base his certainty of Shakespeare's longevity. Yet, after the passing of four centuries, the success of Stratford's revered playwright raises Jonson's tribute to the level of prescience. The presence of Shakespeare's works internationally in school curricula, in worldwide theatres and in amateur playhouses, not to mention the sheer volume of academic writing dedicated to all manner of subjects centred on his oeuvre, attests to both their endurance and popularity – whether through the impetus of tradition or otherwise.

To be sure, throughout history there have always been detractors and naysayers who have decried the attention given to Shakespeare's works. Charles Darwin was 'nauseated' by how 'dull' the plays were when he read them,[1] and Leo Tolstoy found them 'trivial and positively bad'.[2] The *Observer* columnist Killian Fox put together a list of those who had remonstrated against any elevation of England's foremost playwright. He noted that, for Voltaire, the works were a 'giant dunghill', and that a vehement George Bernard Shaw wrote of his desire to exhume Shakespeare only to hurl rocks at his remains.[3] Fox's interest in the cynics was triggered by more recent criticism. After a performance of *King Lear*, Ira Glass, respected radio host of *This American Life*, tweeted: '@JohnLithgow as Lear tonight: amazing. Shakespeare: not good. No stakes, not relatable. I think I'm realising: Shakespeare sucks.'[4] Whilst these individual opinions do not seem to pose too much of a threat to the ongoing presence of Shakespeare, there is a question as to whether we have already plumbed the depths of his works, whether their all too familiar shape and structure has left nothing of value, or at least nothing new, for the modern scholar, reader or audience.

Like a palaeontologist adding flesh and form to the bones of a fossilised skeleton, this book has, in many ways, worked to define the indefinable, to explore Shakespeare's stable interest in unstable spaces that challenge and subvert conventional power structures. In so doing, this study has also worked to find stability in the unstable spaces of academia, revealing the ways in which the tides of new critical movements have often returned the same flotsam to the same shores. Returning to the work of the new historicists and cultural materialists is not an exercise in picking at the already clean bones of Shakespeare's plays, but rather an exercise in fleshing out these bones by considering how liminality had the potential to complicate previously held ideas of how the playwright engaged with power. In doing so, I have sought to do more than simply dust off or reignite theoretical approaches to Shakespeare that went out of circulation or fashion shortly after their inception in the 1980s. New historicism and cultural materialism offered, and still offer, profoundly influential methods of looking at power and its manifestation in cultural expression. Yet despite cultural materialists' focus on early modern contexts and social structures, and the insistence of new historicists on shutting out or disengaging from any such associations due to their potential pollution through modern perspectives, they are inevitably a product of their time. Their condemnation of Bradley, Tillyard and earlier Shakespearean scholars as by-products of a world at war is ironic as both new historicism and cultural materialism emerged from Cold War mentalities and fear of the radical elements of literature and drama that had the potential to upset the status quo. As the first chapter argued, these were the same fears that curbed Bakhtin's academic commitment to the inherent subversion of carnival expression, albeit his reservations potentially arose from the very real threat the Soviet academic system posed to those who ventured too far from the prescribed norms.

Until now, literary geography has developed as a field of studies that is both heavily embedded in Marxist-inflected cultural materialism and new historicism, yet has not seen the potential in joining two fields of Shakespearean theory together to answer the question of whether the early modern stage was more than simply a sanctioned mode of entertainment or if indeed it was a means to channel resistance and change. Viewing the liminal less as a subscribed transition and more of a radical or subversive process opens up new avenues of literary criticism and theory when it comes to early modern theatre. What I have argued is that liminal landscapes open the way for carnivalesque reversals of natural order and the established hierarchies of power. Such settings amplify human agency and licence, allowing a safe space in which to express individual desires and enthusiasms. In turn, the fundamental values and systems which form the foundation of societal structures begin to compromise and shift due to the pressures exerted from the peripheries. These subversive challenges may indeed appear to be absorbed or contained by these centralised organisations, yet in this interchange or dialogue of power they inadvertently negotiate a new centre that has moved, sometimes imperceptibly, from the previously held dogmatic stance.

Change is inevitable. Yet the cause of change is a slippery issue. Michel Foucault noted this ambiguity when he addressed the 'problem of causality', admitting, 'it is not always easy to determine what has caused a specific change', his self-confessed perplexity and embarrassment over his inability to articulate the complex and diverse elements that instigated change prompting him to label such processes as 'more magical than effective'.[5] Scientific discovery, religious reform, social revolution, even blind chance might be perceived as causal factors that facilitate change. Foucault ultimately addressed such phenomena in his other works that attempted to trace the movement of power within systems and social hierarchies.

Change is also central to the plots within Shakespeare's plays. Yet it is not simply the developments that unfold to bring intrigues to a happy conclusion but rather the way power is negotiated that is of vital importance. It is how systems of authority undergo pressures from the edges of society or how independent mental or spiritual energies resist control from approved religious and social beliefs. Furthermore, it is the shape or position that these systems take after such confrontation that lies at the heart of subversion.

Can we say that such structures – the Court, the Church and the fabric of patriarchal regulation – remain unmoved? Or are the dissident and transgressive depictions of these social configurations changeful? Shakespeare's liminal settings are where dissension is born and expressed, settings that allow alternative, even rebellious, models of authority to emerge.

As has been demonstrated, the inclusion of these spaces of innate resistance, whether as physical or imagined geographies, represents a stand against established hierarchies and orders. The changeability of such liminal spaces, their tides, the encroachment of woodlands, the susceptibility of gardens to corruption and seasonal change, and the arbitrary nature of battlefields threaten the very idea of clearly demarcated space and remind us that threat is in itself subversive. Yet such spaces embody more than simply a temporary revolt, but the means to trace the changes that were happening within early modern society, as any act of resistance, even one from the limens of society, prompts change in established centralised authority and cultural attitudes.

Notes

1. Charles Darwin, *The Autobiography of Charles Darwin from The Life and Letters of Charles Darwin*, www.gutenberg.org/files/2010/2010-h/2010-h.htm [accessed 17 Dec. 2020].
2. Leo Tolstoy, *Tolstoy on Shakespeare: A Critical Essay on Shakespeare* (Christchurch: Free Age Press, 1906), p. 4.
3. Killian Fox, 'Shakespeare Sucks: A Potted History of Bard-Bashing', *Observer*, 3 Aug. 2014, www.theguardian.com/culture/2014/aug/03/shakespeare-sucks-potted-history-bard-bashing [accessed 17 Dec. 2020].
4. Ibid.
5. Michel Foucault, *The Order of Things: An Archeology of the Human Sciences* (London: Tavistock Publications, 1970), p. xiii.

Bibliography

Abrams, Rebecca, *The Jewish Journey: 4000 Years in 22 Objects from the Ashmolean Museum* (Oxford: Ashmolean Museum Press, 2017)
Alighieri, Dante, *The Divine Comedy*, trans. C. H. Sisson (Oxford: Oxford University Press, 1993)
Ariosto, Lodovico, *Orlando Furioso*, trans. William Stewart Rose, [online access], www.gutenberg.org/cache/epub/615/pg615.html
Attié, Katherine B., '"Gently to Hear, Kindly to Judge": Minds at Work in *Henry V*', in *Shakespeare and Judgment*, ed. Kevin Curran (Edinburgh: Edinburgh University Press, 2017), pp. 93–114
Bacon, Francis, *Of Gardens* (London: Hacon & Ricketts, 1902)
Bakhtin, Mikhail, *Rabelais and his World*, trans. Helene Iswolsky (Bloomington: Indiana University Press, 1984)
Barrett, Chris, *Early Modern English Literature and the Poetics of Cartographic Anxiety* (Oxford: Oxford University Press, 2018)
Barton, Anne, *The Shakespearean Forest* (Cambridge: Cambridge University Press, 2017)
Bate, Jonathan, *Shakespeare and the English Romantic Imagination* (Oxford: Clarendon Press, 1986)
Bate, Jonathan, *The Romantics on Shakespeare* (London: Penguin, 1992)
Bentley, Gerald Eades, ed., *A Book of Masques* (Cambridge: Cambridge University Press, 1980)
Berry, Edward, *Shakespeare and the Hunt* (Cambridge: Cambridge University Press, 2001)
Berry, Ralph, 'Komisarjevsky at Stratford-upon-Avon', *Shakespeare Survey*, 36 (1983), pp. 73–84
Berry, Ralph, *Shakespeare and the Awareness of the Audience* (London: Macmillan, 1985)
Bliss, Lee, '"Plot Me No Plots": The Life of Drama and the Drama of Life in *The Knight of the Burning Pestle*', *Modern Language Quarterly*, 45(1) (1984), pp. 3–21
Boose, Lynda E., and Richard Burt, eds, *Shakespeare, The Movie: Popularizing the Plays on Film, TV, and Video* (London: Routledge, 1997)

Bozio, Andrew, *Thinking through Place on the Early Modern English Stage* (Oxford: Oxford University Press, 2020)
Bracher, Mark, ed., *Lacanian Theory of Discourse: Subject, Structure and Society* (New York: New York University Press, 1994)
Braddick, Michael J., and John Walter, *Negotiating Power in Early Modern Society: Order, Hierarchy and Subordination in Britain and Ireland* (Cambridge: Cambridge University Press, 2001)
Bradley, A. C., *Shakespearean Tragedy: Lectures on Hamlet, Othello, King Lear, Macbeth* (New York: St Martin's Press, 1978)
Brayton, Dan, 'Sounding the Deep: *Shakespeare and the Sea* Revisited', *Forum for Modern Language Studies*, 46(2) (2010), pp. 189–206
Bristol, Michael D., *Carnival and Theatre: Plebeian Culture and the Structure of Authority in Renaissance England* (New York: Methuen, 1985)
Bruckner, Lynne, and Dan Brayton, eds, *Ecocritical Shakespeare* (London: Routledge, 2011)
Bruster, Douglas, and Robert Weimann, *Prologues to Shakespeare's Theatre: Performance and Liminality in Early Modern Drama* (Abingdon: Routledge, 2004)
Burnett, Mark Thornton, *Masters and Servants in English Renaissance Drama and Culture* (Basingstoke: Macmillan, 1997)
Callaghan, Dympna, *Shakespeare without Women: Representing Gender and Race on the Renaissance Stage* (London: Routledge, 2000),
Carter, Sarah, *Ovidian Myth and Sexual Deviance in Early Modern Literature* (Basingstoke: Palgrave Macmillan, 2011)
Chaucer, Geoffrey, *The Canterbury Tales* (London: J. M. Dent, 1939)
Cicero, Marcus Tullius, *De Re Republica*, trans. G. W. Featherstonhaugh (New York: G. & C. Carvill, 1829)
Comito, Terry, *The Idea of the Garden in the Renaissance* (Hassocks: Harvester Press, 1979), pp. 23–54
Comito, Terry, 'Caliban's Dream: The Topography of Some Shakespeare Gardens', *Shakespeare Studies*, 14 (1 Jan. 1981), pp. 24–40
Davies, John, *The Complete Poems of Sir John Davies*, ed. Alexander B. Grossart (London: Chatto & Windus, 1876)
Dillon, Janette, *Shakespeare and the Staging of English History* (Oxford: Oxford University Press, 2012)
Doebler, John, 'Beaumont's *The Knight of the Burning Pestle* and the Prodigal Son Plays', *Studies in English Literature, 1500–1900*, 5(2), *Elizabethan and Jacobean Drama* (Spring 1965), pp. 333–344
Dollimore, Jonathan, and Alan Sinfield, eds, *Political Shakespeare: Essays in Cultural Materialism* (Manchester: Manchester University Press, 1996)
Donaldson, Peter S., 'Taking on Shakespeare: Kenneth Branagh's *Henry V*', *Shakespeare Quarterly*, 42 (1991), pp. 60–71
Drakakis, John, ed., *Alternative Shakespeares* (London: Methuen & Co., 1985)
Duncan-Jones, Katherine, *Shakespeare: An Ungentle Life* (London: Methuen Drama, 2010)

Dutton, Richard, *Mastering the Revels: The Regulation and Censorship of English Renaissance Drama* (London: Macmillan, 1991)
Dutton, Richard, ed., *A Midsummer Night's Dream: Contemporary Critical Essays* (London: Macmillan Press, 1996)
Eagleton, Terry, *Sweet Violence: The Idea of the Tragic* (Oxford: Blackwell, 2003)
Edelman, Charles, *Brawl Ridiculous: Swordfighting in Shakespeare's Plays* (Manchester: Manchester University Press, 1992)
Elden, Stuart, *Shakespearean Territories* (Chicago: University of Chicago Press, 2018)
Ellacombe, Henry N., *The Plant-Lore and Garden-Craft of Shakespeare* (London: W. Satchell & Co., 1884)
Elyot, Thomas, *The Boke of the Governour*, ed. H. H. S. Croft (London: Kegan Paul, 1883)
Falconer, A. F., *Shakespeare and the Sea* (London: Constable & Co., 1964)
Ferguson, Margaret, Mary Jo Salter and Jon Stallworthy, eds, *The Norton Anthology of Poetry*, 5th ed. (New York: W. W. Norton & Co., 2005)
Finkelpearl, Philip J., *Court and Country Politics in the Plays of Beaumont and Fletcher* (Princeton: Princeton University Press, 1990)
Fitter, Chris, ed., *Shakespeare and the Politics of Commoners: Digesting the New Social History* (Oxford: Oxford University Press, 2017)
Fitzpatrick, Tim, *Playwright, Space and Place in Early Modern Performance* (Farnham: Ashgate Publishing, 2011)
Forshaw, Peter J., 'The Hermetic Frontispiece: Contextualising John Dee's Hieroglyphic Monad', *Ambix*, 64(2) (2017), pp. 115–139
Foucault, Michael, *The Order of Things* (London: Tavistock, 1970)
Foucault, Michael, *The Archaeology of Knowledge* (London: Tavistock, 1997)
Fox, Adam, *Oral Tradition and Literate Culture in England, 1500–1700* (Oxford: Clarendon, 2000)
Freedman, Paul, *Images of the Medieval Peasant* (Stanford, CA: Stanford University Press, 1999)
French, Peter J., *John Dee: The World of the Elizabethan Magus* (Abingdon: Routledge, 2002)
Freud, Sigmund, *The Ego and the Id*, trans. Joan Riviere (London: Hogarth Press, 1927)
Frye, Northrop, *Anatomy of Criticism* (Princeton: Princeton University Press, 1957)
Frye, Northrop, *A Natural Perspective: The Development of Shakespearean Comedy and Romance* (New York: Columbia University Press, 1965)
Garcia, Pedro Javier Pardo, 'Parody, Satire and Quixotism in Beaumont's *The Knight of the Burning Pestle*', *Sederi*, 10 (1999), pp. 141–152
Gerard, John, *Herball, or Generall Historie of Plantes* (1597)
Gilles, John, *Shakespeare and the Geography of Difference* (Cambridge: Cambridge University Press, 1994)
Gordon, Andrew, and Bernard Klein, eds, *Literature, Mapping and the Politics of Space in Early Modern England* (Cambridge: Cambridge University Press, 2001)

Grady, Hugh, *Shakespeare, Machiavelli, and Montaigne: Power and Subjectivity from* Richard II *to* Hamlet (Oxford: Oxford University Press, 2002)
Gray, Patrick, *Shakespeare and the Ethics of War* (Oxford: Berghahn, 2019)
Greenblatt, Stephen, *Renaissance Self-Fashioning: From More to Shakespeare* (Chicago: University of Chicago Press, 1980)
Greenblatt, Stephen, *Shakespearean Negotiations* (Oxford: Oxford University Press, 1999)
Greenblatt, Stephen, *Tyrant: Shakespeare on Politics* (New York: W. W. Norton & Co., 2018)
Guneratne, Antony R., *Shakespeare and Genre: From Early Modern Inheritances to Postmodern Legacies* (New York: Palgrave Macmillan, 2011)
Habicht, Werner, 'Tree Properties and Tree Scenes in Elizabethan Theater', *Renaissance Drama*, ns 4 (1971), pp. 69–92
Harp, Richard, ed., *Ben Jonson's Plays and Masques* (New York: W. W. Norton & Co., 2001)
Harrison, Robert Pogue, *Forests: The Shadow of Civilization* (Chicago: University of Chicago Press, 1992)
Hartmann, Uwe, 'Sigmund Freud and his Impact on our Understanding of Male Sexual Dysfunction', *Journal of Sexual Medicine*, 6(8) (Aug. 2009), pp. 2332–2339
Hattaway, Michael, *Elizabethan Popular Theatre: Plays in Performance* (London: Routledge & Kegan Paul, 1982)
Hattaway, Michael, ed., *A Companion to English Renaissance Literature and Culture* (Oxford: Blackwells, 2003)
Hattaway, Michael, '"Thou Laidst No Sieges to the Music-Room": Anatomizing Wars, Staging Battles', *Shakespeare Survey*, 72 (2019), pp. 48–63
Haydn, Hiram, *The Counter-Renaissance* (Gloucester: Charles Scribner's Sons, 1966)
Hazlitt, William, *Characters of Shakespeare's Plays* (London: Oxford University Press, 1966)
Hegel, G. W. F., *Phenomenology of Spirit*, trans. A. V. Miller (Oxford: Clarendon Press, 1977)
Hill, Tracey, *Pageantry and Power: A Cultural History of the Early Modern Lord Mayor's Show, 1585–1639* (Manchester: Manchester University Press, 2010)
Holinshed, Raphael, *Chronicles of England, Scotland, and Ireland*, vol. 6 (1587)
Honour, Hugh, and John Fleming, *A World History of Art*, 7th ed. (London: Lawrence King Publishing, 2009)
Hopkins, Lisa, *Shakespeare on the Edge* (Aldershot: Ashgate Publishing, 2005)
Hopkins, Lisa, *Renaissance Drama on the Edge* (Abingdon: Routledge, 2014)
Husband, Timothy, *The Wild Man: Medieval Myth and Symbolism* (New York: Metropolitan Museum of Art, 1980)

Jackson, Russell, ed., *The Cambridge Companion to Shakespeare on Film* (Cambridge: Cambridge University Press, 2020)
Johanyak, Debra, and Walter S. H. Lim, eds, *The English Renaissance, Orientalism, and the Idea of Asia* (New York: Palgrave Macmillan, 2009)
Jonson, Ben, 'Eulogy to Shakespeare', *Shakespeare-Online* www.shakespeare-online.com/biography/firstfolio.html [accessed 15 Nov. 2017]
Jorgensen, Paul A., *Shakespeare's Military World* (Berkeley, CA: University of California Press, 1956)
Keegan, John, *A History of Warfare* (London: Hutchinson, 1993)
Keenan, Jillian, *Sex with Shakespeare* (New York: Harper Collins, 2016)
Kern, Edith G., 'The Gardens in the *Decameron* Cornice', *PMLA*, 66(4) (June 1951), pp. 505–523
Kernan, Alvin, 'Place and Plot in Shakespeare', *Yale Review*, 47 (1977), pp. 48–61
King, Ros, 'Shakespearean Narratives of War: Trauma, Repetition and Metaphor', *Shakespeare Survey*, 72 (2019), pp. 64–74
King, Ros, and Paul J. C. M. Franssen, eds, *Shakespeare and War* (London: Palgrave Macmillan, 2008)
Kott, Jan, *Shakespeare our Contemporary* (London: Routledge, 1991)
Law, Robert Adger, 'Shakespeare in the Garden of Eden', *Studies in English*, 21 (1941), pp. 24–38
Lefebvre, Henri, *The Production of Space* (Oxford: Blackwell Publishers, 1991)
Lenman, Bruce, *England's Colonial Wars 1550–1688: Conflicts, Empire and National Identity* (Harlow: Pearson Education, 2001)
Lesser, Zachary, 'Walter Burre's *The Knight of the Burning Pestle*', *English Literary Renaissance*, 29(1) (Winter 1999), pp. 22–43
Lévi-Strauss, Claude, *Structural Anthropology*, trans. Claire Jacobson (London: Basic Books, 1963)
Loomba, Ania, *Shakespeare, Race and Colonialism* (Oxford: Oxford University Press, 2002)
McAvoy, Liz Herbert 'The Medieval *Hortus Conclusus*: Revisiting the Pleasure Garden', *Medieval Feminist Forum*, 50(1) (2014), pp. 5–10
McCarthy, Dennis, and June Schlueter, *A Brief Discourse of Rebellion and Rebels by George North: A Newly Uncovered Manuscript Source for Shakespeare's Plays* (Cambridge: D. S. Brewer, 2018)
Machiavelli, Niccolò, *The Prince*, trans. Tim Parks (London: Penguin, 2009)
MacIntyre, Jean, 'Shakespeare and the Battlefield: Tradition and Innovation in Battle Scenes', *Theatre Survey*, 23(1) (1982), pp. 31–44
Mallory, Thomas, *Le Morte d'Arthur* (London: J. M. Dent, 1947)
Manningham, John, *The Diary of John Manningham* (Westminster: J. B. Nichols & Sons, 1868)
Manwood, John, *A Treatise and Discourse of the Lawes of the Forrest* (London: Adam Islip for Thomas Wight and Bonham Norton, 1598)
Marvell, Andrew, *The Complete Poems*, ed. George Lord (London: Random House, 1993)

Mentz, Steve, *At the Bottom of Shakespeare's Ocean* (London: Continuum, 2009)
Miller, Ronald F., 'Dramatic Form and Dramatic Imagination in Beaumont's *The Knight of the Burning Pestle*', *English Literary Renaissance*, 8 (1978), pp. 67–84
Montrose, Louis, *The Purpose of Playing: Shakespeare and the Cultural Politics of the Elizabethan Theatre* (Chicago: University of Chicago Press, 1996)
Moskina, Oksana, 'The Garden Scene in *Romeo and Juliet*: Its Representation on Stage, Canvas, and Screen', *Riscritture dell'Eden: Il ruolo del giardino nei discorsi dell'immaginario*, 8 (2015), pp. 75–108
Mueller, Janel M., and David Loewenstein, eds, *The Cambridge History of Early Modern English Literature* (Cambridge: Cambridge University Press, 2002)
Mullaney, Steven, *The Place of the Stage: License, Play, and Power in Renaissance England* (Chicago: University of Chicago Press, 2000)
Nardizzi, Vin, *Wooden Os: Shakespeare's Theatres and England's Trees* (Toronto: University of Toronto Press, 2013)
Nelson, Alan H., and John R. Elliott, Jr., *Inns of Court Records of Early English Drama*, 3 vols (Cambridge: Cambridge University Press, 2011)
Nora, Pierre, 'Between Memory and History: *Les Lieux de Mémoire*', *Representations* (Spring 1989), pp. 7–27
Orgel, Stephen, *The Illusion of Power: Political Theatre in the English Renaissance* (Berkeley, CA: University of California Press, 1975)
Owen, Hugh, *Some Account of the Ancient and Present State of Shrewsbury* (Shrewsbury: P. Sandford, 1808)
Partridge, Eric, *Shakespeare's Bawdy* (London: Routledge & Kegan Paul, 1968)
Parvini, Neema, *Shakespeare and New Historicist Theory* (London: Bloomsbury Arden, 2017)
Playford, John, *The Dancing Master: Or, plain and easie Rules for the Dancing of Country Dances, with the Tune to each Dance, to be play'd on the Treble Violin* (London: John Playford, 1653)
Rabkin, Norman, *Shakespeare and the Problem of Meaning* (Chicago: University of Chicago Press, 1981)
Roberts, Jeanne Addison, *The Shakespearean Wild: Geography, Genus, and Gender* (Lincoln, NE: University of Nebraska Press, 1991)
Roe, John, *Shakespeare and Machiavelli* (Cambridge: D. S. Brewer, 2002)
Rowland, Beryl, *Animals with Human Faces; A Guide to Animal Symbolism* (Knoxville, TN: University of Tennessee Press, 1973)
Ruff, Julius R., *Violence in Early Modern Europe, 1500–1800* (Cambridge: Cambridge University Press, 2001)
Salgado, Gamini, ed., *Cony Catchers and Bawdy Baskets* (Harmondsworth: Penguin, 1972)
Salgado, Gamini, *The Elizabethan Underworld* (London: Book Club Associates, 1977)

Salkeld, Duncan, *Shakespeare and London* (Oxford: Oxford University Press, 2018)
Sanders, Julie, *The Cultural Geography of Early Modern Drama, 1620–1650* (Cambridge: Cambridge University Press, 2011)
Schneider, Rebecca, *Performing Remains: Art and War in Times of Theatrical Reenactment* (Abingdon: Routledge, 2011)
Scott, Charlotte, *Shakespeare's Nature: From Cultivation to Culture* (Oxford: Oxford University Press, 2014)
Shakespeare, William, *The Comedy of Errors*, ed. Kent Cartwright (London: Bloomsbury, 2016)
Shakespeare, William, *Henry V*, ed. T. W. Craik (London: Routledge, 1995)
Shakespeare, William, *King Henry IV Part 1*, ed. D. S. Kastan (London: Bloomsbury, 2018)
Shakespeare, William, *The Merchant of Venice*, ed. John Drakakis (London: Bloomsbury, 2010)
Shakespeare, William, *A Midsummer Night's Dream*, ed. Trevor R. Griffiths (Cambridge: Cambridge University Press, 2000)
Shakespeare, William, *Othello*, ed. E. A. J. Honigmann (Walton-on-Thames: Thomas Nelson and Sons, 1997)
Shakespeare, William, *The Oxford Shakespeare: The Complete Works*, 2nd ed., ed. John Jowett, William Montgomery, Gary Taylor and Stanley Stewart (Oxford: Clarendon Press, 2005)
Shakespeare, William, *Two Gentlemen of Verona*, ed. Kurt Schlueter (Cambridge: Cambridge University Press, 2012)
Sinfield, Alan, *Faultlines: Cultural Materialism and the Politics of Dissident Reading* (Oxford: Clarendon Press, 1992)
Smith, Joshua S., 'Reading between the Acts: Satire and the Interludes in *The Knight of the Burning Pestle*', *Studies in Philology*, 109(4) (Summer 2012), pp. 474–495
Smith, Peter J., 'A "Consummation Devoutly to be Wished": The Erotics of Narration in *Venus and Adonis*', in *Shakespeare Survey*, 53 (Cambridge: Cambridge University Press, 2000), pp. 25–38
Smith, Peter J., Janice Valls-Russell and Daniel Yabut, 'Shakespeare under Global Lockdown: Introduction', *Cahiers Elisabethains: A Journal of English Renaissance Studies*, 103 (2020), pp. 101–111
Spenser, Edmund, *The Faerie Queene* (London: Penguin, 1987)
Spurgeon, Caroline, *Shakespeare's Imagery* (Cambridge: Cambridge University Press, 1952)
Staley, Lynn, *The Island Garden: England's Language of Nation from Gildas to Marvell* (Notre Dame, IN: University of Notre Dame, 2012)
Stallybrass, Peter, and Allon White, *The Politics and Poetics of Transgression* (New York: Cornell University Press, 1986)
Standish, Arthur, *The Commons Complaint* (London, 1611)
Stevens, Jenny, 'A Close Reading of Chaucer's "The Merchant's Prologue and Tale"', *British Library* (2018) www.bl.uk/medieval-literature/articles/a-close-reading-of-chaucers-the-merchants-prologue-and-tale [accessed 18 Feb. 2020]

Stewart, Stanley, *The Enclosed Garden: The Tradition and the Image in Seventeenth-Century Poetry* (Madison, WI: University of Wisconsin Press, 1966)
Sullivan, Garrett A., Patrick Cheney, and Andrew Hadfield, eds, *Early Modern English Drama: A Critical Companion* (New York: Oxford University Press, 2006)
Sutherland, John, and Cedric Watts, *Henry V, War Criminal? And Other Shakespeare Puzzles* (Oxford: Oxford University Press, 2000)
Theis, Jeffrey S., *Writing the Forest in Early Modern England: A Sylvan Pastoral Nation* (Pittsburgh: Duquesne University Press, 2009)
Thesiger, Sarah, 'The Orchestra of Sir John Davies and the Image of the Dance', *Journal of the Warburg and Courtauld Institutes*, 36 (1973), pp. 277–304
Thomas, Keith, *Man and the Natural World: Changing Attitudes in England 1500–1800* (London: Penguin Books, 1983)
Thomas, Keith, *Religion and the Decline of Magic* (London: Penguin, 1991)
Tillyard, E. M. W., *The Elizabethan World Picture* (London: Chatto & Windus, 1973)
Traversi, Derek, *An Approach to Shakespeare*, vol. 1 (London: Hollis & Carter, 1968)
Traversi, Derek, *Shakespeare: 'Richard II' to 'Henry V'* (London: Hollis & Carter, 1979)
Tricomi, Albert H., 'The Mutilated Garden in *Titus Andronicus*', *Shakespeare Studies*, 9 (1 Jan. 1976), pp. 89–105
Tuch, Richard, 'Murder on the Mind: Tyrannical Power and Other Points along the Perverse Spectrum', *International Journal of Psychoanalysis*, 91 (2010), pp. 141–162
Turner, James Grantham, *Libertines and Radicals in Early Modern London: Sexuality, Politics, and Literary Culture, 1630–1685* (Cambridge: Cambridge University Press, 2002)
Turner, Victor, *Dramas, Fields, and Metaphors: Symbolic Action in Human Society* (Ithaca, NY: Cornell University Press, 1974)
Turner, Victor, *The Ritual Process: Structure and Anti-Structure* (Chicago: Aldine Publishing Co., 1969)
Underdown, David, *Revel, Riot and Rebellion: Popular Politics and Culture in England, 1603–1660* (Oxford: Clarendon Press, 1985)
Vaughan, Alden T., and Virginia Mason Vaughan, *Shakespeare's Caliban: A Cultural History* (Cambridge: Cambridge University Press, 1991)
Viljoen, Hein, and Chris N. Van Der Merwe, *Beyond the Threshold: Explorations of Liminality in Literature* (New York: Peter Lang, 2017)
Weimann, Robert, *Author's Pen and Actor's Voice: Playing and Writing in Shakespeare's Theatre* (Cambridge: Cambridge University Press, 2000)
Weimann, Robert, *Shakespeare and the Popular Tradition in the Theater: Studies in the Social Dimension of Dramatic Form and Function* (Baltimore: Johns Hopkins University Press, 1978)

White, Paul Whitfield, and Suzanne R. Westfall, eds, *Shakespeare and Theatrical Patronage in Early Modern England* (Cambridge: Cambridge University Press, 2002)

White, T. H., *The Book of Beasts* (London: Jonathan Cape, 1969)

Wiles, David, *Shakespeare's Clown: Actor and Text in the Elizabethan Playhouse* (Cambridge: Cambridge University Press, 1987)

Williams, Raymond, *The Country and the City* (London: Chatto & Windus, 1973)

Williams, Raymond, *Marxism and Literature* (Oxford: Oxford University Press, 1977)

Wilson, Christopher R., and Michela Calore, *Music in Shakespeare: A Dictionary* (Bloomsbury: London, 2014)

Wright, Louis B., 'Stage Duelling in the Elizabethan Theatre', *Modern Language Review*, 22(3) (1927), pp. 265–275

Index

Abrams, R. 76n34
Alighieri, D. 36, 94, 100–101
Ariosto, L.
   Orlando Furioso 84
Attié, K. B. 190

Bacon, F.
   Gardens, Of 124–126, 130–131, 146, 154
Bakhtin, M. 8, 13–17, 22–23, 65, 109–110, 136, 139, 193, 205
Barrett, C. ix, 36
Barton, A. 82, 84, 86, 88, 90, 106, 108
Bate, J. 158n11
Beaumont, F.
   Knight of the Burning Pestle xi, 31
Berry, E. 92, 97, 106, 109, 140
Berry, R. 52, 57, 178, 180, 195
Bozio, A. 9
Bracher, M. 79n71
Bradley, A. C. 8, 9, 18, 205
Brayton, D. 41, 53, 158n8
Bristol, M. D. 33n37, 196
Bruckner, L. 158n8
Bruster, D. 25, 31

Callaghan, D. 50
Carter, S. 118n54
Chaucer, G. 100, 118n57
   Merchant's Tale 136–138

Cicero, M. T.
   De Re Publica 124, 144–145, 174, 200n21
Comito, T. 122–126, 132–133, 141, 145, 150

Davies, J.
   Nosce Teipsum 10
   Orchestra 11
Dee, J. 40–44, 56
Dillon, J. 165, 195
directors *see* productions, and directors of
Dollimore, J. xii, 19
Donaldson, P. 187
Drakakis, J. 50–51
Duncan-Jones, K. 107–108
Dutton, R. 29

Eagleton, T. 51
Edelman, C. 165, 183, 194–195
Elden, S. x, 43
Ellacombe, H. 120, 156
Elyot, T. 11

Falconer, A. F. 40, 61
Fitter, C. 21–22
Fitzpatrick, T. 95
Foucault, M. 1, 2, 93, 122–123, 206
Fox, K. 204
Freud, S. 15, 97–102, 109, 118n56
Frye, N. 90–92, 105, 109, 156, 191

Index

Gerard, J. 120
Gillies, J. ix, xv, 37, 51–52, 60
Gray, P. 165
Greenblatt, S. xii, 20, 22, 26, 50, 167–170, 172, 180

Habicht, W. 117n44
Harrison, R. P. 80–81, 100, 106
Hattaway, M. xii, xiii, 95, 185, 190
Haydn, H. 156
Hazlitt, W. 63, 107–108
Hegel, G. W. F. 71, 78n70
Holinshed, R. 174, 176, 188, 198
Hopkins, L. 50, 113–114
Husband, T. 115n14

Johanyak, D. 76n27
Jonson, B. 17, 64, 107, 204
   Bartholomew Fair 11
Jorgensen, P. A. 165, 167, 172, 175, 185

Keegan, J. 178
Keenan, J. 112
Kern, E. G. 158n17
Kernan, A. 110, 111
King, R. 174, 175
Kott, J. 91–92

Law, R. A. 130
Lefebvre, H. 68, 93
Lenman, B. 47, 74n3
Lévi-Strauss, C. 4
Loomba, A. 48, 74n9

McAvoy, L. H. 134, 137, 142
Machiavelli, N. 189–190
MacIntyre, J. 183–184, 188, 189
Mallory, T. 81
Manningham, J. 183
Manwood, J. 80
Marlowe, C.
   Jew of Malta xi, 26
Marvell, A. 139, 150–151, 158n10
Mentz, S. 41, 43, 54
monarchs
   Elizabeth I 11

Henry IV 20, 21, 152, 169, 171–172, 177, 184, 188, 191–195
Henry V 12, 20, 26, 30–31, 96, 106, 126, 166, 176, 178, 180–181, 184–185, 188–190, 201n49
Henry VI 44–45, 57, 126, 131, 146, 170, 179
Henry VIII 25, 45, 183
Richard II 12, 25, 46, 129, 143, 149, 152, 178, 202n54
Richard III 28, 54, 163, 189
Montrose, L. x, 187
Moskina, O. 127
Mullaney, S. 6, 61

Nardizzi, V. 80, 96–97
Nora, P. 197

Orgel, S. 31

Partridge, E. 119n57
Parvini, N. 58
productions, and directors of
   Branagh, K.
      All Is True (2018) 120
      Henry V (1989) 26, 186–187
   Davies, R. T.
      Midsummer Night's Dream (2016) 112–113

Rabkin, N. 190
Roberts, J. A. 102–104, 138–139
Roe, J. 202n58
Ruff, J. R. 33n37

Salgado, G. 61
Salkeld, D. vii, 62, 175
Sanders, J. x, 55
Schneider, R. 169, 198
Scott, C. 23, 123, 157n8
Shakespeare, W.
   Antony and Cleopatra 44, 55, 167
   As You Like It 37, 82, 87–92, 95, 98, 107–108, 136, 140

Index

Comedy of Errors xi, 40,
  52–58, 62–73
Coriolanus 106, 152, 167
Cymbeline 96, 105, 136,
  141, 167
Hamlet 17, 40, 45, 72, 126,
  128–129, 145–146, 198
1 Henry IV 45, 169, 172,
  177–178, 184, 188,
  191–196
2 Henry IV 21, 152, 171
Henry V 26, 31–32, 96, 106,
  126, 166, 176, 178–190
1 Henry VI 44, 131, 146, 179
2 Henry VI 44, 126
3 Henry VI 57, 170–172
Henry VIII 25, 45, 184
Julius Caesar 138, 146, 167–168
King John 106, 147
King Lear 45, 167, 204
Love's Labour's Lost 17, 140
Macbeth 27, 70, 96, 129, 167
Merchant of Venice 39, 40,
  43–45
Merry Wives of Windsor 46, 67,
  117, 140
Midsummer Night's Dream 15,
  30, 72, 82, 86, 91, 105,
  109–113, 167
Much Ado About Nothing 45,
  141, 167
Othello xi, 40, 45–50, 167
Pericles 40, 43, 45, 57–58, 68
Richard II 25, 46, 129, 143–144,
  149, 152, 178
Richard III 28, 54, 189
Romeo and Juliet 95, 129,
  141, 183
Sonnet LXIV 44
Sonnet XCIV 155–156
Tempest xi, 27, 40, 43–48,
  57, 152
Timon of Athens 40, 85–88
Titus Andronicus 88, 97–98,
  102–105, 108–109, 131,
  146, 151–155, 167

Troilus and Cressida 9, 38,
  141, 167
Twelfth Night 15–18, 30, 40,
  54, 141–142, 167
Two Gentlemen of Verona 87–88
Venus and Adonis 98, 101,
  103–106, 137–140
Winter's Tale 16, 40, 96
Sinfield, A. xii, 47
Smith, P. J. vii, xvii, 105, 154
Spenser, E. 84, 127
Staley, L. 123, 143, 150
Stallybrass, P. 71, 151, 169
Standish, A. 81
Stevens, J. 137
Stewart, S. 122–124, 130,
  134–135
Sutherland, J. 187–188

theatres
  Globe 30, 37, 39, 57, 61, 77n53,
    95, 96–97, 175, 184
  Gray's Inn 64, 77n53
  Rose 78n57, 96
Theis, J. S. 93–94
Thomas, K. 67, 83
Tillyard, E. M. W. 8–12, 18, 205
Traversi, D. 8, 12, 25
Tricomi, A. H. 154–155
Tuch, R. 101
Turner, Victor 4–7, 17–21, 32, 51,
  173, 183

Underdown, D. 11, 171, 183

Vaughan, A. T. 46–48, 75n23
Vaughan, V. M. 46–48, 75n23

Weimann, R. xiv, 25, 27–31, 110
White, A. 71, 151, 169
White, T. H. 65
Wiles, D. 29
Williams, R. viii, 7, 19–20,
  90, 127
Wilson, C. R. 184
Wright, L. B. viii, 183

EU authorised representative for GPSR:
Easy Access System Europe, Mustamäe tee 50,
10621 Tallinn, Estonia
gpsr.requests@easproject.com

www.ingramcontent.com/pod-product-compliance
Lightning Source LLC
Chambersburg PA
CBHW051611230426
43668CB00013B/2065